An OPUS Book

Twentieth-Century French Philosophy

ERIC MATTHEWS is a Professor in the Department of Philosophy, University of Aberdeen. He studied philosophy at Oxford with Paul Grice, Gilbert Ryle, and A. J. Ayer, and has taught at Aberdeen since 1963, except for a short period as a visiting lecturer at the University of New Orleans, USA. Apart from articles in philosophical journals, he has published three translations of recent German philosophical texts, and has been invited to speak at a number of international conferences in Europe and North America. He is married, with two sons.

Praise for *Twentieth-Century French Philosophy*:

'It is quite rare to find skilful philosophical argumentation combined with genuine history of ideas in a single volume. Here Matthews shows himself to be both a rigorous philosopher and a sound historical scholar.'
Stephen Priest
University of Edinburgh

Twentieth-Century French Philosophy

—

ERIC MATTHEWS

Oxford New York

OXFORD UNIVERSITY PRESS

OXFORD

UNIVERSITY PRESS

Great Clarendon Street, Oxford OX2 6DP

Oxford University Press is a department of the University of Oxford.
It furthers the University's objective of excellence in research, scholarship,
and education by publishing worldwide in

Oxford New York

Athens Auckland Bangkok Bogotá Buenos Aires Calcutta
Cape Town Chennai Dar es Salaam Delhi Florence Hong Kong Istanbul
Karachi Kuala Lumpur Madrid Melbourne Mexico City Mumbai
Nairobi Paris São Paulo Singapore Taipei Tokyo Toronto Warsaw

with associated companies in Berlin Ibadan

Oxford is a registered trade mark of Oxford University Press
in the UK and in certain other countries

British Library Cataloguing in Publication Data

Data available

Library of Congress Cataloging in Publication Data

Data available

ISBN 0-19-289248-7

5 7 9 10 8 6

Printed in Great Britain by
Cox & Wyman Ltd,
Reading, Berkshire

For Hellen

Acknowledgements

Many people have helped, in one way or another, in the writing of this book. First, I owe a debt to several generations of undergraduate students at the University of Aberdeen who have taken my courses in modern French philosophy, and to a number of graduate students over the years who have pursued research with me into aspects of French philosophy. I have learned at least as much from them as they have from me. Among these many I am particularly grateful to Leigh Clayton and Samantha Holland.

My colleagues, past and present, in the Department of Philosophy at Aberdeen, at New Orleans and at the University of Iceland, especially Pall Skulason, have helped me enormously, by their support, by general philosophical discussion, and by their critical and other comments on papers I have read on topics related to the subject-matter of this book. I am grateful also to the University of Aberdeen Research Committee for awarding me a period of study leave in the academic year 1993–4 which made it possible for me to complete the book, as well as to pursue other lines of research.

I hope it is not too much of a cliché to say that my greatest debt of all is to my wife, Hellen. Cliché or not, it is true: and the debt is an intellectual as well as an emotional one.

Contents

—

CHAPTER ONE

The Frenchness of French Philosophy

1. Philosophy in its Place

According to the traditional conception of philosophy, there is an air of paradox about devoting a study to twentieth-century French philosophy. After all, philosophy is supposed to aspire to universal truth—to produce propositions which would be acceptable to any rational person anywhere at any time. The philosopher has no country. How then can it be important to the understanding of works of philosophy to know in which geographical area they were produced, or the nationality of their authors, or the period in history at which they were written? The appearance of paradox may, however, simply be a sign of the shortcomings of the traditional conception of philosophy, and an important part of the point of writing this book is to demonstrate that that is the case, by showing that the work of the particular philosophers who are to be considered can only be fully understood if one takes into account the fact that they are *French* and that they belong to the *twentieth century.*

What looks like a paradox is anyway easily resolved. Philosophers are, after all, always particular human beings, and as such necessarily live in a particular place at a particular time in history, speaking a particular language, and so belonging to a particular cultural tradition. (Most Western philosophers, at least until very recently, have also belonged to one gender, as recent feminist philosophers, especially in France, have emphasized. Their views will be discussed in a later chapter, but for the most part I shall concentrate on the influences of time and place rather than of gender.) The perspective of our own time and place will necessarily determine what philosophical problems we consider and how we formulate those problems. Only if we can understand the questions which a philosopher seeks to answer, and the ways in which she or he sees those questions can we hope to understand the answers themselves.

There is, however, this element of truth in the traditional conception of philosophy. Unless a philosopher's formulations can be translated (both literally and metaphorically) into language which is intelligible to those who have a different perspective, they cannot be regarded even potentially as a contribution to *philosophy*. The philosopher must indeed have a country, but if anyone's work is to count as genuinely philosophical, it must be universal at least in the sense that it is possible to communicate its content to human beings generally, whatever country they may happen to belong to. On the other hand, this will not be a genuine *translation* unless it conveys the distinctiveness of the original perspective, as determined by the national, cultural, historical, and indeed individual position of its author. The problem of interpreting philosophy is thus to render it intelligible to those of a different background, while taking full account of the context in which the thought was formed.

To come down to a more concrete level, most of the readers of this book (like its author) will not be French: if they have a background in philosophy, it is likely to be in what the French would call the 'Anglo-Saxon' tradition, which in our time means the 'analytic' tradition (again, like the author). Superficially considered, recent French thought and analytic philosophy hardly seem to belong even to the same enterprise: given my own philosophical background and training, that is certainly how much of it seemed to me on first acquaintance. But given my love for France and French culture, I have always been reluctant to share the arrogant and insular dismissal of recent French thought by some on the English-speaking side as 'not really philosophy at all'. To attempt to understand it, for someone with my background, it is necessary to assume that, despite its different style, preoccupations, and methods, twentieth-century French philosophy is part of the self-same enterprise in which analytic philosophy is also engaged. This assumption also means that it must be possible to criticize the positions and arguments of French philosophers in exactly the same ways in which one might criticize an analytic philosopher, and indeed that it is only by critically assessing their arguments that one can properly understand their positions. But to do this does, of course, require that one should take their arguments seriously, however unfamiliar their style may be. Most daring of all, this approach implies that it might even be possible for analytic philosophers to learn something from their French colleagues!

It may, of course, be that this assumption is completely unjustified, or even that treating French 'philosophy' as the same sort of enterprise as 'philosophy' in the English-speaking world only distorts our understanding of it—like treating French *boules* as the same game as English bowls. But how else is it possible to proceed in a work such as this? *Boules* may be a different game from bowls, but the only way in which a bowls-player can even begin to grasp what the French game is about is by fixing on those elements which the two have in common: this is a precondition even for understanding what is different about the other game. In the case of philosophy, as I shall try to show, the assumption that French philosophers are engaged in the same project as the 'Anglo-Saxons' works very successfully at least until the 1960s and even the deviations from that project since then can be seen to have their roots in the earlier common tradition.

My aim is not to give an account of every important work of philosophy produced in France in this century. That would be neither possible (for practical reasons of space), nor desirable from the point of view of bridging the gap between French and Anglo-Saxon philosophy. Some philosophy which happens to have been written in French could equally well have been written in any language and forms part of international movements in philosophy: we might think of the contributions of Poincaré and Duhem to the philosophy of science, for example, or of the work of the neo-Thomist Jacques Maritain, which has distinctively French elements in it, but which fundamentally belongs to an international school. Many French philosophers, again, have devoted most of their energy to scholarly work in the history of philosophy, which may embody certain particularly 'French' features in its style and approach, but is not intended as an original contribution to the development of philosophy. A relatively small number of French philosophers have even adopted the approach of English-speaking analytic philosophy, in the style of Austin and Ryle or more recent figures. What I shall attempt to do is rather to isolate a *distinctively* French tradition in twentieth-century French philosophy from whose very foreignness those such as myself who have a different formation can hope to learn.

The Frenchness of this tradition in philosophy is not necessarily compromised by the influences from non-French sources which have undoubtedly played some part in shaping it, nor indeed by the fact that not all those who have contributed to it are French by birth. The effect of non-French influences is hardly surprising. French culture as a whole, after all, is ultimately inseparable from that of the rest of Europe, and French philosophy in particular has always responded to currents of ideas originating from Germany, Austria, and the British Isles. In the twentieth century, it has been German-speaking philosophy, above all, which has provided the main external source of inspiration (Hegel, Marx, Nietzsche, and Heidegger: perhaps one can also add Freud, though he was not strictly speaking a philosopher). French philosophy remains French, however, in that it has assimilated such external influences and given them a particularly Gallic gloss. Again, to write philosophy primarily in France and in French is necessarily to place oneself within a particular cultural tradition, whatever the writer's own original nationality may be.

The twentieth-century French philosophy to be considered, then, will not include everything philosophical written by French authors since 1900, but only the work of those who can be described as belonging to this characteristically French tradition. The aim will be to trace the development of a line of thought which I believe to be the outcome of a specifically French style of philosophy at a certain stage in its history. I shall not even discuss all those philosophers who can be counted as belonging to this tradition, but only those who seem to me to have played a particularly significant role in advancing this development. There are several thinkers who are very important in themselves, such as Paul Ricoeur, who will nevertheless, with regret, have to be omitted by this criterion, and others, such as Emmanuel Lévinas, who will receive only cursory treatment. My choice of significant figures will inevitably be somewhat subjective, and I must apologize in advance if I have omitted authors who may be considered by some readers to be more important than those whom I have included. It is perhaps some excuse that my purpose has not been to produce an encyclopaedic reference book, but to make it possible to understand the present situation of French philosophy by retracing the route which it has followed.

This, then, is a work which is primarily addressed to those, like me, who have been formed in a different philosophical tradition from that of the authors to be considered within it. Its aim is to attempt to bridge the gap between these two traditions. To do this will require a 'translation' which, like all good translations, both respects the otherness of the original and makes clear what in that original is not 'other'. Only then can we see what we can learn from the French and what they can perhaps learn from us. This can be done only if we take recent French philosophy seriously *as philosophy*. We must at all costs avoid the temptation to see it as a mere reflection of wider French culture, as a kind of sociological phenomenon, to be understood in terms of external developments in French life. We must treat it as an activity with at least some degree of autonomy, developing under the pressure of *arguments* which can be critically examined. That means that we must be willing to subject it to critical appraisal of exactly the same kind that we might apply to any kind of philosophy: but that critical appraisal, to repeat, can be applied to it only once we have fully *understood* what is being said in its own terms.

2. A Peculiarly French Tradition?

More recent French philosophy was described earlier as the outcome of an older French national tradition. Any consideration of it must begin, therefore, by an examination of what is specifically French about that tradition. It has become something of a cliché to describe the French as 'Cartesian', and there is certainly an element of truth in that (as in most clichés). But such descriptions need careful handling: the legacy of Descartes is ambiguous, and some aspects of that legacy have been more prominent in specifically French philosophy than others. Descartes was both an 'Augustinian' philosopher of subjectivity[1] and a 'Galilean' advocate of a modern physical science based on mathematics and a mathematically conceived logic. The latter element in his thought has certainly not been without its French followers, especially in the seventeenth and eighteenth centuries, but it is essentially something to be shared by scientifically inclined philosophers (whether rationalist or empiricist), regardless of nationality. The line of descent from it passes through such figures as Malebranche, Locke, Leibniz, Spinoza, Condillac, Hume, Kant, Comte, and Mill to the logical empiricists and positivists of our own century.

More characteristic of the peculiarly French tradition has been the influence of the other element of Descartes's thinking: the return to subjectivity seen in Descartes's choice of the *cogito* or 'I think' as the Archimedean point on which a stable system of beliefs could be balanced after the destructive process of methodical doubt. Other authors of the sixteenth and seventeenth centuries, such as Montaigne and Pascal, made the *spiritual* relevance of sceptical doubt and the withdrawal into subjectivity much more explicit than did Descartes himself. In both of them, the beginning of wisdom is the rejection of the impersonal spirit of geometry. In Descartes, by contrast, this return to subjectivity was connected to the scientific rationalism, with which, as is clear, he was primarily concerned, by the construction of arguments for the existence of a benevolent and truthful God, who guaranteed the reliability of our 'clear and distinct' perceptions. But the weakness of these arguments was such that it is easy to see how the two strands in his thought could become separated. A search for truth in the inner man does not sit easily with a desire to find a basis for an objective physical science, and the kind of philosopher who is attracted by the former quest is therefore unlikely to be interested in the latter.

My claim is that what is distinctively 'French' about much of French philosophy, and certainly about much of the French philosophy of the twentieth century, is that it springs from the Augustinian Descartes rather than the Galilean. Indeed, under the influence of the Augustinian elements in Descartes, the philosophers in this tradition have usually regarded themselves, paradoxically, as *anti*-Cartesian. The French philosophers whom I shall be considering have by and large not been particularly interested in mathematics or the physical sciences. In so far as science has featured in their philosophical interests at all, it has been in the 'softer' form of biology, or psychology, or the social sciences, or even in the form of psycho-analysis, a practice which many Anglo-Saxon philosophers would not regard as scientific in any sense at all. Philosophy has certainly not been seen as the 'handmaiden of the [physical] sciences', as it has usually been regarded in the English-speaking tradition since Locke (and to a lesser but still significant extent in the German tradition since Leibniz). The natural affinities of philosophy have rather been taken to be with literary and artistic culture, and the concerns of the philosopher have centred on moral, literary, spiritual, socio-political, and cultural questions rather than on the logic of the sciences.

Although the non-scientific or even anti-scientific strain in French philosophy is most noticeable in our own century, it has always been the case that the primary concerns of French philosophers have been with moral, social, and personal issues rather than with the impersonal truths of physical science. Their question has been Montaigne's first-person 'What do I know?' rather than Locke's more generalized inquiry into 'the original, certainty and extent of human knowledge'. Because of this, philosophy has played a crucial role in the general cultural life of France, to an extent which is simply inconceivable in any English-speaking country. In part, this is because, since the Revolution, it has been taught as a key element in the secondary-school curriculum, as a secular substitute for religious education. But this cannot be the sole explanation for the prominence of philosophy in French culture: indeed, even the choice of philo-sophy to serve this educational function itself implies that it was already regarded as having a peculiar status. I want to suggest that it was precisely because French philosophy had already taken the direction it had, towards a primary concern with the nature of humanity and with moral and social questions, that it seemed particularly suited, in the eyes of the anti-clerical Left in French post-Revolutionary society, to take on a special educational role. For the same reason it has always found its home as part of the general literary and artistic culture of France.

This remains true in the twentieth century. It is not possible fully to understand French literature, drama, cinema, or visual arts, or the course taken by French political life, in this century without some awareness of contemporary developments in philosophy. Conversely, the understanding of philosophical developments is impoverished if they are not seen in the context of the wider changes in French culture. Any discussion of recent French philosophy must therefore make at least some effort to relate philosophical to wider cultural developments, and I shall certainly attempt to do that as far as space allows. To say this may sound like accepting the view rejected earlier that French philosophy is a mere reflection of general culture. But that is not what is intended. On the one hand, it cannot be understood *as philosophy* unless it is seen as developing in response to its own internal pressures of argument and the intellectual criticism of argument. And on the other its role in relation to general culture can be properly understood only if it is seen as philosophy: it is related to the rest of French culture precisely by being a philosophical argument about problems thrown up in that culture.

3. The End of 'Humanism'?

The outstanding feature of the development of French philosophy in the twentieth century has been the deepening crisis of the Cartesian synthesis of Augustine and Galileo, and of the rationalistic and humanistic view of the world which was based on it. The narrative of this book will thus be the story of the development of this crisis. It has affected above all the Cartesian concept of the human subject, as a universal being of pure reason divorced from its own body and so from any position in space, time, and history. One of the great paradoxes of Descartes's thought is that, despite his free use of the first person pronoun

(*I* think, therefore *I* am), the subject or mind of which he speaks is in fact curiously impersonal. This is inevitable, given that his starting-point was a concern with the foundations of knowledge. Knowledge is essentially impersonal—what I can know is not especially *mine*, to do with me in particular as an individual person, but rather what can be known by anyone whatsoever in the appropriate position, no matter who they are. In that sense, the subject of knowledge is a universal subject, a 'one' rather than an 'I'.

Thus, in his zeal to overcome the sceptic's doubt that knowledge is possible at all, Descartes plays the sceptic at his own game, by doubting everything that it is possible to doubt. In the final phase of this doubt, he even doubts the existence of his own body and of the material world itself, and draws the conclusion that the only thing which it is impossible for even the most determined sceptic to doubt is his own existence as a thinking being. Given that the preceding doubts had stripped away everything which could have particularized this thinking being, identified it with a particular human person (René Descartes or whoever), the use of 'I', however, seems peculiarly inappropriate. The conclusion should not be that *I* exist as a thinking being, but just that *thinking* or perhaps *a thinking subject* exists. The subject whose existence is the foundation of all knowledge is not and cannot be any particular human being living in a particular place at a particular time in history, but must be a universal or abstract subjectivity or 'consciousness in general', as Kant was later to express it. In contrast to this transcendental subjectivity, actual, embodied, human subjects then became just parts of the objective world, which, according to Cartesian dualism, operated in a purely mechanistic fashion, in accordance with the laws of physics.

The fullest development of this Cartesian abstraction or depersonalization of the subject was thus paradoxically in nineteenth-century 'positivism', which saw itself precisely as the abandonment of metaphysics in favour of an empirical scientific study of biology and of human individual and social behaviour, modelled on what were believed to be the methods of physics. Auguste Comte, in the first half of the nineteenth century, laid the foundations for a positivistically conceived social science, or 'sociology'; in the latter half of the century, Émile Durkheim built a sophisticated theoretical and empirical structure on those foundations. Durkheim, significantly, preferred the term 'rationalism' to 'positivism'. 'Indeed our main objective', he said, 'is to extend the scope of scientific rationalism to cover human behaviour by demonstrating that, in the light of the past, it is capable of being reduced to relationships of cause and effect . . . '[2] In a parallel development in the biological sciences, Claude Bernard (who also disliked the *term* 'positivism', but thought in thoroughly positivistic ways), in his *Introduction à l'étude de la médecine expérimentale* (*Introduction to the Study of Experimental Medicine*) of 1865, advocated the abandonment of metaphysical preconceptions in the study of living organisms and the search for empirically verifiable generalizations about the connection between one phenomenon and another. Thus the ultimate outcome of Cartesian rationalism was a unified scientistic world-picture in which the human mind, living organisms, and the physical realm were all conceived of as subject to timeless laws, discoverable by an impersonal and universal reason.

Even before this, there had been the beginnings of a reaction against Cartesianism, most notably in the work of Maine de Biran (1766–1824), who saw the foundation of learning as lying not in intellect or cognition, but in the experience of willing one's own body to move. To make the human subject primarily the subject of *action* in this way, rather than the subject of thought or knowledge, is already to make it less plausible to represent the essential human being as disembodied or impersonal. The reaction against positivism which set in at the very end of the nineteenth century and in the present century took up this emphasis on the essential embodiment of the self, which in turn came to be seen as implying the impossibility of fully transcending the limitations of the time and place at which one happens to exist. Thus, the first stage in the crisis of the Cartesian synthesis was marked mainly by the rejection of the abstraction and disembodiment of Descartes's conception of the self.

More recently still, as we shall see in the later part of the book, the crisis in Cartesianism has deepened further. The insistence on the necessary involvement of the self with a body implies a denial of another characteristic Cartesian doctrine, that of the 'transparency' of the human subject, that is, its full accessibility to consciousness. 'I know plainly', Descartes says, 'that I can achieve an easier and more evident perception of my own mind than of anything else.'[3] The rejection of transparency, besides following from the philosophical criticism of disembodiment, was also reinforced by the influence of Freudian conceptions, by the growth in historicist modes of thought, especially those derived from Hegel and Marx, and later by ideas derived from structural linguistics and anthropology which were somewhat in conflict with historicism.

As the focus of philosophical criticism switched from Descartes's mind–body dualism to his doctrine of the fully transparent subject, outside time and history, so the emphasis came to be more on the problems in Cartesian rationalism. The conception of universal principles of rationality becomes harder to sustain if the human mind cannot extract itself from its position in a particular time, place, and culture. The insistence on the essentially embodied character of human beings led naturally to a conception of human rationality as limited by the bounds of history and culture. For a time, the 'structuralist' thinkers led a deviation from this increasing historicism, insisting on the existence of universal structures of thought. But this was not really a return to Cartesian rationalism, since these structures were not a priori principles of reason but empirically discoverable patterns of human thinking. In the 'post-structuralist' reaction against their views, French philosophy moved further towards a thoroughgoing cultural and historical relativism.

There is a sense in which this deepening crisis of Cartesianism was a crisis of philosophy itself, especially as it was traditionally conceived in France: namely, as a secular humanist substitute for revealed religion. The role of philosophy, on this conception, was to work out, on the basis of human reason alone, a set of ideas and values by which human beings could govern their lives: being rationally based, these ideas and values were supposed to apply universally, to all human beings at all times and in all places, just like the religious ideas and values which they were to replace. Once human reason began to be historicized, the notion that the philosopher could by means of reason discover universal truths and values in this sense became more difficult to sustain: but at least philosophy could continue to affirm human dignity, in the form of the capacity for free choice of values possessed by the fully conscious self.

When the notion of self-transparency also came under fire, however, then the final link between philosophy and this kind of rationalistic humanism was broken. Furthermore, the very concept of philosophy itself, as an independent and foundational discipline, could be called into question. For the claim to independence and foundational status rested on philosophy's alleged purely a priori access to the universal rational structures inherent in the conscious human mind: but if the actual structures of human thought were outside consciousness, in realms accessible only to empirical disciplines such as psychology, linguistics, or anthropology, then the very basis for such a claim was undermined. Philosophy, if it survived at all, could do so only on the margins of these empirical disciplines (and also of literature and the other arts), thereby occupying a much more subordinate place in the culture as a whole. This crisis in the Western philosophical tradition is not, of course, confined to France: Richard Rorty has argued that the whole Western idea of philosophy as a foundational study has to be called in question, and that philosophy should occupy a more modest role as a branch of literature, playing its small part in 'the conversation of mankind'. But it has perhaps been made more explicit and felt more intensely in twentieth-century French philosophy than in the cosier world of English-speaking philosophy. Since these are problems with which all philosophers must grapple, we in the English-speaking world can gain something from considering what the French have had to say on them.

The account of French philosophy in the twentieth century must begin by considering the work of Henri Bergson, both because he is chronologically the first important representative of the tradition I wish to consider (indeed, his first published works appeared at the end of the nineteenth century) and because he has a right to be regarded as the founding father of this tradition.

If it is true, as Whitehead said, that the whole of Western philosophy can be seen as a series of footnotes to Plato, then it is equally true that most of twentieth-century French philosophy can be seen as a series of footnotes to Bergson. Bergson is little read nowadays, and that is hardly surprising in view of his tendency to verbosity and the very turn-of-the-century atmosphere of rather unfocused 'spirituality' and a belief in general progress which pervades many of his writings. That he was more than a fashionable society thinker of the Edwardian or *belle époque* period, however, is indicated by the remarkable number of references to him in later French philosophers, which we shall note in the appropriate places. Whether they agreed with his views or not, it was Bergson who in many ways set the agenda for the kind of French philosophy with which this book is concerned: the insistence on the importance of embodiment and concreteness, the rejection of a concept of rationality modelled on mathematics and the physical sciences, the recognition of time and becoming—all these themes of later French philosophy were developed in a particularly compelling and original way by Bergson. The work of these later philosophers is in large part the development of traditions begun by Bergson. One of his successors in the Chair of Philosophy at the Collège de France, Maurice Merleau-Ponty, said of Bergson in his Inaugural Lecture: 'Now we can bear witness to the vitality of his works only by saying how he is present in our own, showing the pages of his works in which, like his listeners in 1900, we with our own preferences and partialities think we perceive him "in contact with things".'[4]

It is with Bergson, then, that our discussion of twentieth-century French philosophy must begin.

CHAPTER TWO

Bergson

1. Life and Works

The life of Henri Bergson straddles the division between the
nineteenth and twentieth centuries, and his complex thought
likewise marks the transition from the scientifically minded
positivism of such essentially nineteenth-century philosophers as
Auguste Comte, Claude Bernard, and Émile Durkheim to the
more suspicious attitude towards the mathematically based
physical sciences characteristic of the twentieth century. His own
philosophy combined respect for mathematics and physics with
a sense of their limitations as keys to metaphysical reality. His
arguments make frequent reference to scientific findings, but the
science in question is usually *biology*, and his account of biology
itself is founded in intuition rather than mathematical reason.
The atmosphere of most of his writings is that of the turn of
the century, but the themes which caught his interest were
largely those which were to preoccupy more recent French
philosophers—the nature of the self, its essential embodiment,
the assertion of human freedom against the claims of scientific
determinism, the sources of moral value, change, and becoming,
and the concreteness of human existence.

Bergson was born in Paris in 1859, the year, significantly, of
the publication of Darwin's *Origin of Species*, which was to
dominate so much of the thought of the later nineteenth century
and to provide the themes for Bergson's own philosophy. He
came of a Jewish family, his father having been born in Poland
and his mother in England (he continued to have considerable
sympathy for English life and culture). At his secondary school
(the Lycée Condorcet), he distinguished himself in both mathematics and literature. In 1878, he enrolled as a student of

philosophy at the École Normale Supérieure, from which he graduated in 1881. In the French style, he became a teacher of philosophy in *lycées*, or secondary schools, first in Angers and Clermont-Ferrand, and later in Paris.

In 1897, he was appointed a *maître de conférences* (a senior teaching post) at the École Normale Supérieure, and taught there until 1900, when he was appointed to the distinguished Chair of Philosophy at the Collège de France. His lectures at the Collège de France, from 1900 to 1924, became enormously fashionable with wider Parisian society, especially after the publication of his *Creative Evolution* in 1907, and many of his ideas greatly influenced current thinking in the arts, literature and politics, on both left and right.[1] At the same time, he was regarded with some suspicion by many of his academic colleagues: his disciple, the writer Charles Péguy, who assiduously attended the lectures himself, says that he saw all kinds of people there, 'except for academics . . . Above all, I did not see to my knowledge any professors of sociology or philosophy.'[2] Nevertheless, in 1914 Bergson was elected to the Académie Française, and in 1928 was awarded the Nobel prize for literature.

Bergson's life, however, was not entirely taken up with academic and literary activity. During the First World War, for example, he travelled to the United States on a diplomatic mission, to try to persuade the Americans to enter the war. After the war he became chairman of a League of Nations body called the Commission Internationale de Coopération Intellectuelle, which seems to have been a sort of precursor of UNESCO; but he had to retire from this position in 1925 on health grounds.

Although his earlier philosophical works had been placed on the Catholic Church's *Index of Prohibited Books* in 1914 (because of their tendency to encourage theological 'modernism'), and despite his Jewish origins, Bergson grew more and more sympathetic to Catholicism. In his will, which was written in 1937, he said that the only thing which was keeping him from being received into the Catholic Church was his desire to identify with his own Jewish background at such a time of anti-Semitic persecution (it has been alleged that he was in fact converted on his death-bed). He died in occupied Paris in 1941, from pneumonia contracted while he was queuing in bitterly cold weather to register as a Jew: there is an indication in all this of his nobility and integrity of character.

2. Being and Becoming

Bergson's philosophy is a reaction against the scientific positivism of the nineteenth century: unlike the positivists, he regarded metaphysics not only as possible, but as the central concern of philosophy, indeed of humanity as a whole. But what he meant by 'metaphysics' shows him as in revolt, not only against positivism, but against the whole mainline tradition of Western philosophy since Plato. Metaphysicians in that tradition have held that the ultimate reality which underlies the world of sense-perception (the world of 'appearances') is timeless and unchanging, a world of Being, rather than of Becoming, a world of abstract Forms of kinds of things, rather than of concrete particulars. Access to it is by means of reason or intellect, conceived of on the model of mathematical logic (which also deals with timeless, necessary truths about general classes of entities). For Bergson, by contrast, the ultimate metaphysical reality was to be found precisely in what is alive and constantly changing, in the world of Becoming and concrete particularity, and our mode of access to that ultimate reality was by means of what he called 'intuition' rather than by mathematical reason (because of this, Bergson is sometimes accused, for instance by Bertrand Russell, of 'irrationalism': but this rather vague charge seems to depend only on an excessively narrow definition of rationality).

Intuition is supposed to be the basis of metaphysics because intuition grasps things from the inside, and therefore *absolutely*, rather than from some merely relative point of view. In his essay *An Introduction to Metaphysics*, which first appeared as an article in the *Revue de Métaphysique et de Morale* in 1903,[3] Bergson defines 'intuition' as 'the kind of *intellectual sympathy* by which one places oneself within an object in order to coincide with what is unique in it and consequently inexpressible' (p. 6). He uses the analogy of the difference between an abstract consciousness of Paris, based on a mere collection of sketches of the city from different points of view, and the awareness of Paris possessed by someone who has really been there and so has had an intuition of the place as a unified whole. But this is just intended as an analogy, to illustrate Bergson's point: the best example of real intuitive awareness is, according to Bergson, our consciousness of ourselves, of 'our own personality in its flowing through time' (p. 8). We are aware of ourselves 'from the inside': we do not contemplate ourselves, as we might contemplate an object, from some external point of view; and our grasp of our essential nature is not arrived at, as it has to be with an object, by putting together the different perspective views (as we might put together different pictures of parts of Paris to try to get some kind of picture of the city as a whole).

In *Introduction to Metaphysics*, Bergson uses 'analysis' as the contrasting term to 'intuition' (in other works, he uses other terms, such as 'intellect', to make the contrast). Where intuition gets at what is absolute, inward, concrete, inexpressible, analysis (intellect) is always relative, external, abstract, and expressible in words. Whereas intuition is the method of metaphysics, analysis is the method of mathematics, the physical sciences, and practical common sense. The knowledge gained by analysis is *propositional*, that is, it is knowledge *that* something or other is the case, in contrast to intuitive knowledge, which consists in *coinciding with* what is known and so is not knowledge of a proposition about something but a direct acquaintance with the inner essence of the thing itself.

Hence analytic knowledge is of a kind which can be expressed in symbols: linguistic, mathematical, or other. To use symbols is essentially to classify things in some way or other, and so involves thinking of the thing referred to, not in its concrete individuality as *itself*, but simply in respect of what it has in common with other things of the same sort. Thus, to say that Bergson was a French philosopher is to consider him as just one instance among others of the class of French philosophers. It is precisely for this reason that scientific knowledge is analytic, since science is essentially concerned with formulating generalizations about classes of entities, and so with considering individuals simply as instances of those general truths. For practical purposes we need to think about things in these general terms: the usefulness of things (for instance the suitability of a particular material for a particular task) has to do with the properties which they have in virtue of being members of a class, not with anything intrinsic to the individual simply as an individual. Scientific knowledge, and the common sense knowledge which we pursue in everyday life, are thus closely connected for Bergson with our practical dealings with the world, rather than with pure theoretical understanding.

Intuitive knowledge, by contrast, is supposed to be divorced from such practical considerations and directed simply to the deep understanding of the essences of things which we seek in metaphysics. There is, however, a problem here for Bergson. The most plausible (indeed, it might be said, the *only* really plausible) case where an awareness of something 'from the inside' might be possible is our consciousness of our own inner selves. (Though perhaps, as Bergson suggests, this might be extended to include our grasp, by imaginative empathy, of the inner lives of other human beings, including the fictional human beings we encounter in literature). But a metaphysics whose only possible subject-matter was the metaphysician's own inner life, or even one whose only subject-matter was the inner lives of human beings in general, real or fictional, would seem, to say the least, somewhat impoverished. We shall discuss a little later Bergson's attempts to overcome this limitation: for the moment, however, let us concentrate on what he has to say about our awareness of our own inner selves.

We can have analytic knowledge about ourselves as much as about anything else. Clearly, we can approach our own bodies scientifically, as simply one specimen amongst others of a human organism, which we can study as physiologists or anatomists and to which we can apply our knowledge of the general laws of physiology, biochemistry, genetics, or whatever. But we can even have analytic knowledge of our own mental lives, of our thoughts, feelings, motives, desires, and so on. This will be knowledge of them, not as specifically *our own* thoughts etc., but simply as instances of a general *kind* of thought, of the properties of thoughts of that kind and their characteristic relations to other kinds of thought, feeling, wish, desire, or whatever. The knowledge we shall acquire in this way is thus not self-knowledge, but knowledge of certain psychological generalizations about 'the human mind' (whether the psychology in question is strictly scientific or is of the more common-sense kind which some modern philosophers call 'folk psychology'). And, like all analytic knowledge, its value in Bergson's view will be principally practical—it will help us, for instance, in manipulating our own behaviour or that of other people in order to secure certain aims.

Furthermore, these psychological generalizations, like all scientific generalizations, will be in a certain sense 'timeless'. They may well, of course, describe certain temporal relations between states of mind, as when it is said that a particular kind of feeling (say, hunger) tends to cause a particular kind of thought (say, 'I want to eat something'): the cause comes *before* the effect. But the conception of time involved here is not, in Bergson's eyes, real time at all—not time as we actually experience it, flowing from the past through the present into the future, but an abstract version, modelled on the properties of space, which may be useful for certain limited purposes but does not capture the true essence of time. Spatial relations hold between discrete entities, and are essentially reversible. If my coffee-cup is currently situated approximately five centimetres from my computer, then that relation is, first, purely external (that is, it does not affect the character of either the coffee-cup or the computer) and, secondly, is reversible in the sense that it could equally be said that my computer is five centimetres from my coffee-cup.

When we speak of relations of 'earlier than' and 'later than', we are, Bergson would argue, thinking of time in spatialized terms. If A is earlier than B, then that does not affect the character of either A or B, which thus remain discrete events; and the relationship is reversible in that there is no reason in principle why B should not have been earlier than A. Spatialized time does not have any necessary direction. However, when I reflect on my own inner experience as an individual, (that is, not just as an instance of the class of human beings, or of a particular type of human being), then, Bergson would say, I am aware of that experience as 'in time' in a much more truly 'temporal' sense—in a time which has quite a different character from space. I am aware of certain of my experiences, for instance, as being 'in the past' and of certain others as 'in the future', still to come. Describing them in these ways involves an essential reference to the 'present', to where I now am: what is past or future is so only relative to the perspective of the present, which is the perspective of a particular human consciousness and which is constantly changing, as what was future becomes present and then falls in turn into the past.

The time of inner experience, the time of past, present, and future, which Bergson calls *durée* or 'duration', is, he contends, different in important respects from the spatialized time in which we locate external objects (including our own selves when we treat them as if they were objects external to us). First of all, it has an intrinsic direction, from the past, through the present, to the future. This direction is in principle irreversible: what is future could not come before what is past. In becoming past, an experience changes its character as an experience: it becomes the object of *memory*, in which we recall the past experience in all its pastness. Moreover, we recollect it as part of *our own* past, which acquires a personal significance for us as part of that unique life history which gives us our identity as individuals.

Secondly, time in this sense is not precisely measurable: it cannot be divided into discrete units and measured by the number of those units which have passed. Objective, spatialized time can be, and is, so measured, just as space itself is: we can divide spatialized time into hours, minutes, seconds, to be measured, significantly by the movement of something through space, e.g. the movement of the hands of a clock round a clockface. But duration cannot be so divided and measured: a boring conversation may take exactly twenty minutes by the clock, but to the bored person the time which the experience takes cannot be pinned down so precisely—it just seems interminable.

Thirdly (and connected with the second point) there are no sharp boundaries in inner time, no precise line between what is past and what is present, or what is present and what is future. Duration flows on like a stream, the past mingling with the present and flowing on into the future. Bergson makes no distinction between our inner experience and the duration 'in' which that experience occurs: our self *is* duration, and that is what gives its peculiar unanalysable and wholly individual character to each self. For my self is what it is because it has had the particular past which it has had, and which it does not share with any other self. We can form generalizations about particular thoughts or feelings which I may have, provided that we consider them only in abstraction from their context in my life history: abstractly considered in this way, they can be shared with others, general concepts can be applied to them, and so they can form the subject of generalizations, of scientific psychology for instance. But considered in the fullness of their concrete reality, with the meaning which they have as part of *my* individual experience, no general terms can be applied to them—they are unique and unshareable.

Strictly speaking, duration is identified only with the deepest and most personal layer of the self. For Bergson sees personality as many-layered. We are at our most superficial and least personal when we are functioning as purely practical and social beings. At this level, our thoughts, feelings, perceptions, etc. are closest to being merely general and so communicable to others: though even here our thoughts and so on will be 'impregnated' (as Bergson puts it) with the memory-images which complete and interpret them. Even at its most impersonal, that is, my self is still *my* self, the self which has had the particular life history which I have had. As one gets closer to the heart of a self, however, so this individuality becomes more and more marked; until, at the deepest and most personal level, my thoughts, feelings, wishes, etc. are so intensely *mine* that they are essentially incommunicable to others, inexpressible in the public language which we use to communicate with each other for practical and scientific purposes.

3. Individuality and Freedom

This view of the uniqueness and individuality of each self, at least at its deepest level, enabled Bergson to present an original case for human free will, which avoids the problems both of the kind of absolute libertarianism which treats human actions as essentially random (and so not genuinely *chosen*) and the determinism which treats them as fully caused (and so again not genuinely chosen). Determinism is the doctrine that human thoughts, and so human actions, are subject to general causal laws, just like all other processes in nature: if that is the case, the argument goes, then whenever a relevant cause occurs, the appropriate effect necessarily occurs. Thus human beings can no more avoid having a particular thought in certain circumstances, or acting in a certain way when they have an appropriate thought, than an unsupported boulder can help falling downhill.

In a sense, Bergson would agree, as we have seen, that human thoughts can be treated as being subject to general laws: but only, as we have also seen, when we consider them in their most abstractly expressible form—the form in which they are not the thoughts *of anyone in particular* but just generalized types of thought. To take a simple example, if I am depressed by the sight of yet another rainy day, then the general aspect of my thought, the aspect in which anyone else in any circumstances might have it, is expressible in the words 'Oh no, not another rainy day!' But my deepest personal feelings about the situation, the feelings which I have in virtue of being me, with my unique life history, will not be fully expressible in language at all (at most, I may convey something of them to those sympathetic to me by such things as the tone of voice in which I say the words).

Generalizations can be formulated, Bergson would accept, about the general aspects of thought in this sense, and these will provide the subject-matter of a scientific psychology, which will allow predictions of future thoughts and actions in just the same way as the laws of any science. These predictions, however, given what was said above about the many layers of the self, will apply strictly only to the most superficial and least personal aspects of human thought and action. At the deepest and most personal level (which is also the most concrete level, the one at which we are talking about the actual actions which individuals perform in particular situations), thoughts, feelings, perceptions, desires, and so on flow into each other in such a way that it is impossible to separate 'cause' from 'effect' in the way that scientific prediction requires.

Bergson gives a marvellous example in *Time and Free Will* to illustrate this point, one which makes it plain why writers such as Proust found his philosophy so congenial. His discussion of the example is so illuminating that it is worth quoting from it at some length. The example concerns the way in which the smell of a rose evokes for him recollections of childhood. 'Associationists' in psychology might see this as just an instance of an 'association of ideas', a case of a general law that certain kinds of smell evoke certain kinds of memory. In one respect, Bergson accepts, it may be considered in this way: but this way of treating the example leaves out of account one of its most important features.

The crucial part of Bergson's discussion of the example is this:[4]

To others it [the rose] will smell differently. —It is always the same scent, you will say, but associated with different ideas. —I am quite willing that you should express yourself in this way; but do not forget that you have first removed the personal element from the different impressions which the rose makes on each of us; you have retained only the objective aspect, that part of the scent of the rose which is public property and thereby belongs to space. Only thus was it possible to give a name to the rose and its perfume. And you now say that our different impressions, our personal impressions, result from the fact that we associate different recollections with rose-scent. But the association of which you speak hardly exists except for you, and as a method of explanation.

The association of the scent of the rose with recollections of childhood, in other words, is an essentially *personal* one: it is an association *for Bergson* of this scent with memories of *his own* childhood. To treat it as simply a particular instance of a generalizable association is to miss this essential feature. It is to look on it entirely from the outside, as something to be causally explained in terms of generalizations about human behaviour. But from the inside, the person himself is not concerned to give a causal explanation: he already understands it as part of the flow of his own life history, which he can grasp by intuition simply because it is his own.

The same kind of account can be given of the relation between motives or reasons and actions. Suppose, for instance, that I am uncertain how to act in a particular situation (this example is adapted and expanded from one of Bergson's own[5]). Perhaps I hesitate about whether to tell the truth to a friend about her illness or to keep quiet and spare her feelings. I go through agonies of deliberation: on the one hand, I feel I owe it to her to be honest about her chances of recovery, but on the other a kind of moral cowardice (backed up by rationalizations about being kind) makes me reluctant to face what I fear may be her utter devastation on being told the truth. Eventually, perhaps, my sense of my duty as a friend overcomes my rather cowardly scruples and I find a way of telling her.

As actually experienced by someone, this is thought and felt in an intensely personal way: it is *my* feelings about *this particular* friend, based on the life we have shared with each other, which incline me to tell the truth, and equally it is my own particular brand of moral cowardice, dealt with in my own way, which inclines me in the other direction. At no point in the deliberation can I *predict* what the outcome will be: the deliberation, as I experience it, is not directed towards prediction, but towards decision. Even so, the decision which I reach (*whichever* decision it is) will be intelligible in the light of my past history: it will, as it were, flow from that past history. But it will not be *causally determined* by it, since cause and effect, as Hume taught us, must be distinct existences, and nothing in someone's life history, as lived from the inside, exists in isolation from anything else in that history. My past feelings about my friend give its particular flavour to my present sense of responsibility to her. My present thought is not a distinct existence from my past feelings: it has the character it does only because of its relation to those past feelings. And in turn it is because of the relation between one aspect of my feelings for my friend (my sense of responsibility to her) and others (such as my desire to spare her feelings) that my decision takes the form it does.

A psychological determinist could present this whole process very differently. The so-called process of 'deliberation', the determinist might say, is really just a causally determined interaction between conflicting tendencies in an individual: on the one hand, the socially inculcated belief in the duty of truth-telling, and on the other the fear of the emotional distress resulting from telling the truth. Which of these tendencies triumphed in a particular case would, on this view, depend on the personality-type to which the individual in question belonged, and that would in its turn be determined by biochemistry, by upbringing, or by similar factors. The whole story would thus be presented in causal terms, in terms of the application to the particular case of generalizations about the relation between factors of type A and factors of type B.

The determinist can give such an account, however, as Bergson would argue, only because he or she is considering the process purely from the outside. The thoughts which go through my head when I am deliberating are separated out from their context in *my* life history, and treated abstractly, concentrating only on those elements in them which make them thoughts *of a certain kind*, such as anyone at all might have. The thought of a responsibility to tell the truth to a friend, for instance, is stripped of any purely individual elements derived from my personal experience of relations with *this* friend and considered purely in its most general and abstract form. As such, it can be distinguished from the equally abstract 'decision to tell the truth', and so can have an external, causal relation to that decision. If there is a well-confirmed generalization that 'People with a strong sense of duty will give preference to their duty over any other feelings which they may have,' then it can be predicted that I, as such a person, will obey the duty to tell my friend the truth about her condition in these circumstances.

These abstract formulations of the thoughts and decisions involved, however, necessarily omit those features which make them the thoughts which *I* have and the decisions which *I* make in connection with *this particular friend* in this particular situation. The description of me as an example of a person with a strong sense of duty does not do justice to the particularity of my case: the way in which *I* feel a sense of duty and the particular kind of sense of duty which *I* feel. Because of this lack of fit to the concrete particularities of the case in question, the prediction, like all scientific predictions based on general laws, can only be reliable to a certain degree of approximation. It may turn out to be correct, but if so it will only be by good fortune. And that is not sufficient to provide the sort of necessity of outcome which is required for strict determinism.

Bergson's account, however, is meant to provide a reply, not only to determinism, but also to a common objection to libertarianism. If the libertarian denies that human actions have causes, the objection goes, then that implies that my actions have no connection with me as an individual. They do not spring from my character, or my desires or wishes, or from anything about me, since that would mean that they were *caused* by these things, and libertarianism holds that actions have no causes. But if they do not spring from anything about me, then there is no real sense in which they are *my actions*: they are simply random movements, like the movements of a subatomic particle in quantum theory, and are no more the outcome of *choice* than those particle-movements. In a nutshell, the notion of free choice contradicts itself, since to be free is to be uncaused and to make a choice is to have a cause for one's actions.

The key premiss in this argument is the claim that my actions can be truly mine only if they are caused by my character or something else about me. Bergson's account of decision-making as we actually experience it from the inside enables him to refute this premiss, for it shows that there is only one way in which actions can be truly mine, and that is when they are not *caused* by my thoughts, but belong with them in the total flow of my life history. In that context, they can be understood after the event, but they cannot be causally explained or strictly predicted beforehand.

4. Myself and my Body

This account of the self and its many layers also makes it possible for Bergson to develop a view of the relations between a self and its body which deviates in important respects from Descartes's mind–body dualism (even though, in the introduction to *Matter and Memory*, he describes his views in that book as 'frankly dualistic'[6]). In so doing, he was also preparing the way for one of the most characteristic concepts of twentieth-century French philosophy, that of human beings as necessarily 'embodied' or 'incarnate'. Cartesian dualism is the view that the mental and the physical aspects of human existence are not merely different from each other, but belong to radically different 'substances', where what is meant by a 'substance' is something capable of independent existence. Thus, if human beings are composed of a 'mental substance' and a 'bodily substance', then it follows that they could exist as minds alone, without bodies, and (as is anyway obvious) also as bodies alone, without minds.

Bergson is 'frankly dualistic' only in the sense that, in his own words, he affirms both 'the reality of spirit' and 'the reality of matter'. But his presentation of his views does not suggest that he was a dualist in the full-blown Cartesian sense who believed that the realm of 'spirit' was in principle separable from that of 'matter'. Rather, he sees the spiritual as gradually shading into the material. Our innermost selves are most purely spiritual, and their existence can only be understood as unfolding in 'duration', in Bergson's sense. In our most intimate selves, on his view, we are furthest removed from the practical demands of action, and the memory which we have of our own pasts at this level is most purely memory—the pure contemplative (though emotionally charged) recollection of past experience *as* past, divorced from any connection with our present needs for action. Their very personal and individual character means that they cannot be readily expressed, or expressed at all, in the language which we share with others and which can never therefore convey what is peculiar to one individual (except perhaps in the form of metaphor or imagery).

As we move to more superficial layers of ourselves, so the connection with action and its needs becomes stronger. Our thoughts at this more superficial level are geared more to active intervention in the world around us, and for that very reason are necessarily fully expressible in the ordinary language which we use for communicating with others in the practical pursuits which we carry on together. Because they are still parts of our selves, memory still permeates them, but now it is what Bergson calls 'habit-memory', the relatively impersonal sort of memory of how to act, acquired by repetition of the same effort or the same gesture. This is impersonal in the sense that there is nothing particularly *mine* about the skills which I happen to possess: my ability to speak French does not differ essentially from anyone else's.

The connection with action makes the link between self and body peculiarly close at this level, so close that we cannot draw a boundary-line between them. I *use* my body, including my brain, to cope with the environment in which I am placed. This talk of my self using my body is certainly dualistic in its implications in one way: but in another it implies an involvement of thought with matter which is far from classical dualism. Because my link with my body is made by action, I cannot regard my own body as simply another *object*, another lump of matter which just happens to be closer to me than others. My body *is* me, in the sense that it is the way in which I act on the world around me and am acted on by it. The interaction between myself and the material world takes the form of perception, above all. Pure perception would be something entirely physical, a direct response of the sense-organs and the nervous system to an independently existing physical object. (Bergson will have no truck with the notion that the immediate objects of perception are mental 'representations', or with the idealist attempt to reduce matter to collections of such representations.)

But pure perception does not exist as such: 'Perception is never a mere contact of the mind with the object present; it is impregnated with memory-images which complete it as they interpret it.'[7] What we see (or hear, or smell, or taste) is never just the outcome of the impact of stimuli on our sense-organs, but always that outcome as interpreted by our past experience, stored in our memories. At the very least, we shall have to fit it under a certain concept, if we are to describe it or manipulate it for practical purposes: this will be the work of habit-memory. But we may also interpret it more in terms of its emotional or personal significance, in which case it will be pure memory, operating at deeper levels of our selves, which will be involved. (Looking at the matter from the other end, we might say that the present object of perception may evoke these emotionally or personally charged memories, as in the example of the smell of the rose, cited earlier, or in that of Proust's madeleine). This necessary interplay between perception and interpretation means that Bergson can no more be a simple realist, believing that the mind plays no part in perception, than he can be a philosophical idealist, holding that our minds constitute the objects of perception.

5. Intuition and Metaphysics

Bergson's account of human personality—his treatment of such problems as those of personal identity, of free will and determinism, and of mind–body relations—is thus distinctive and original. The common thread running through his treatment of all these problems is his notion of 'intuition', as a direct, non-perspectival, inner comprehension of something. But this notion was introduced as the basis, not simply for our conception of ourselves, but of a general metaphysics, a source of truths which would be *absolute*, as opposed to the relative and perspectival truths supplied by 'analysis' to science and common sense. There is plainly a tension between 'intuition' as the name for the method of metaphysics, the apprehension of the absolute, and 'intuition' as the name for the way in which each of us apprehends himself or herself 'from the inside'.

This tension can be described in various, related ways. First, although our internal awareness of ourselves may be *non-perspectival* or *non-relative*, it cannot properly be called *absolute*. For it is only non-perspectival in the sense that we *are* ourselves: that is, we *are* our perspectives on other things, and so cannot meaningfully be said to have a perspective on ourselves. But that is not the same thing as having a non-perspectival grasp of the *truth* about ourselves: to *be* me is different from *grasping the truth about* myself. To talk of the *absolute*, in the sense which is relevant to metaphysics, is precisely to talk about absolute *truth*. In short, metaphysics is meant to be a form of knowledge of what is true: but simply coinciding with oneself is neither knowing what is true nor believing what is false about oneself. As was said earlier, intuition is not supposed to be knowledge of true propositions, but direct acquaintance with one's own existence.

Secondly, and even apart from that, no metaphysics worthy of the name, as was suggested earlier in the chapter, can be simply knowledge of what is true about oneself. Metaphysics seeks the absolute, in the sense of knowledge about the ultimate nature of reality as a whole. Bergson himself clearly recognized that. Indeed, his first thoughts about the inadequacy of a spatialized conception of time were inspired, not by reflection about the inner self, but by problems in thinking about the motion of physical objects. The ancient Greek philosopher Zeno had propounded a number of paradoxes about the idea of motion, the upshot of which was supposed to be that there were serious difficulties in the whole concept of motion, and it was his reflections on these paradoxes of Zeno which first set Bergson on the road to his distinctive philosophical positions.

Perhaps the best-known of Zeno's paradoxes is contained in the story of Achilles and the tortoise. Achilles and the tortoise had a race, but Achilles generously agreed to give the tortoise a start, let us say of 50 metres. Now suppose that Achilles runs ten times faster than the tortoise: then in the time that he takes to cover that fifty metres, the tortoise will have advanced a further 5 metres. In the time that Achilles takes to cover that 5-metre gap, the tortoise will have advanced a further 0.5 metres. And so on: every time that Achilles covers a previous gap between them, the tortoise will have advanced a little further, creating a new gap, however vanishingly small. Thus, this analysis of the story seems to show, paradoxically, that Achilles will never succeed in overtaking the tortoise—that the tortoise will always be ahead, though the gap between the two will become so small as to be undetectable.

That this is a paradox is clear: in the real world we should of course expect Achilles to overtake the tortoise. But mathematical analysis of the motion of the two competitors seems to lead to the opposite conclusion. Perhaps, however, Bergson reasoned, that is just the point: that a mathematical analysis of motion is incapable of capturing its reality. The mathematical analysis involves treating movement *through* space on the analogy of the spatial distance which is traversed. Just as the space between two points can be divided into an infinite number of discrete points, so the mathematical analysis regards the motion of Achilles and the tortoise (and the time which that motion takes) as if it were made up of an infinite number of units, which could then be added together to make the continuous motion. But a unit of motion would have to be a point of time in which no motion occurred—a point of stillness or motionlessness (otherwise it could be further divided). So Zeno's paradoxes arise from thinking of motion as consisting of the addition of an infinite number of points of motionlessness, which is a contradiction.

The only way to avoid paradox, Bergson concluded, was to cease to think of motion and the time which motion takes in this mathematical, spatial way, as divisible into discrete units, and to think of them rather as *continuous*, not really divisible, which is, after all, the way in which we actually experience both motion and time. Whether or not this is a satisfactory way of dealing with Zeno's paradoxes is not strictly relevant to our present concerns: but what is relevant is that Bergson's account of the motion of physical objects can hardly expand the range of his metaphysics beyond the inner self. For we can hardly have an 'intuition', in his sense, of such motion. 'Intuition' is defined, it will be remembered, as 'the kind of *intellectual sympathy* by which one places oneself within an object in order to coincide with what is unique in it and consequently inexpressible'.[8] But we surely cannot meaningfully 'place ourselves inside' the bodies of Achilles or the tortoise in motion, in order to coincide with that motion. We may be able to *imagine* ourselves as Achilles or the tortoise taking part in the race, but that is not the same as really 'coinciding' with them; nor will it give us any better grasp of how Achilles was able to overtake the tortoise than the mathematical analysis of Zeno.

Perhaps under the unconscious influence of such thoughts, Bergson's focus of attention moved away from the physics of motion and more towards a general picture of ultimate reality as consisting not in the static Being of a Platonistic or mathematically based metaphysics but in change and Becoming. The primary instance of this he found, as we have seen, in the inner life of the self. Another plausible-seeming candidate, however, especially in view of the dominance in the late nineteenth and early twentieth century of ways of thinking inspired by evolutionary biology, was biological life, both in the individual organism and in the biosphere as a whole. The most promising way in which Bergson could extend the scope of his metaphysics, therefore, was to produce a biologically and evolutionarily based account of reality as a whole, into which his existing account of the self could be fitted: the close connection which, as we have seen, Bergson made between the life of the mind and of the body made it easier to take this further step.

6. Evolution and Philosophy

The fullest example of Bergson's vitalist metaphysics, and his best-known and most influential work, was his *Creative Evolution*, first published in French in 1907 and in English translation in 1911. Bergson saw the general idea of the evolution of life as in harmony with his own concept of duration, but he was dissatisfied in many ways with Darwin's mechanistic theory of natural selection—that species evolved merely because some chance mutations had a differential survival value. Such a theory could not, in his view, explain the way in which the course of evolution seemed to lead in the direction of greater complexity:

a simple organism, after all, could be as well adapted, or better adapted, to its environment, as capable, or more capable, of survival as a more complex one. Bergson could not accept that the course of evolution could be determined in this way by pure chance, or by the mere rearrangement of what was there already. Contemplation of the present state of things made it seem to him that evolution must be both more *purposive* than that and also more *creative*, more productive of genuine novelty. Evolution must lead, as it were, to surprises, to changes which could not have been predicted beforehand, even though their emergence from what had previously existed was completely intelligible in retrospect. And if so, then the Darwinian account of evolution as the directionless outcome of chance responses to the environment must be inadequate.

The view of evolution as emergent and creative also seemed to him to be incompatible with a *teleological* conception, a view of evolutionary development as the fulfilment of a predetermined plan. Such a view would make the present as much determined by the past as the mechanistic conception. A truly creative evolution had to be conceived rather on the analogy of Bergson's own account of the development of the individual human personality. Thus he says at the beginning of Chapter 1 of *Creative Evolution*[9] that each of us has an 'internal and profound' perception of his or her own existence as constantly changing, but not in the mechanical way of merely replacing one fixed state by another. The change is continuous, and the continuity is secured by memory: 'My memory is there, which conveys something of the past into the present. My mental state, as it advances on the road of time, is continually swelling with the duration which it accumulates: it goes on increasing—rolling upon itself, as a snowball on the snow.' Memory, as Bergson uses it here, does not necessarily mean conscious recollection, only the preservation of the past in us, even without conscious recall. Thus he says:[10] 'What are we, in fact, what is our *character*, if not the condensation of the history that we have lived from our birth—nay, even before our birth, since we bring with us prenatal dispositions?' It is this extended sense of memory which allows Bergson to move with seeming legitimacy from the realm of human consciousness to the biosphere as a whole—to suggest that the evolution of living things might have the same form as the psychological development of an individual human being. For biological evolution can be seen as preserving its past in its present: the present form of a species depends on what has happened to the species in the past.

Thus, the whole universe, to the extent that it is living anyway, can be seen as having 'duration', in Bergson's sense, rather than existing in objective, reversible, physical time. What it is now incorporates what it has been, but goes beyond it: just as an individual human personality at any stage in its life incorporates but transcends its past. In this way, biological evolution can be said to have a direction, to be going somewhere, without the need to postulate any *extrinsic* purpose for it or to know *where* it will eventually end up. And it can be seen as genuinely creative of novelty, new forms which go beyond what has existed in the past and are not simply determined by that past: nature itself is not mechanistically determined, but is *free* in much the same sense that human beings are. It is hardly surprising that Bergson's contemporaries found this sort of biologistic, yet also spiritualist, metaphysics exciting.

We, however, can ask more critical questions about it. Most importantly, we can ask whether the analogy which Bergson makes between human memory and the preservation of the biological past in the present will really stand up to close examination. It is surely part of the essence of what we mean by memory, and certainly of memory as interpreted by Bergson himself in earlier works, that it is *conscious recollection*. My past influences my present, according to Bergson, because I recall it as my own past, that is, I see it as having a certain significance for me in relation to my present experience. The relation between past and present created by memory is thus not a *causal* one, in which cause and effect are distinct existences: my remembered past is in this sense a *part* of my present experience. But it is only as preserved in memory that the past can be said to be a part of the present in this sense: where there is no possibility of conscious recollection, as in biological evolution, the past is dead and gone and must be a separate existence from the present. The past is not literally 'preserved': it simply has had a causal influence on the character of the present. It is thus merely playing with words for Bergson to say 'Its [the living organism's] past, in its entirety, is prolonged into its present, and abides there, actual and acting.'[11]

The importance of this is that it undermines Bergson's attempt to assimilate biological evolution to the psychological development of an individual person, and thus invalidates one of his principal arguments for denying that evolution can be explained mechanistically, i.e. causally. Equally importantly, this frustrates a major element in his attempt to liberate his metaphysics of duration from its confinement within the individual psyche, to make it a true metaphysics in the sense of an account of the whole of reality. This attempt at a vitalistic metaphysics, which saw all reality as alive, and all life as inherently purposive, as striving towards some yet-to-be-defined goal, was not by any means compatible with Christian orthodoxy. The *élan vital*, or vital impulse, which was held, in the metaphysics of *Creative Evolution*, to be the driving force of all living activity, could not be equated with God, since it was not a conscious being. Nevertheless, the move to thinking of nature in purposive terms at all was consistent with Bergson's own spiritual development towards an acceptance of Catholicism, and with the increasingly religious tone of much of his later writing. (It was also influential on the thought of such later unorthodox Catholic writers as Teilhard de Chardin.)

7. Morality and Religion

The last of Bergson's major works to be published was separated by twenty-five years from *Creative Evolution*. This was his long study of *The Two Sources of Morality and Religion*, published in 1932. It has been well said that this title is something of a misnomer: Bergson is not really talking about the two *sources* of morality and religion, but about two different *types* of morality and religion: Bergson talks of 'closed' and 'open' morality, and correspondingly of 'static' and 'dynamic' religion. Much of the work reads more like a study in anthropology than in philosophy: it is full of descriptions of what actually happens in so-called 'primitive' and 'more advanced' societies. But the descriptions are not given primarily to convey anthropological information or to expound an explanatory anthropological theory, so much as to provide material for a philosophical analysis.

Broadly speaking, 'closed' morality and 'static' religion are said to 'follow from the original structure of human society'.[12] Both morality and religion, Bergson argues, have an original function in human society, namely, to substitute for animal instinct another way, more in accordance with human intelligence, of restraining human desires and wishes. Closed morality consists therefore of rigid customs, which we come to think of as analogous to laws of nature: cf. the expression 'These things just *aren't done.*' They are imposed on us by the pressure of other members of society, and this is the origin of our sense of obligation. Any closed morality is thus the code of a particular social group, and will probably include injunctions to treat members of other groups as enemies. Since this function of social control is part of the very nature of human society, closed morality will be a feature of all human societies, even the most sophisticated, though it may be more obvious in the morality of less-developed societies.

In much the same way, static religion will be a feature of all societies, but will be most clearly found in simpler societies, in which it has not yet been overlain by more sophisticated beliefs and practices. The beliefs of static religion, fulfilling as they do many of the same functions as instincts, will be based on imagination rather than reason, and will often appear merely absurd and superstitious to rational minds. The faculty of imagination is a faculty of *myth-making*, rather than of abstract speculation. Human beings have such a faculty, Bergson argues (in line with his 'creative' view of evolution), for a purpose: it is there to control the dangers of excessive intellectualism. Intelligence is an evolutionarily useful capacity, but if over-developed, or developed in the wrong way, it poses a threat to the survival of society, the threat of excessive individualism and atomization, which it is the function of the myths of static religion to avert.

Nevertheless, human beings cannot escape from the fact that they have intelligence and reason. There are rational principles inherent even in closed morality and static religion, and it is more or less inevitable that human beings will reflect on them and produce more rationalized versions of morality and religion. These are what Bergson calls 'open' morality and 'dynamic' religion. In open morality, the sense of obligation which is found in closed morality is retained, but the instinctive sociability on which it rests is seen to extend to all human beings, not just to the fellow-members of one's own local community. Obligations under open morality may thus conflict with those under the closed morality of our own tribe, for example when we are required to show kindness to human beings from another community which may be an actual or potential enemy of our own. Open morality thus depends on human intelligence, and the consequent ability which human beings have to break away from rigid rule-following. It is the sign of life itself in human beings that they are not bound by repetitious routines. Already, in a much earlier work, *Le Rire* (*Laughter*), published in 1900,[13] Bergson had seen the essence of the comical as lying in situations where living human beings behave in the repetitious and mechanical ways of inanimate objects, and the social function of our laughter at the comical as a corrective to this imperfection in our humanity—this 'absentmindedness' (i.e. absence of intelligence).

In much the same way, dynamic religion embodies the sense that the ties which bind us to other members of our own community are really just an instance of the ties which bind all human beings together just in virtue of being human. In order to make the break from static to dynamic religion, Bergson thinks, we need 'heroes', charismatic figures (like Christ or Mohammed) who will exercise the emotional power over us which is needed to liberate us from the ties of our own special community and its myths. These heroes will be 'mystics', their thought will express intelligence with a 'fringe of intuition'. The soul which is strong enough to make this effort, Bergson says, will 'feel itself pervaded . . . by a being immeasurably higher than itself' and 'Its attachment to life would henceforth be its insep-arability from this principle, joy in joy, love of that which is all love.'[14] Mysticism is to dynamic religion what myth is to static.

Dynamic religion and open morality are plainly modelled on Christianity: but it is significant that Bergson describes them in terms of his evolutionary metaphysics. Open morality evolves from closed, and both are essentially in the service of biological necessities: closed morality serves to ensure the survival of human communities, open morality results from reflection on closed morality by an intelligence which is itself seen as a biological endowment. The necessity of this development, and the clear implication that it is a development towards something better, reveal the work of the *élan vital* which is the blindly purposive force which drives evolution. Much the same could be said of static and dynamic religion and of the development from the former to the latter.

Even dynamic religion is a long way from Catholic orthodoxy, of course, but it embodies a general religiosity and an antipathy to mechanistic ways of thinking and the intellectualism without 'a fringe of intuition' which inspires them, which make it easier to see why Bergson ended his life at least on the threshold of the Roman Catholic Church. It also makes it easier to see why Bergson had such an appeal for many French intellectuals who inclined towards Catholicism but found difficulties in reconciling a purely orthodox traditional Catholic faith with modern developments such as the theory of evolution. Jacques Maritain himself was, for a time, one of these, although he was eventually to reject Bergson in favour of a Thomism which was more obviously acceptable to the Church. Others who continued to feel the influence of Bergson, while remaining practising Catholics, included Charles Péguy, Emmanuel Mounier, and Gabriel Marcel, as we shall see in the next chapter.

The reverberations of Bergson's ideas in the thought of these men were not, however, simply a result of their connection with religion. His preoccupation with time, with memory, with life as opposed to mechanism, with our essential embodiment, with the reality of individual difference, was to be taken up, not just by them, but by many other French writers and thinkers in this century. In philosophy, apart from the authors already mentioned, his ideas influenced Merleau-Ponty and Sartre, even if only in these writers' reactions against them. In literature, perhaps their greatest resonance was in Proust's *À la recherche du temps perdu*, which starts from the image of memory being provoked by a present sensory experience and unfolds the idea of understanding a life by retracing its past.[15] But the themes of memory and individuality continue to recur in French culture, for example in Alain Resnais's films *Hiroshima mon amour* and *L'Année dernière à Marienbad*. It cannot be often that the preoccupations of a single philosopher have coincided in such an all-pervasive way with those of a whole culture.

—

CHAPTER THREE

Two Religious Philosophers

1. Introduction

Culturally, France is undeniably a Catholic country. This is true despite the fact that an increasing proportion of the population is indifferent or even hostile to religion, or that, of those who are religious in some way, significant minorities are non-Catholic—Protestant, or Jewish or Muslim. In the realm of ideas, however, for obvious historical reasons, Catholicism remains, as it has always been, a dominant force, and for much of this century, it was, along with Marxism, one of the two major options for French intellectuals. The reasons for this are not purely historical: Roman Catholic theology has always been expressed in an intellectualistic and theoretical form, in which the attempt has been made to codify all aspects of human life, from the details of social organization and personal morality to the most abstract speculations of metaphysics, in a single, at least apparently coherent, system. In this respect, it competes in the same market as Marxism, and it is precisely in this market that French intellectuals like to shop.

Many French Catholic intellectuals, of course, find enough intellectual satisfaction simply in carrying on the central philosophical traditions of the Church, above all those of Thomism. This is true of perhaps the greatest French Catholic thinker of this century, Jacques Maritain. Just because of this, however, as was said in Chapter 1, a discussion of Maritain's thought would not be appropriate in a book such as this, dedicated to what is specifically *French* about French twentieth-century philosophy. It would not be true to say that there were no distinctively French elements in Maritain's Thomism, but in general his work is a very distinguished contribution to an international philosophical movement. For this reason, I have preferred to take as examples of recent French Catholic thought two other philosophers who were more distinctively French, in the tradition deriving from Bergson—Emmanuel Mounier and Gabriel Marcel.

2. Emmanuel Mounier

Emmanuel Mounier was born in Grenoble in 1905, of relatively humble and devoutly Catholic parents. He studied philosophy at Grenoble from 1924 to 1927, where his teacher, Jacques Chevalier, was a devoted follower of Bergson, who sought to combine Bergsonism with Catholic orthodoxy. After being successful in the *agrégation*, the qualifying examination for becoming a teacher, in Paris in 1928, Mounier contemplated an academic career, and taught philosophy in secondary schools during 1931–2. During this time, he was also working on a study of the thought of Charles Péguy, already mentioned in the previous chapter as a Catholic disciple of Bergson: this was published as *La Pensée de Charles Péguy* in Paris in 1931.

Mounier always had an overriding concern for social issues, a desire to apply his Catholicism to the overwhelming social problems created by capitalism and liberal individualism, without falling into the opposite trap of Communist totalitarianism. These had also been the concerns of Péguy, and, together with a group of friends of similar inclination, Mounier decided in 1932 to set up the review *Esprit* to propagate this approach to social and religious questions. The review was to be both very influential and the object of bitter criticism, on the one hand from those more conformist Catholics who felt that it came close to abandoning Catholicism for Marxism and on the other from many Communists who saw it as a ruse by the bourgeoisie to seduce the workers.

Mounier taught at the French *lycée* in Brussels from 1933 to 1939, while continuing to edit *Esprit* and to play an active part in the political life of France and Europe in those critical years. At times in the 1930s he was perhaps a little too inclined to give a benevolent interpretation of the more communitarian aspects of Fascist and Nazi thought and practice, but such naïvety was excusable when so little was known of the dark underside of

Nazi Germany, and it would never be true to describe Mounier as a Fascist. In 1939, he was called up to serve in the French Army, from which he was demobilized after the fall of France in 1940. He then went to live in the unoccupied zone of France governed by the Pétainist puppet regime in Vichy. For a time, he cherished somewhat naïve hopes that the Pétainist new national order might be the vehicle for creating the kind of simple, traditional, Catholic, and communitarian society which he himself had been advocating, and gave broad support in *Esprit* to the Vichy government.

He was, however, soon to be disillusioned, when that same government banned *Esprit* for publishing what it regarded as a subversive article, and imprisoned Mounier himself for subversion in 1942. He was eventually acquitted after a few months in prison, but this experience showed him the hopelessness of pinning his faith on the 'national revolution'. He spent the rest of the war quietly with his family, in rather poor health, in Montélimar. At the end of the war, he returned to Paris and was active in writing books and articles, and in reviving *Esprit*, which he continued to edit until his death in 1950.

3. Personalism and Individualism

The principal focus of Mounier's interests, as was said earlier, was on practical and concrete social action. He felt many aspects of modern society to be destructive of human values—its egoistic individualism, both as expressed economically in the competitive market system and as embodied in the spiritual élitism and contempt for ordinary people of many modern intellectuals. But he was equally opposed to the totalitarian denial of the value of the individual which had arisen as a reaction to the problems created by this competitive individualism. The true worth of the individual, he felt, could be expressed only when that individual was part of a community, but a genuinely worthwhile community could be created only by recognizing the worth of its individual members.

Being a French intellectual, Mounier sought to support these social values with a general philosophical theory—which is why he is of interest from our present point of view. The philosophy which he developed belongs in the tradition of 'personalism', though Mounier's version has a number of distinctive characteristics, and he is probably the best-known of personalist philosophers. In his main post-war philosophical work, simply called *Personalism*,[1] Mounier describes personalism as 'a philosophy but not a system' (p. xv). It cannot be a system, he says, because its central claim is that there exist free and creative persons, and so 'it introduces into the heart of its constructions a principle of unpredictability which excludes any desire for a definitive system' (p. xvi).

At the heart of personalism, and clearly showing the influence of Bergson, is a resistance to the excessively abstract ways of thinking about human beings promoted ultimately by Cartesian rationalism and the central place which that gave, in its account of the nature of reality, to mathematical physics. Mind–body dualism is an essential feature of that account: the object of physical enquiry is a material universe which is entirely devoid of any 'mental' characteristics—of purpose, meaning, or value— and in which individuality can be defined only in terms of location in space and time, that is, of the possession of a particular quantitative extension. If there is to be any place at all for 'mind' in such a universe, it must be as something which is entirely divorced from any necessary connection with any material object, even a human body.

Such a dualism, however, fails to correspond with a realistic assessment of what human beings are. What we are is both bodies and spirits, and our existence as spirits is inseparable from our existence as bodies. My body is not an object distinct from me, but makes it possible for me to exist as a person. To exist as a person in the full sense is not just to be a disembodied intellect (which after all would have nothing particularly individual about it), but to have needs, wishes, desires, emotions, all of which depend on being embodied; and to be recognizable as a person by other persons, which again requires embodiment. Hence any proposal for human welfare cannot neglect the needs of the body, or the needs of relations with others. Our material existence, moreover, like all material existence, is 'irreducible and autonomous': it is just *there*, not something which is either created by our thought or which can be willed away by taking thought, creating a permanent obstacle to any attempt by human beings to live a purely 'spiritual' life.

At the same time, we become persons in the full sense only by transcending our physical nature: to be a person is to be *both* a physical *and* a spiritual being. The physical universe, including our own bodies, by its very nature tends towards the impersonal: it creates, as was just said, a permanent constraint on our necessary striving to become fully personal. Thus, in order to become persons, we have to subdue physical nature to our human purposes and values, and the universe is personalized to the extent that we are able to do that. But the whole history of the universe, Mounier says, can be seen as preparing for this creation, by human beings, of a personal universe out of that 'natural history' from which it never entirely escapes. (We can clearly see here the influence of Bergson's doctrine of creative evolution, given a slant which makes it somewhat closer to Catholic orthodoxy.)

To become a 'person' in this sense, however, is different from becoming an 'individual' in the sense espoused by modern liberalism. The fundamental nature of the person, for Mounier, lies in *communication* with other persons, whereas liberal individualism sees human beings as essentially *isolated* from each other. The person, on Mounier's view, grows as a person only by 'making himself *available* (Gabriel Marcel) and thereby more transparent both to himself and to others'.[2] (The explicit reference here is to Marcel's doctrine of 'availability', which will be discussed in more detail later in the chapter.) The maintenance of a *society* is thus at the heart of our lives as persons. Each of us has to accept the sheer 'otherness' of other persons, and that requires seeing each other as inexhaustible and indefinable. Real love, Mounier claims, is gratitude to the other person simply for being an *other*, and this is the basis for the 'existential *cogito*' which Mounier wants to substitute for Descartes's more intellectualistic one: instead of 'I *think*, therefore I am', the foundation of personalism is 'I *love*, therefore I am, therefore being is and life has value . . . '

Values exist only in so far as they are affirmed in human action in community: 'The person could therefore be defined as a movement towards a transpersonal condition which reveals itself in the experience of community and of the attainment of values at the same time.'[3]

The definition of persons as 'a movement towards values' is implicitly a rejection of the concept of human beings as a mere species of physical objects, subject to causal laws. This in turn implies that persons are thought of as essentially free and creative, and we have already seen that Mounier puts this freedom and creativity at the centre of personalism. The account of persons as necessarily embodied, however, entails that this freedom cannot be absolute. Our freedom to act must be constrained by the limitations which inevitably follow from embodiment—a restriction to a particular place and time, with all that that involves, a limit to our physical capacities for action, perhaps even the inescapability of certain desires connected with our bodily needs. We have to win our freedom by straining against these limitations: but being constituted as we are we cannot avoid striving to increase our freedom in this way, and thus to become more fully personal.

Thus, personalism is a doctrine which both declares that personal existence is the highest form of existence possible and claims that the whole universe is striving towards transforming itself into a personal universe. This movement of universal history, however, can only really take off when human beings come on the scene—beings who are essentially embodied but who also by nature have the capacity to transcend their physical condition in the direction of a more personal existence. Human beings can become personal only in communication with others of their own kind, that is, in society. So the creation of a personal universe is also the creation of a society in which persons can exist as persons, in communication with each other, with their bodily needs provided for and with activities in which they can realize themselves in free creativity.

Mounier, as the story of his life makes clear, was primarily interested in changing society rather than metaphysics. The philosophical works seem to have been important to him only as providing a background or a framework for his analysis of what was wrong with contemporary society, which he attributed, not ultimately to its economic system or its social structure, but to the legacy of Cartesian metaphysics. But this means that his metaphysical views were adopted largely because they were required by his social concerns rather than as a result of independent philosophical argument, of which there are few obvious examples in his writings. From a philosophical perspective, this is a serious weakness in his doctrines. Nevertheless, he deserves a place, if only a relatively minor one, in a book such as this, in part because of his general influence, through *Esprit* and its associated activities, on French cultural and political life before and immediately after the Second World War; and in part because the philosophical account of human beings and their place in the scheme of things which he gave has sufficient genuine interest as part of the anti-Cartesian movement of modern French philosophy to make its lack of argumentative support excusable.

4. Gabriel Marcel

There is a great deal in common between Mounier's ideas and those of Gabriel Marcel, though Marcel developed his thought independently and, since he had more of a primary interest in philosophy than Mounier, in a much more genuinely 'philosophical' style. Although he became a friend and associate of Mounier's during the early days of *Esprit*, Marcel was in fact a good deal older than he was, having been born in Paris in 1888. His mother died when he was only 3, but his father subsequently married Gabriel's aunt, to whom Gabriel was much attached. His father was in the French diplomatic service and in 1898 was posted as French minister to Stockholm, so that Gabriel spent some of his childhood in Sweden. He returned to Paris for schooling, during which he discovered philosophy, which he came to love. In 1906 he enrolled as a student of philosophy at the Sorbonne. The teacher who made the strongest impression on him as a student was Henri Bergson, but in this early period Marcel's main philosophical interests lay elsewhere, in the works of the Anglo-American Idealist philosophers such as Bradley and Royce. He studied for the *agrégation*, and when he had passed it became a teacher of philosophy at the Lycée de Vendôme in Paris (1911).

During the First World War, Marcel worked for the Red Cross, dealing with cases of missing persons—an experience which had a profound emotional effect on him. He had a profound love of music, and after the war married a musician, Jacqueline Boegner. He resumed work as a teacher of philosophy at a *lycée* in Sens, outside Paris, during which time he also wrote plays, and after three years asked for indefinite leave of absence from his teaching duties so that he could move back to Paris and seek to have his plays professionally produced. To support himself and his wife, he took a job as a publisher's reader.

In 1927, he published his first important philosophical work, the *Journal métaphysique* (*Metaphysical Journal*). This early work showed him moving towards Catholicism, though he had been brought up in an atmosphere of liberal agnosticism and he felt some attraction towards Protestantism. In 1929, prompted by the novelist François Mauriac, he was received into the Catholic Church (his wife remained a Protestant for many years, though she eventually joined him in his Catholicism). It is somehow typical of Marcel, and significant for understanding his thought, that he always had some misgivings about Catholicism and never subscribed to the Thomist philosophy.

During the 1930s, he wrote more plays, several philosophical essays, and book reviews, and in 1935 published one of his major works, *Être et avoir* (*Being and Having*),[4] which took the *Metaphysical Journal* up to October 1933 and added four essays, on the phenomenology of having, on the irreligion of today, on faith, and on the nature of piety. During the Second World War, which he spent for the most part in the country at Corrèze, he maintained a neutral stance, supporting neither Vichy nor the Resistance. In 1944, he published another of his major works, *Homo Viator*;[5] and in 1949–50 he was invited to give the Gifford Lectures at Aberdeen, the text of which was later published as *The Mystery of Being*.[6] In the following years he published many books and articles on philosophy, social issues, literature and music, and in 1961–2 gave the William James Lectures at Harvard on 'The Existential Background to Human Dignity'.[7] He died in 1973.

5. Problems and Mysteries

Marcel is often described as a 'Christian existentialist', but he was not fond of the label 'existentialist', mainly because of its associations with the atheistic thought of Sartre. Although Marcel was willing to admit that Sartre's philosophy was 'powerful and important', he classified it among 'the "techniques of vilification", by which I mean techniques which result, deliberately or not, in the systematic vilification of man'.[8] His own preferred label was 'Socratic philosophy' or 'concrete philosophy'. After his youthful flirtation with Idealism, to which he was attracted by the suggestion that ultimate reality was to be found only by working through appearances, but which repelled him by its systematic character, he rejected the idea of philosophy as a system. Calling his own philosophy 'Socratic' or 'concrete' was a way of emphasizing that, for him, to philosophize was not to construct an all-embracing system of final truth, but to engage in a 'search', an 'investigation', or a 'quest.'[9] He compared philosophical activity to making tracks across unexplored territory: the philosopher's virtue was a dedication to finding one's way, not logical rigour.

What was wrong with systematic philosophy was above all that it saw philosophy as modelled on science, as a kind of 'super-science', pursuing the same kinds of truths but at an even more general level. Marcel was not hostile to science, as long as it remained in what he regarded as its proper province, but he did want to draw a sharp distinction between the tasks and methods of science and philosophy. Science, like common sense, seeks to solve what Marcel calls *problems*: that is, to answer questions which can be clearly defined, whose answers can therefore be clearly defined, and which do not involve the questioner's own personal feelings or values in any way. Science, by its very nature, must be *impersonal*: scientific questions are questions which can be asked by anyone whatsoever, no matter what their individual situation, and the answers to which can therefore be accepted as correct by anyone whatsoever who is qualified to understand them. Scientific investigation can therefore yield results, which can be considered separately from the investigation which gave rise to them—for instance, they can be incorporated in a general theory of the domain in question, applied technologically, and so on.

Philosophical or metaphysical questions are not, according to Marcel, like that. They do not arise from an impersonal problem, but arise *for particular individuals* from the unease which they feel in their personal situation. 'A situation', Marcel says,[10] 'is something in which I find myself involved.' That is, one is involved, not simply in being located at a particular time and place, but in the sense that one's own responses to the situation are part of the situation itself—'the situation is not something which presses on the self merely from the outside, but something which colours its interior states . . . ' (ibid.). Philosophy does not have 'problems' in the sense in which science has them, but 'mysteries'. 'A mystery is a problem which encroaches upon its own data, invading them, as it were, and thereby transcending itself as a problem.'[11] Mysteries in this sense present themselves to us when we become aware of a problem as a problem *for us as individuals*: that is, any problem whatsoever can in principle become a mystery, provided it is perceived as having some personal significance. The distinction is thus not one between the nature of the difficulties in each case, but between the ways in which we see and handle them.

Corresponding to the difference between problems and mysteries is a distinction between the kinds of reflection required for thinking about them. *Primary* reflection is the kind of practical, instrumental, rather impersonal, thought required for dealing with problems of the kind which could arise for anyone—the practical problems of everyday life, such as finding a lost watch, or the kinds of theoretical problems which arise in science, such as that of investigating the particular parts of the brain involved in different mental functions. *Secondary* reflection, on the other hand, is the sort of personal, involved thought required for dealing with mysteries, in Marcel's sense. Primary reflection works analytically, dividing up problems into their component parts in order to clarify them: because the terms of the problem can thus be made clear, the aim is to achieve a *solution*. Secondary reflection, by contrast, requires immersion in the problem as a whole: the problem, in a sense, *is* oneself, one cannot be detached from it and so cannot in principle see clearly what the issue is. Solutions are not to be expected: but what one can hope for is to recover one's own sense of inner unity which had been disturbed by the problem. 'Roughly, we can say that where primary reflection tends to dissolve the unity of experience which is first put before it, the function of secondary reflection is essentially recuperative; it reconquers that unity.'[12]

Traditional philosophy, in Marcel's view, had confused itself with science, and had seen itself as dealing with problems rather than mysteries. Thus, Descartes (and later philosophers) have approached our relation to our own bodies as a problem—the 'mind–body problem', as if it were an impersonal, purely intellectual, problem like the problem in neurophysiology of the relation between the brain and the rest of the nervous system. If the question is seen in this light, then our own bodies come to be seen as just one kind of object, a lump of matter which might just as well 'belong' to anyone else. If, instead of engaging in this kind of primary reflection, however, we see philosophy as a species of secondary reflection, then the issue here ceases to be impersonal, and becomes the question of how each of us individually relates to his or her own body. The body is no longer considered as just a lump of matter like any other (which may be a perfectly useful way of seeing it for the purposes of science or medicine), but is seen as being for each of us our way of being in the world, as giving us a location in the world, an identity and a means of acting on the world. Then I and my body cease to be treated as distinct entities: I am essentially incarnate, and my body is not a mere 'instrument' which I use.

My relation to my own body, on this view, is not detached and intellectual, it is one of feeling or sensation, of direct participation in the world and so in the society of other people. To exist as a human being is essentially to be embodied, to interact with other things in the world and to have at least the possibility of communing with other human beings. (This notion of the self as essentially embodied is, as has been said already, one of the key themes of twentieth-century French philosophy, and was to be taken up and developed, most notably, by Maurice Merleau-Ponty, as will be shown in a later chapter.)

6. The Mystery of Being

The ultimate object of the philosophical quest, the supreme 'mystery', was for Marcel the 'mystery of Being'. Philosophers trained in the analytic tradition often find it hard to take seriously discussions of Being (despite the long and respectable history of such discussions in Western philosophy since Plato). It seems to them that to talk of 'Being as such' is simply to be misled by the grammatical possibility of forming a noun from the verb 'to be'. Whether a philosopher who makes use of that possibility is thereby being *misled*, however, surely begs the question of whether there is some serious philosophical point to doing so. Alternatively, or in addition, philosophers may object on Wittgensteinian grounds that we cannot simply assume that all those things which are called by the same name must have something in common. To the extent that Wittgenstein's contention was that we cannot *assume* this to be the case, he was of course completely correct: his own example of 'games' is a clear instance where this is not so. But to go further and claim that we can assume that this is *never* the case seems completely unjustified. Whether or not all things to which the same term is applied have some common characteristic is a question which has to be decided case by case.

Those philosophers who discuss Being do so because they consider that all particular 'beings', that is, all those things which 'are' in some sense, must have something in common, Being or reality, and that therefore the nature of that common Being must be worthy of philosophical investigation. Whether they are right in that must be judged by the fruitfulness of their discussions of the question. Certainly, it is true that, if there is a meaningful question of Being at all, then it must, in Marcel's terms, be a 'mystery', transcending the limits of a merely technical 'problem'. For we, as beings ourselves, are necessarily one of the data of the problem, and cannot therefore regard it as something detached from ourselves which we can consider in an impersonal and unemotional way. We are not, furthermore, if the view of the self as essentially embodied is correct, merely detached intellects on the Cartesian model: our own mode of being is that of *participation* in the world—our being is involved in Being as a whole. The quest for Being is thus a quest for a sense of our own existence and identity as consisting in that involvement.

To see Being as a mystery in this sense is thus to see Being as a personal *need* (Marcel speaks of *'l'exigence ontologique'*—the 'ontological requirement', where 'ontology' refers to the study of Being as such). In order to be fully ourselves, as human beings, we need to have a sense of our participation in Being as a whole—of ourselves as not merely atomistic or isolated individuals, but as participants in nature and in a human community. Conversely, it is the loss of such a sense of Being in modern society which Marcel sees as responsible for the fragmentation of that society and the increasingly functional conception of human beings. The dominance in modern society of science and technology, with their inherent requirement to deal with manageable and purely technical 'problems', means that the issues of human existence also tend to be reduced to such problems, to be handled in a detached and instrumental fashion. Human beings are then identified purely in terms of their function in society—the consumer, the producer, the citizen, or in terms of their job—the railwayman, the professor, the clerk, etc. They are in effect seen simply as machines, or as cogs in the wider machine which is society or the economy as a whole. Like machines, they are overhauled to make them function effectively for as long as possible: death is simply the cessation of the machine's functions.

The quest for Being is therefore, for Marcel, not simply an interesting intellectual exercise, but the basis for a wide-ranging critique of a society in which science and technology have strayed beyond their proper boundaries and have begun to infect the ways in which we think about human beings and human existence. We discover what Being is in proportion as we become clearer about the connection between our own identity as individuals and our participation in Being as a whole, and so in proportion as we change the value which we put on ourselves and on others. For to see our own identity as necessarily bound up with our participation in a wider Being is to see that it cannot be imposed on us from the outside (since there *is* no outside). Our identity cannot therefore be that of a mere functionary, which is imposed from the outside. Again, to the extent that our identity is in part constituted by our citizenship or by the job we do, it will only be in the sense that we ourselves identify ourselves with that citizenship or that occupation.

7. Myself and Others

Paradoxically, therefore, the mystery of Being as a whole cannot be separated from the mystery of one's own identity and relation to others. The primary way in which we establish ourselves as an 'I', Marcel argues, is in the act of drawing attention to ourselves. He gives the example of a child who brings his mother flowers and cries 'Look, I picked these!'[13] The very fact that this is the primary use of 'I' indicates, for Marcel, that we cannot draw a sharp distinction between myself and my body, or even between myself and other people: there is a sense in which I am my body, and in which I exist only in relation to others. The conclusion which Marcel thinks we should draw is that our own identity as individuals entails a commitment to something which transcends our separate individual existence, so that our lives can be seen as the realization of a project which goes beyond ourselves. We are, as Marcel puts it, as it were witnesses giving testimony about our lives to a supreme court which he calls 'transcendence'.

To become a person in the full sense is thus to accept one's involvement with the world and with others and to take responsibility for one's own life. The essential characteristic of a person is what Marcel calls '*disponibilité*' (the English version translates this as 'availability'). What he means by this is: 'an aptitude to give oneself to anything which offers, and to bind oneself by the gift. Again, it means to transform circumstances into opportunities, we might even say favours, thus participating in the shaping of our own destiny and marking it with our seal.'[14]

'Availability' thus seems to involve a combination of openness to what existence offers and willingness to use those offers in order to realize one's own projects. Both of these seem to be inherent in the idea of oneself as something to be created, not in a void or from nothing but in response to the demands of a wider Being in which one is simply one participant. The self created in that way is not a mere isolated ego, but a *person* involved in relations with others and therefore fully accepting their reality as other selves. Hence, becoming a person for Marcel cannot be separated from developing the capacity for *love* (or 'charity' in the Christian sense), where love means no more than the acceptance of the full reality of other human beings, rather than regarding them simply as machines to be manipulated for one's own ends.

Creating oneself as a person in this sense is a never-ending process. We are defined by our aspiration towards something which we never in fact achieve. The consequence of this is to give a particular significance to the concept of hope. When we are thinking scientifically or technologically, 'hope' must rest on the certainty of the predictions we can make about the looked-for benefit: it is, in Marcel's words, 'frantic' because it is beset by anxiety that our predictions may be wrong and our expectations frustrated. It is, he says, really only a 'pseudo-hope'. Genuine hope comes rather from the confidence that we are a part of Being and that therefore Being is not ultimately hostile to what is most central to us. This is not mere passive quietism, indeed it is a liberation to active life. To be at the mercy of one's own technology is to be deprived of control over one's own life: genuine hope frees us from that dependency and so enables us to have a truly human existence. Death itself ceases to be merely the ultimate breakdown of the human machine and becomes instead that which sets a boundary to our projects and so delimits our lives as *our* lives.

The 'ontological mystery', therefore, which is the heart of philosophy on Marcel's conception, is the mystery of the ultimate unity of Being, including our own being as individuals. In secondary reflection on our own existence and identity as individuals and our relation to the world of other human beings and of things, we become aware of that ultimate unity and of our own necessary relation to what transcends ourselves. We then cease to see ourselves as separate 'subjects', detached from the problems which confront us externally and which must be solved by the application of analytic reasoning of the kind found in science: we come to see ourselves rather as elements in that unity, linked to each other and to reality as a whole.

8. A Critique of Marcel

The religious undertones of this way of thinking are obvious, and it is easy to see how thinking along these lines could have led Marcel from his agnostic background into some form of religion (though not necessarily Christian, and certainly not necessarily Catholic—his reasons for choosing Catholicism seem to have been largely pragmatic and strangely abstract and unemotional). At the same time, the more sceptical reader may well feel that perhaps an underlying personal need to identify with some established form of religion led Marcel to overlook the width of some of the logical gaps across which he leapt so boldly, and to express what are often in themselves illuminating ideas in rather misleading terminology.

One can accept, for instance, that it is a legitimate philosophical concern to investigate Being as such, what is common to all particular beings, without sharing Marcel's conception of Being as some sort of meaningful unity in which all particular beings, including ourselves, are related in some sense other than that they are all beings. One can agree with Marcel's insight that a person's identity is defined at least as much by what he or she aspires to be as by what he or she is or has been, and that in that sense someone's identity is never complete, without glossing that to mean that each of us is responsible for his or her life before some tribunal of 'transcendence'. Equally, that insight does not seem to provide any grounds for thinking that a 'hope' which is not based on any rational predictions about the future may nevertheless be justified (however much one's capacity for action may be increased if one is buoyed up by such groundless hope).

Again, it is certainly possible to accept that in modern society there is a persistent tendency to regard human beings as isolated individuals rather than sharing in a community and to reduce individuals to their social roles or functions. But that does not commit one either to going along with Marcel's rhetorically exaggerated claims of the extent of these tendencies or to sharing his attribution of them to the analytic modes of thought associated with science and technology (rather than, say, to deep-seated social and economic changes). Still less should it lead one to the implied conclusion that the way to correct these tendencies is to recreate a sense of community based not on rational dialogue between individuals but on some kind of unanalysable mystical bond.

In all these cases, there is detectable an urge to leap straight from insights and positions which are true and even valuable in themselves to conclusions which are certainly not entailed by these insights. And in every case, the motive for that urge seems to be a desire for a mode of expression which will support the religious position which Marcel wished to arrive at. His acceptance of that position is worthy of respect: he was a man, plainly, of deep spirituality and religious feeling. What is not so respectable, however, is the unseemly haste with which he arrived at it. His own distinction between the primary reflection or analytic thinking on which science is based and an allegedly different, though ill-defined, secondary reflection which is appropriate to philosophy is in part what makes this possible. That philosophical problems may involve the thinker personally in a way that scientific problems do not, clearly does not entail that there is not an important place for analytic reasoning in philosophical thought. Without the disciplines of such analytic reasoning, it becomes only too easy to present as the conclusions of deep reflection what is really only the expression of the thinker's personal needs.

There is plainly much in common between Mounier and Marcel, both in their analysis and critique of modern technological society and in the type of philosophical thought which underpins them. That Marcel's thought is elaborated in a much more recognizably 'philosophical' style is equally plain, even from the relatively brief summaries of the two men's views which have been given in this chapter: he goes into the philosophical issues in greater depth and shows greater reflective power. He is much less inclined than Mounier to make unsupported assertions, even if the force of his arguments is sometimes weakened, as has just been said, by his own obvious desire to make his conclusions fit his own preconceived opinions. The wider cultural influence of both men can be seen mainly in their effects on French religion and politics, both in their journalism and philosophical writings and, in Marcel's case, in his plays (though these do not seem to be much performed now). They opened up to intellectual Catholics in France a possible way of thinking about their faith which was less rigid than Thomism and more in tune with the modern world, and an option for Catholic social action which could be located to the left of the centre of the political spectrum, and which thus helped to transform the French political scene as a whole, especially after the Second World War.

—

CHAPTER FOUR

Phenomenology and Existentialism: 1. Sartre

1. Sartre and Existentialism

Of all the philosophies which have been advocated in France in the twentieth century, existentialism is probably the one which is most familiar to the average educated person in the English-speaking world. And of all the French existentialists, it is almost certain that Jean-Paul Sartre is the best-known (apart, perhaps, from Albert Camus, who was not, in the technical sense, a philosopher at all). This is partly, of course, because Sartre is known for his novels and plays, and for his political stances, at least as much as for his works of philosophy in the narrow sense. His novels and plays, however, are intensely philosophical, just as his philosophical writing is clearly the work of someone who is also a novelist and playwright. Existentialism is a kind of philosophy which is naturally expressed in literary form, since it gives philosophical significance to the concrete and particular: in that sense, it could be seen as the culmination of that specifically French philosophical tradition spoken of in Chapter 1, which relates philosophy to literature, politics, and the human studies rather than to the generalities and abstractions of mathematics and the physical sciences.

Sartre is currently out of fashion in France (though he may be due for a revival) and so tends to be devalued, both as a writer and as a philosopher. But he is a philosopher of considerable originality and insight. Although there are other distinguished philosophers who are labelled 'existentialist', such as Kierkegaard, Nietzsche, or Jaspers, it was really Sartre who created existentialism as we know it, by taking Husserlian phenomenology and filtering it through the French philosophical tradition and his own personal preoccupations to produce something essentially new—a technically developed and articulated philosophy which incorporated many of the insights of such unsystematic thinkers as Kierkegaard and Nietzsche into something which could be described as a system. In order to see how Sartre arrived at this position, we need first to say something about his life and intellectual development.

Jean-Paul Sartre was born in Paris on 21 June 1905, the son of a French naval officer who died when Jean-Paul was a little over a year old. Through his mother, Jean-Paul was related to the same family to which Albert Schweitzer belonged, and it was his maternal grandfather, Charles Schweitzer, who took over responsibility for his upbringing after his father's death. Charles had been trained for the Protestant ministry, but having been expelled from the seminary because of his relationship with a woman, he became instead a teacher of German. In his autobiographical essay *Les Mots* (*The Words*), published in 1963, Sartre recalled how his grandfather had transferred his religious attitudes from 'the Divine' to 'Culture': he was the author of a number of books about music and literature, as well as of a text-book on German. In this household, Jean-Paul was adored and indulged, and was blissfully happy: in *Les Mots* he looked back on his childhood as 'Paradise'. But he was also a somewhat solitary child, living very much in his own imagination and early acquiring his enduring love of words.

At the age of 19 he entered the École Normale Supérieure to study philosophy, and it was there that he met his lifelong companion Simone de Beauvoir and became friendly with Raymond Aron, later to become one of France's leading liberal political thinkers (and to be estranged from Sartre). What thrilled Sartre most in his philosophical studies was the work of Bergson, especially his *Time and Free Will* (*Essai sur les données immédiates de la conscience*)—once again we see the truth of the point made earlier about the towering influence of Bergson on the whole of twentieth-century French philosophy. After failing to gain the *agrégation* at the first attempt in 1928, he came out at the head of the list of candidates in the following year, and then became a teacher of philosophy, first at various provincial *lycées* (including one in Le Havre, which later became the model for the town of 'Bouville', or 'Mudtown', in Sartre's first published novel *Nausea*) and eventually at the Lycée Condorcet in Paris.

Sartre began to develop his characteristic modes of thinking from a very early stage: the idea of the 'contingency' of existence—the denial that anything which exists, including human beings, has any reason for existing—which is so central to his later philosophy was already a preoccupation when he was still a student and a young teacher. It was during the early 1930s, however, that he made the discovery which was to set him definitively on the road to his mature philosophy. In the second volume of her autobiography, *The Prime of Life*, Simone de Beauvoir describes the incident which led to this discovery: Raymond Aron had been spending a year at the French Institute in Berlin and there had become acquainted with Edmund Husserl's 'phenomenology'. During an evening together at the Bec de Gaz in the Rue Montparnasse, Aron told his friends Sartre and de Beauvoir about this exciting development in German philosophy, using the speciality of the house, an apricot cocktail, to illustrate it. 'You see, my dear fellow, if you are a phenomenologist, you can talk about this cocktail and make philosophy out of it!' Sartre, de Beauvoir tells us, 'turned pale with emotion at this', and immediately went out and bought Lévinas's book on Husserl which he leafed through as they walked along.[1] The result was that he was inspired to spend a year in Berlin himself (1933/4) studying Husserl.

2. Existential Phenomenology

Why did Husserl's phenomenology excite Sartre so much? De Beauvoir suggests that it was because it appeared to offer a chance for philosophy to find a concrete basis for itself in actual lived experience. 'Phenomenology' is so called because it is the study (*logos*) of 'phenomena', a term which literally means 'appearances': Husserl himself says that 'The word "phenomenon" is ambiguous in virtue of the essential correlation between *appearance and that which appears*.'[2] 'Phenomena', in other words, are both the objects of our consciousness and the way in which they 'appear' or are 'given' to consciousness.

The phenomenologist, however, in studying phenomena, did not do so in the same way as the empirical scientist, who assumes, as we all do in the common-sense attitude, that there is a world 'behind' phenomena whose character explains what is presented to our consciousness. 'I am to treat all sciences only as phenomena, hence not as systems of valid truths, not as premises, not even as hypotheses for me to reach truth with.'[3] In the 'phenomenological reduction', all such assumptions about a 'transcendent reality' are to be set aside, so that we can concentrate on seeking 'the meaning of the absolutely given'.[4] Phenomenology is thus far from being an explanatory science, and still further from being any kind of grand metaphysical theory: it aims at achieving clarity about the meaning of the concrete contents of our consciousness—in Husserl's slogan, it seeks to return 'to the things themselves'.

According to the principle of the 'intentionality of consciousness' which Husserl accepted, all consciousness is *intentional*: that is, all consciousness is consciousness *of something* (its 'intentional object'). The principle of the intentionality of consciousness is central to the existential phenomenology which Sartre developed out of his study of, and reflections upon, Husserl in the early 1930s, although Sartre put his own interpretation on it, which was significantly different from Husserl's. In his essay 'Intentionality: A Fundamental Idea of Husserl's Phenomenology,'[5] Sartre says:

Husserl never tired of affirming that things cannot be dissolved in consciousness. You see this tree here, let us say. But you see it in the very place it is in: at the edge of the road, in the midst of the dust, alone and twisted in the heat, eighty kilometres from the Mediterranean coast. It could not enter into your consciousness, for it is not of the same nature as it.[6]

The sense of things as existing *outside* consciousness and incapable of being absorbed into it (which Sartre also finds in Bergson) is at the heart of Sartre's existentialism. It made it possible, as he goes on to say in the same essay, to be 'delivered from Proust', that is, to be delivered from 'the fondlings of our inner selves'. 'It is not in some kind of retreat', he concludes, 'that we shall discover ourselves: it is in the street, in the midst of the crowd, a thing amongst things, a man amongst men.'[7]

Although Sartre presents himself here as expounding Husserl, however, the realism of Sartre's interpretation of intentionality differs markedly from Husserl's own view. According to Husserl, the phenomenologist's task is to investigate 'phenomena', which, as we have seen, are both the objects of consciousness and the way in which these objects are presented to consciousness. Phenomenology therefore requires a 'transcendental reduction', in which we mentally separate off, or 'put in brackets', any assumptions about what is external to consciousness in order to concentrate on consciousness itself: we have, in effect, to set aside the question of whether the objects we seem to experience really exist, so that we can concentrate only on our own experience and discover its essential structures. The 'intentional objects' of consciousness cannot be things outside consciousness, but must be identified with the contents of consciousness itself. This leads Sartre to say: 'Due to this fact he [Husserl] never passed beyond the pure description of the appearance as such; he has shut himself up inside the *cogito* and deserves—in spite of his denial—to be called a phenomenalist rather than a phenomenologist. His phenomenalism at every moment borders on Kantian idealism.'[8]

A further important difference between Sartre and Husserl follows from this. If, as Husserl says, everything is thus within consciousness, then the consciousness in question cannot be *my* consciousness or *yours*: for 'I' and 'you' are particular human beings, and so are themselves phenomena, items given to consciousness. The consciousness to which phenomena are presented must therefore be an *impersonal* consciousness, or, as Husserl calls it following Kant, a 'transcendental ego'. Sartre rejected this notion very early in his career as a phenomenologist, while he was still studying in Berlin. During his time there, he wrote a short study called 'La Transcendance de l'ego' (to be published a few years afterwards, in the journal *Recherches philosophiques*, 6 (1936/7) ,[9] in which he argued that there could not be such a transcendental ego. If, following Sartre's interpretation of intentionality, everything is 'outside' consciousness, then that includes even the self: the ego or self is not, as it were, an inhabitant of consciousness, because nothing is. We discover ourselves, not by looking within, but by looking outside consciousness: 'in the end', he says in the 'Intentionality' essay cited earlier, 'everything is outside, everything, even including ourselves: outside, in the world, among others'.[10]

What I call 'myself' is an object in the world, like other objects: it consists, not in any alleged 'inner life', but in the actions which I perform in the world, in my dealings with other selves. It might also be said that my 'self' is an object which I must *construct* by my actions in the world. Heidegger, whose work Sartre began to discover in his year in Berlin, but which he only read in any depth during his period in a German prisoner-of-war camp after the French collapse in 1940, provided Sartre with a phrase to describe this sense of what a human being was: our being, said Heidegger, is 'being-in-the-world'. It follows, Sartre argued, that what is 'inside' consciousness is literally *nothing*. A consciousness or self is not, as Descartes had said, a 'mental substance'—that would imply that a self was *something*, that it had some positive properties. But a consciousness has 'being' only in the paradoxical sense that it does not: it exists only as a kind of opening on to things which do have being—the objects of which we are conscious.

3. Being and Nothingness

This is the key to Sartre's thinking in his 'existentialist' period, which received its fullest expression in his major work of that period, *Being and Nothingness*,[11] published in Paris during the Occupation, in 1943. It was this work which above all made Sartre's name as a philosopher, which indeed made him the dominant French thinker, and 'existentialism' (often only partly understood) the prevailing intellectual fashion in Paris after the Liberation. In it Sartre divides reality into two categories—the objects of consciousness (which have 'Being') and consciousnesses themselves (which are 'Nothingnesses'). The subtitle of the work describes it as 'An Essay in Phenomenological Ontology': it is ontology in that it is an account of the fundamental structure of reality as a whole, and phenomenological in that the division it proposes is based on the fundamental structure of our experience of reality.

To say that the human mode of existence is 'Being-in-the-world' implies that neither consciousness nor its objects can exist without each other: consciousness, as we have seen, exists on Sartre's interpretation of intentionality only by being conscious *of* objects, and objects are necessarily objects *for* some consciousness or other. The two sorts of reality are both utterly distinct from each other and necessarily related to each other. And both, as *existents*, or beings which exist, are different from those abstract realities, such as mathematical entities (numbers, triangles, and so on), which do not strictly exist at all, but have being only as concepts or essences. The world of abstractions, just because it is abstract, is a world of necessity: numbers, circles, or triangles have their properties necessarily, because they are just concepts, and their properties follow logically from the definition of their concepts. We, however, and the objects we experience in the messy world of existence, are merely *contingent*: what we are, and what they are, has no necessity about it and might equally well have been otherwise. It is not a necessary truth that there should ever have existed someone with the properties which I happen to have. The room I am working in might have been differently decorated, in a different building, in a different town—indeed, I might not have been working on this book now at all, in this room or any other. The world of existence is, Sartre argues, *absurd* or meaningless: there is no logically compelling reason why it must be the way it is rather than any other way.

In *Being and Nothingness*, Sartre normally represents his basic distinction between consciousness and its objects in a more positive way. Conscious beings such as ourselves, he says, have 'being-*for*-ourselves'; the objects of our consciousness (*as* objects) have 'being-*in*-themselves'. We have being 'for' ourselves to the extent that what we are is inseparable from what we think of ourselves as being. Sartre would, of course, accept that many things about us are true of us quite independently of anything we may think: this is what he calls our 'facticity', the element in our situation which we cannot change. I, for example, am male, white, middle-aged, a University graduate whose mother-tongue is English. All these things are true about me whatever I may think about them: they are determined, not by my self-conception, but by my biology or my past history. Nevertheless, these 'facts' about me give only an outline of who I am: who I am in a less schematic sense is determined by how I *think* about my situation, including how I think about my facticity. How do I *think* about my maleness, about my whiteness, about my age or my Englishness? There is clearly an enormous variety of ways in which I can think about these things, and each of these ways will entail that I become, in an important sense, someone different.

The objects that I am aware of, on the other hand, have a character which is shaped entirely by things outside themselves. Natural objects are what they are in virtue of the workings of natural laws: the boulder on the hillside is where it is, and is shaped as it is, because of the forces which have brought it there and have acted on it. Artefacts are what they are in virtue of human action, under the constraints imposed by natural laws. The chair I am sitting on, for instance, was made what it is by the human being or human beings who produced it: they gave it its shape, its size, its colour, in accordance with their thoughts about what a chair should be in order to fulfil its function in human life. The situation of the boulder or the chair is entirely constituted by these facts: they are what they are, as Sartre puts it. That is what is meant by having 'being-in-itself'.

Other people have an ambiguous position in all this. As far as I am concerned, they are also objects of my consciousness, and to that extent they have being 'in themselves' (as do I for them). But I become aware, Sartre says, when some other conscious being *looks at me*, that they are not quite like other objects of my consciousness, since they have being *for themselves*. What they are for me (as what I am for them) can perhaps be pinned down in a definition, an 'essence', as in the case of an object such as the boulder or my chair. But unlike such objects, there is something else to be considered, namely, what they are for themselves, how they themselves see what they are. There is thus a third kind of being, or perhaps it is simply an aspect of the being of consciousness resulting from the fact that there is more than one consciousness in the world, which Sartre calls 'being-for-others'. Sartre's account of this 'being-for-others', as we shall see later, is incredibly bleak: but before that account can be fully intelligible something further must be said about being-for-one-self.

4. The Ambiguity of Human Existence

If a consciousness is a 'nothingness', and there is therefore no inner life, then it clearly follows that all of a human being's life is on the outside. It consists only in what we *do* (in a broad sense of 'doing' which includes 'saying', 'expressing' thoughts and emotions and so on). In all these cases, the outward action does not 'express' something inner in the sense of being the visible sign of something which is not visible: there *is* nothing inner, if Sartre is right—what you see is what you get. And for the same reason, we cannot say that what we do or say, or even the emotions we express, are caused by something inner (which may itself be caused in turn, by biology, by social conditioning, by past history, divine predestination, or whatever). There is no inner 'essence' or 'nature', however constituted, which *makes* us act the way we do: we are not made to act at all, we just act without determinant causes, in total freedom. To put it another way, our consciousness, our self, as a 'nothingness' or pure negation, is removed from the deterministic causal system to which all 'beings' belong, and so acts in absolute freedom.

To say that our freedom is absolute is not, for Sartre, to deny that we always act in a situation, defined in part by our facticity. Unless we were in a situation, we could not act freely at all, since we should have no specifiable alternatives between which to choose. As a citizen of a relatively wealthy European country, for instance, I am faced with choices which simply could not confront someone living in an impoverished country in Africa (just as conversely he or she faces choices which could not face me). But if I did not live *anywhere* in particular, if I had no particular level of wealth, if I were not of some particular gender, if I had no particular cultural background, if I had no past life—in short, if I were not in *some* specifiable situation or other, then I could have no choices at all, since there would be nothing to define any alternatives between which I could choose. This is not incompatible, however, with a belief that my freedom is absolute, in the sense that no situation could in principle remove all alternatives. At the very least, as Sartre would put it, I have the choice between 'living my situation' in one way and in another: I could 'live' my citizenship in a rich country by wallowing in selfish indulgence, or by finding ways to utilize that wealth to relieve suffering in poorer countries, or by taking political action to change the world economic system, or—and so on.

To say that my freedom is absolute is thus to say that there is nothing outside myself which can make me act in one way rather than another (and nothing inside myself either, of course, since there is nothing inside myself anyway). Since I am only what I do, and since I choose without external or internal determination to act as I do, I literally create myself from nothing. Freedom is inescapable for conscious beings, since having consciousness makes it impossible to be determined by anything outside oneself. But this inescapability of freedom is not to be seen as a joyful liberation so much as a source of anguish: we are, as Sartre puts it, '*condemned* to be free'. It would be much more comfortable for us if we were determined, since then the external determinants of our actions could always be made the scapegoats or the excuses if we acted wrongly or stupidly or pettily. We love to make excuses for ourselves: if we act greedily or lecherously, we say 'It's only human nature,' or 'I just couldn't help myself, that's just the kind of person I am.' Accepting that freedom is inescapable and total removes all possibility of such excuses: no human or individual nature makes me act greedily— if I do so, it is because I choose to do so, and the responsibility is therefore all mine.

The human situation is thus for Sartre fundamentally ambiguous: it is necessarily determinate in character, made so by certain objective and contingent facts which we cannot change, but at the same time its factitious character does not and cannot take away our power to choose not only what we shall do but even what we shall be. This ambiguity of existence is inescapable. To live is to choose, and to choose, in a given situation, is to choose oneself as a person of a certain kind, by choosing to act in one way rather than another. Thus we cannot avoid always acting as if we were giving ourselves an 'essence', that is, making ourselves into an object. But this object which we seek to make of ourselves is an object which is at the same time a subject: it has an essence which makes it what it is, and which is the ground of its values, but at the same time it *chooses* to act as it does.

This is the nature ascribed to God in traditional theology: God is conceived of as a being who both has an essence (he is a necessary being, one whose existence follows from his essence) and yet is entirely free and creative. In making ourselves by our choices, we are in effect aspiring to be God, to create our own worlds and our own values, but at the same time to ground those values, to make them objectively justifiable. But the concept of a being who both has an essence and is absolutely free is self-contradictory, logically impossible. So Sartre concludes both that the concept of God is a logical impossibility, that God necessarily cannot exist, and that we, in seeking to become such a self-contradictory being, are necessarily condemned to an impossible task. 'Everything happens as if the world, man, and man-in-the-world succeeded in realizing only a missing God.'[12]

5. Bad Faith

There is thus an inevitable tension between our freedom and our facticity, and the human response to this tension is to fall into what Sartre calls '*mauvaise foi*' or 'bad faith'. Bad faith refers to the cultivated illusion by which we seek to conceal from ourselves the uncomfortable ambiguity of our position—that we must and can choose, and yet that the only real choices we can make are those presented to us by the situation in which we happen to find ourselves. The best way to explain what Sartre means by this central concept in his thought is probably to examine the examples he gives to illustrate it in *Being and Nothingness* (pt. 1, ch. 2, s. 2).[13]

He there considers three main examples: the woman who goes out with a particular man for the first time, the waiter in the café, and the homosexual. The woman in the first example knows that her partner wants to seduce her. She, however, wants neither to be regarded as a mere sexual object, nor equally to be regarded with 'a respect which would be only respect'.[14] She attempts to solve this problem by denying to herself the sexual character of the man's behaviour and remarks and by distinguishing herself from her own body: her 'hand rests inert between the warm hands of her companion—neither consenting nor resisting—a thing'.[15] She is in bad faith.

What does her bad faith consist in? Clearly, above all, in her attempt to refuse to make a decision which she nevertheless cannot avoid making. She must either accept the man's advances or reject them: this is the choice which actually confronts her in the situation which she presently finds herself in. She tries to avoid the choice by divorcing herself from her situation: by, on the one hand, giving a non-sexual interpretation to the man's behaviour,[16] in defiance of what she herself *knows* to be the case; and, on the other, treating her body as in the situation in just the way that an object is. In both respects, she is seeking to conceal from herself the ambiguity of her existence as a human being: she is not simply an object, and so must make choices, but at the same time that choice must be a response to the given facts of her situation (in this case, the man's real intentions with regard to her).

The waiter in the café tries to refuse to make choices by adopting a different strategy. The waiter, as Sartre describes him, is a little *too* perfect in his 'waiterly' movements, as if he were playing the role of a waiter in a play or as if he were some kind of robot-waiter, programmed to perform a waiter's actions flawlessly. This man, Sartre says, plainly wants to *be* a waiter, in the way that an inkwell *is* an inkwell. That is, he wants to identify so completely with his role as a waiter that he can forget that awkward capacity which he has to be conscious of what he is doing and so to make choices about doing it. The inkwell lacks that consciousness and that choice, and so cannot decide whether or not to be an inkwell, or what should happen to it in the course of its existence. To use the Sartrean phrase cited earlier, the inkwell 'is what it is'. The waiter, however, as a conscious being, 'is what he is not'—by which paradoxical phrase Sartre means that he 'is' a waiter, not in virtue of some pre-existing definition of what he is, but only because he himself chooses so to define himself and thus always transcends any such definitions. His bad faith consists, not in denying the given facts of his situation as the woman in the first example did, but precisely in affirming them as if they were *more* than mere facts, as if they constituted an 'essence' of what he is which could determine what he did and so remove from him the need to choose.

The third example, that of the homosexual, is the most complex of all, involving as it does two people who are in bad faith in contrasting ways. The two people in the example are the homosexual himself and his friend who is 'his most severe critic' and a 'champion of sincerity'. The homosexual in the example falls into bad faith precisely by *denying* that he is really a homosexual at all: 'the mistakes are all in the past; they are explained by a certain conception of the beautiful which women can not satisfy; we should see in them the results of a restless search, rather than the manifestation of a deeply rooted tendency, etc. etc.'.[17] He is right to deny that he is a homosexual in the sense 'in which this table *is not* an inkwell',[18] but he is in bad faith in denying any connection with his own past, with his facticity. His critical friend urges him to 'come out' as a homosexual—to acknowledge that that is what he is. The friend is in bad faith in the sense that he regards him as 'a homosexual' in the same sense in which an inkwell is an inkwell, as if he was defined once and for all by what he had been in the past. So the homosexual himself attempts to avoid the need to make the actual concrete choices which he must make by denying the facts of the situation which set those choices before him; while his friend affirms the facts of the situation, but seeks, like the waiter, to make those facts into an 'essence', something which his friend *is* and which determines his actions in the way that the movements of an unconscious thing are determined.

Sartre's discussion of these three examples show that his concept of bad faith is considerably more complex and subtle than the account given of it in most commentators. To be in bad faith is not simply to regard oneself as a 'thing', a 'being-in-itself' (though that is one form which it may take). It is rather to refuse to come to terms with the ambiguity of the human situation, which is the condition for the exercise of human freedom. To be free agents, for Sartre, is at once to acknowledge the constraints of our situation—of our place in space and time, of our physical characteristics, of our individual past, and of the point in history in which we exist—and to transcend these constraints in our actions. Unless the constraints are acknowledged, we cannot transcend them; but if we do not transcend them, we become entangled in them in the same way that inanimate objects are entangled in *their* situations. For the homosexual in Sartre's example (to take that case as an illustration of the general point) to deny or to misrepresent the facts of his own past is to refuse to face up to the real choices which he has to make, and so is to refuse to take responsibility for his own future actions every bit as much as if he treats himself as defined once and for all by that past. To avoid bad faith, to be 'authentic', as Sartre would express it, would be to accept that he is (i.e. has been) a homosexual who must therefore now choose whether to continue in the same style of life or not.

6. Values and Choice

If human beings cannot (without self-deception) escape the need to choose how to act, then it follows that they must also choose their values. For to choose to act in one way rather than another is necessarily to regard that way of acting as preferable to the other, that is, as a value. To choose to be a teacher rather than a civil servant, for example, is implicitly to affirm that teaching is a better occupation than being a civil servant, at least as far as one is concerned. One form which bad faith takes is therefore to deceive oneself about the necessity to choose one's own values: to pretend that one's values are not chosen at all, but are somehow imposed upon one by someone or something outside oneself, whether by God, or by an impersonal reason, or by the nature of things, or by human nature. In his popular lecture of 1946, *L'Existentialisme est un humanisme*,[19] Sartre recounts an episode from his own experience to illustrate this point. During the Occupation, a student had come to Sartre to seek advice about a personal dilemma: should he try to escape to England to join the Free French forces in the hope of eventually assisting in the liberation of his country, or should he stay and look after his mother, who was emotionally and practically dependent on him? The young man's father had betrayed his mother and was something of a collaborator: his brother had been killed by the Germans, and the young man longed to avenge his death. Both these considerations gave him a strong motive for wishing to free his country from German occupation, but the emotional devastation which they had caused his mother also gave him a good reason for staying with her.

Sartre points out that no doctrine of objective values, whether religious or philosophical, could help the young man to make his decision. The Christian doctrine that we should love our neighbour, for instance, could give no guidance about whether his fellow-countrymen were, or were not, more deserving of his love than his mother; the Kantian principle that we should treat others never simply as means but only as ends could not help him to decide whether he should treat his mother as a means to his fellow-countrymen's ends or vice versa; and utilitarian considerations of social benefit left it open whether benefiting his compatriots was better or worse than benefiting his mother. In the end, he could not escape the necessity to make his own choice: even if Sartre or anyone else gave him advice, he would still need to choose whether to act on that advice or not.

To make a choice is to regard one set of considerations as having more weight than another—in this case, to regard love of country as having more weight than love of one's mother, or vice versa. But the example seems to show that there can be no rational or objective grounds for attributing greater weight to one consideration than to any other. Even if we could show that, for example, it followed from Kantian principles that the young man should prefer, say, love of his mother to love of his country, we should still have to ask why we should prefer to act on Kantian principles than any other. And, if Sartre is right, it seems that there is no answer that we can give to that question.

Values do not exist independently of our consciousness of them: 'human reality is that by which value arrives in the world'.[20]

This denial of the objective reality of values has led many commentators to conclude that Sartre could not in principle make good his promise, at the very end of *Being and Nothingness*, to 'devote . . . a future work' to questions which 'can find their reply only on the ethical plane'.[21] The very nature of Sartrean existentialism, they argue, makes values purely arbitrary and subjective, and so rules out anything which could be described as a philosophical ethics, in which the rational basis of certain values could be demonstrated. Sartre himself, however, clearly attached great importance all his life to certain ethical values. His obvious contempt for the bad faith of the bourgeoisie of Bouville, in *Nausea*; his opposition to French colonialism, and to the war in Algeria in particular; his participation with Bertrand Russell and others in the International Tribunal to condemn alleged war-crimes in Vietnam (to name but a few examples)—all reveal his passionate attachment to certain moral values. Philosophically, too, there are hints in the works published during his lifetime of at least the outlines of a moral theory; and it is evident from his posthumously published *Notebooks for an Ethics*[22] and from numerous still unpublished notebooks that the question of ethics continued to preoccupy him. (It has to be said, however, that the later attempts to develop an ethics show Sartre moving away from the existentialism of *Being and Nothingness* towards the kind of *rapprochement* with Marxism found in his later works, in which the social and historical context of human action comes to the fore.)

Is there any way in which something describable as an ethics is possible within the framework of the ontology of *Being and Nothingness*? That is, is it possible to show that values are in some sense subjective without drawing the conclusion that they are therefore entirely arbitrary? One attempt by Sartre to show this can be found in *Existentialism and Humanism*. Sartre begins by claiming that 'the subjectivity which we thus postulate as the standard of truth is no narrowly individual subjectivism'.[23] Descartes was wrong, he argues, to think that it was only *one's own* existence which one discovers in the *cogito* ('I think, therefore I am'): in becoming aware of one's own existence, one necessarily becomes aware also of the existence of others, and of others furthermore as the conditions of one's own existence:

Under these conditions, the intimate discovery of myself is at the same time the revelation of the other as a freedom which confronts mine, and which cannot think or will without doing so either for or against me. Thus, at once, we find ourselves in a world which is, let us say, that of 'inter-subjectivity'. It is in this world that man has to decide what he is and what others are.[24]

Because I have to make my decisions in this 'inter-subjective' context, Sartre argues, I have to recognize that the fundamental conditions which define *my* situation are also those which define the situation of *any* human individual. Every human purpose is thus, he goes on, intelligible to me, whether or not I happen to share it: all human purposes have in this way an intrinsic universality about them. So, he concludes, in choosing for myself I am also implicitly choosing universally: in realizing myself, I am also realizing 'a type of humanity'. If I choose to get married, for instance, I am implicitly recommending monogamous marriage as a value for all human beings. Thus, my choice, though purely subjective, has 'nothing to do with caprice': in short, it is not entirely arbitrary, but represents my serious reflection on what is important in human life. We have to invent our values, but this invention is more like an artistic creation, which adds something permanent to human life, than a mere individual *jeu d'esprit*.

What are we to make of this argument? It rests on the claim that to discover myself is to reveal the other as a freedom with which I must reckon. No support for this claim is offered here by Sartre, and the account of human relations which is given in *Being and Nothingness,* as we shall see in the next section, is inconsistent with any view that we must *respect* the freedom of others. Nevertheless, similar claims have been argued for by other philosophers,[25] so that perhaps we can accept it as a premiss here for the sake of argument. Even if we do so, however, what follows from it? Certainly, that in making my decisions I have to take account of the likely reactions of others to them. But does it follow, as Sartre thinks, that the values which inform my choices must implicitly be recommended as universal values for all humanity? Does this follow even when we add to the argument the further, and in itself persuasive, premiss that at any rate some of the most fundamental purposes which one human being can have must be intelligible to any human being because of the common character of the human condition? It is, to say the least, not obvious that it does.

If we take the concrete case of getting married, this may make the point clearer. In choosing to marry someone, my existing in an inter-subjective world implies that I must recognize that my actions will have an effect on others besides myself—on my spouse, obviously, on her and my relations and friends, on our potential children, even on the national economy and on society at large. To the extent that I care about the others in question, these considerations may have an effect on the decision I take, and my reflection on them may alter my conception of marriage and its value. The ultimate human needs which underlie a decision to get married are common to all human beings (though they may not, in all societies, result in the kind of monogamous marriage with which we are familiar): in this sense, they will be ultimately intelligible to other human beings, no matter what their culture. But it does not seem in the least to follow that, in deciding to get married, I am in the end doing anything more than satisfying my own individual needs and desires. I can regard monogamous heterosexual marriage as something good for me without thereby regarding it as a good independent of my choice of it. This particular argument, therefore, does not seem to justify the claim that values can be subjective without being arbitrary: if there is no reason prior to my choice why, say, monogamy is a good thing, then there can be nothing about the circumstances of my choice itself which confers on it such a universal value.

In *Being and Nothingness* itself, there are hints of a different sort of argument for the non-arbitrariness of values. There Sartre says: 'Value in its original upsurge is not *posited* by the for-itself; it is consubstantial with it—to such a degree that there is no consciousness which is not haunted by *its* value and that human reality in the broad sense includes both the for-itself and value.'[26] Here the implication is that values, though they 'arrive in the world' through 'human-reality', do not do so because they are *chosen* or *created* by human beings. Rather, they are a necessary part of our being-in-the-world. Conscious human beings exist in the world as a 'lack', as a negation of the situation in which they find themselves. The lack consists in an 'internal relation' between the negation and what it negates: that is, a relation which constitutes both the related terms in their being. Thus consciousness is constituted in its being by what it is not.

What we lack, and so what we are, is precisely *value*: 'Value is the self in so far as the self haunts the heart of the for-itself as that for which the for-itself *is*.'[27] We might translate this by saying that, for conscious human beings, what we are is defined, not by our factual state, but what we 'are-to-be', that is, by what values our lives are directed towards. But these values, Sartre appears to be saying here, are inseparable from what our factual situation happens to be, since they express our negation or transcendence of that particular factual situation. The self which we 'have to be' is defined by what is lacking in what we factually are, and vice versa. (As, in Sartre's own analogy, what the crescent moon lacks, and so what defines it as a *crescent moon*, is what it would take to make it a full moon.) So, for example, an oppressed worker, in becoming conscious of himself as exploited, is negating what he actually is and conceiving the value of overcoming that form of exploitation which he actually endures.

This view of values would still make them 'subjective', in the sense of being relative to the situation of the particular individual concerned. But they would only avoid being 'arbitrary' if they were not ultimately *chosen* by that individual: if they were intrinsic to his or her situation. If the individual could freely choose how to regard his or her situation, we should be back with the same problem as before. Although making values intrinsic to our situation might solve the problem of making values a mere matter of 'caprice', however—of people saying to the existentialists, 'Then it does not matter what you do'[28]—it would do so only at a serious cost. To deny that we choose our own values, after all, is to contradict the basic doctrine of existentialism that, because we are ultimately nothingnesses, because we have no being-in-ourselves, what our situation is can only be what we freely choose it to be. The exploited worker's situation cannot, for the existentialist, *determine* that he regard it as one of oppression, to be overcome by revolution: how he regards it must be his free choice.

7. Existentialist Individualism

Thus, Sartre does not seem to be able finally to reconcile, within the framework of *Being and Nothingness*, his belief that values must be a matter of individual choice with his desire to deny that they are matters of mere caprice. It is open to him to say that our values are what we ourselves regard as ultimately most serious in our lives, but that does not remove their arbitrariness, since there is nothing, other than our own individual choice, on which this ultimate seriousness can be grounded. The problem arises for him because of something very fundamental about his existentialist philosophy, namely, its complete individualism. It has already been mentioned that Sartre's distinction between being-for-itself and being-in-itself makes it difficult for him to fit in the being of other people. I certainly have being for myself, in that I am directly conscious of my own existence; inanimate objects equally clearly do not have consciousness of their own existence, and so they plainly have only being in themselves. But other people have an ambivalent status: I do not have direct consciousness of their existence, and so it ought to follow that for me they are in the same position as inanimate objects, mere beings-in-themselves, things in a world which centres on my consciousness.

The complication, however, is that I enter into certain sorts of relationship with others which depend on attributing self-consciousness to them, even though their self-consciousness is not accessible to me. Sartre's favourite example of such a relationship (significantly) is the Look. When someone else *looks at* me, especially when I am doing something shameful, then I become conscious of them as more than a mere object in my world, as a centre of a world of their own in which *I* am a mere object amongst others: the shame which I feel is an expression of this consciousness of another conscious being who is reducing me to a mere object in his or her world. It is significant that Sartre chooses this sort of example, because it reveals that he conceives of relations between human beings as necessarily hostile: indeed, he explicitly says that 'The essence of the relations between consciousnesses . . . is conflict.'[29]

The same picture of human relations can be found in his wartime play *Huis Clos* (variously translated as *No Exit*, *In Camera*, and *Vicious Circle*), in which three characters are condemned to spend eternity together in a Hell which is depicted as a small, rather elegant room, without doors and windows. The three people—Joseph Garcin, a journalist who has been executed for political activities, Incz Serrano, a Lesbian who has committed suicide, and Estelle Rigault, a rather conventional young married woman who has died of pneumonia—suffer the torments, not of fire and brimstone, but of existing only as objects in the mind of others. They are reduced to 'being-for-others', of which, as just said, conflict is the essence, and no longer have that 'being-for-themselves' which makes it possible freely to determine one's own situation, one's own world. Each of the three has guilty secrets, and these become manifest under the constant scrutiny of the others. It is this which provokes one of Sartre's best-known lines, when Garcin exclaims, 'Hell is other people.'

But why is this the 'essence' of relations between conscious beings: why is no other kind of relation possible? The answer is that if I can relate to the other person only as an object in my world, and can see his consciousness of me only as an awareness of me as an object in his world, then I can retain my own subjectivity, my freedom and power to control my own existence, only in so far as I can resist being reduced to such an object. But I can do that only to the extent that I can deny the other's subjectivity, his or her status as a conscious being, that is, to the extent that I can reduce the other to a mere object in *my* world. My attempt to do that, however, will similarly be resisted by the other. This is why the only possible relations between consciousnesses, if Sartre is right, will take the form of battles to the death in which each consciousness strives to assert its mastery over the other in order to reduce it to a mere object.

In this situation, there can be no room for what Heidegger called *Mitsein*, a sense of community, of being 'we' rather than a collection of unrelated 'I's. In sexual relations, which Sartre discusses in a brilliant, if depressing and thoroughly sexist, section of *Being and Nothingness*,[30] there is no room for anything that could be called 'love', only for an attempt to possess the other's consciousness by possessing his or her body and so reducing her/him to an object. In sex as in other human relations, moreover, the battle between consciousnesses is doomed to futility, since neither side can ultimately succeed in reducing a subject to an object. This, as said earlier, is a peculiarly bleak picture of human relations, and one which it is surprising to find coming from someone as eminently sociable as Sartre. But it is important to see that Sartre was compelled to see human relations in that way because it follows directly from his initial principles.

Sartre's conception of consciousness necessarily implies both that consciousnesses have no individuality and that two consciousnesses cannot share anything with each other, that is, cannot genuinely communicate. For if a consciousness is a 'nothingness'—if it has no determinate content of its own—then there is literally nothing to distinguish one consciousness from another. A consciousness cannot be individuated by being connected to a particular body, or by existing in a particular historical situation, since consciousness exists only by *negating* its body or its historical situation. This consciousness cannot be identified with 'me', since the ego is, as we have seen, just another object in the world. Indeed, paradoxically, there is nothing to make it *this* consciousness rather than *that*. Thus, Sartre ends by implying the very doctrine which he rejects in *The Transcendence of the Ego*. Consciousness exists only as an indeterminate 'subjectivity-in-general', and everything outside it, including other subjectivities, including even my own self as an individual person, becomes from its point of view an object.

By a peculiar twist, therefore, the very impersonality of consciousness on the Sartrean view, its very lack of individuality,

makes it impossible to build any bridges between one consciousness and another. For individuals can share things with each
other only if they have something to share: if there is something
peculiar to each which they can then communicate to the other.
On the other hand, if there is nothing peculiar to each, then that
very indistinguishability makes it impossible for them to come
together. If they are solitary individuals in the sense that they
cannot communicate with each other, then plainly they cannot
form shared values as a result of such communication: they can
have only the values which they choose for themselves. There
can be no question of the kind of *universal* values of which Sartre
speaks in *Existentialism and Humanism*, since that would require
appeal to some sort of common humanity, necessarily shared by
all human beings as such. But there is not and cannot be any
such sharing (except perhaps as a purely contingent fact about a
particular group of human beings).

To end up in this position was clearly not what Sartre
intended. Indeed, in many ways his final position contradicts his
starting-point. As stated earlier, Sartre took over from Heidegger the concept that the human mode of being was 'being-in-
the-world'.[31] That view followed from the intentionality of
consciousness, and indeed was a necessary part of the emphasis
on concreteness and individuality which is central to existentialism. By emphasizing the conception of consciousness as a
'nothingness', however, he was, despite what he says in the
passage quoted earlier, breaking off the connection between
consciousness and its situation, and so between one consciousness and another. For a 'nothingness' can have no internal
connection with any particular situation. But, surely, to be
consciousness *of* a particular situation is to have a certain
determinate character. If my situation, for instance, is that of a
male human being, then there is a sense in which my consciousness is male: it is not a total nothingness, with no specific
characteristics. And the fact that my consciousness has specific
characteristics is what makes it possible for me to communicate
with other consciousnesses: there is something about me to be
communicated. Furthermore, it is only if my own being is
inseparably linked with my situation in this way that we can

make the connection between freedom and facticity which is, as we have seen, the basis of that ambiguity of human existence from which we seek to escape in 'bad faith'.

There is another sense in which Sartre's conclusion conflicts with his starting-point. The driving force behind his thinking was essentially moral, or even political. As he became more politically involved, first through the Resistance and later through his attempts to participate in far-left politics after the war, so his opposition to the bourgeoisie and its ways developed from the traditional largely aesthetic distaste of French intellectuals for the class from which most of them came into a political hostility to the economic and social system which they dominated. We can see this development reflected also in his novels of the 1930s and 1940s. In *La Nausée* (*Nausea*) (1938), the central character, Antoine Roquentin, is represented as living a life of almost total social isolation, and this fact about him is surely not unconnected with his fundamentally 'existentialist' view of the world. His own existence, for instance, appears to him in existentialist fashion to be essentially meaningless: his alienation from others makes it impossible for him to find a meaning in any shared human project which, as such, would give his individual life some sense outside any attempt on his part to *impose* one upon it. Similarly, he sees the attempts of others to find an objective meaning for their lives as, not simply mistaken, but the result of seeking to read their own petty estimates of their importance into the very structure of the universe. Even his own keeping of a diary, and so seeking to impose a narrative structure on the random sequence of real events, is exposed as an example of what Sartre was to call, in *Being and Nothingness*, 'bad faith'.

By the time he came to write his novel-sequence, *Les Chemins de la liberté* (*The Roads to Freedom*: *The Age of Reason* (1945), *The Reprieve* (1947), and *Iron in the Soul* (1949)), Sartre, while still retaining the central existentialist concepts, had already begun to place his accounts of individual existence in a much more social and historical context. There are still in the later novels examples of bad faith, such as Daniel, the homosexual who allows himself to be fixed in his character by the imaginary gaze of God and wallows in the guilt which this induces, or

Brunet, the Communist who sinks his individuality in a total unquestioning commitment to the Party. Or again, the existentialist preoccupation with human freedom remains the primary theme of all three novels (as shown in the overall title of the sequence). The principal character, Mathieu Delarue, a philosophy teacher (surely modelled on Sartre himself), wrestles throughout the three novels with the need to make choices, which he is unwilling to confront. But all this is now set against a historical background—the period from the summer of 1938, when the prospect of war was only a distant cloud, through the months following the Munich agreement with its illusion of preventing war, to 1940 and the reality of French defeat and occupation. And the characters themselves move from a preoccupation, in the first novel of the sequence, with purely private concerns— personal relationships, intellectual discussions, entertainment, work—to an increasing realization of the need to make choices related to the wider political situation.

This seems to have been the course of Sartre's own development at this period. But such political choices had to provide a basis for collective action, and so to appeal to something more than the tastes of particular individuals. Furthermore, political activity implied the abandonment of individualism and the acceptance of the possibility of real 'togetherness', or *Mitsein*, to use Heidegger's term—a sense of being 'we' rather than simply 'I'. It was this increasing political involvement which led Sartre himself to become dissatisfied with strictly 'existentialist' views of the kind embodied in *Being and Nothingness*, and to look for some kind of fusion between existentialism and Marxism. Further discussion of that development, and of the later period of his life, is, however, appropriately left to a later chapter, in which it can be placed in the context of the wider debate about Marxism in French philosophy.

8. Simone de Beauvoir and Albert Camus

Others besides Sartre shared in this development, including Sartre's lifelong companion Simone de Beauvoir. De Beauvoir was by no means a secondary figure in existentialism: indeed, some have suggested that it was she, rather than Sartre himself, who was ultimately responsible for the ideas for which he is known. Although that claim is scarcely credible, it is undoubtedly true that Sartre's conversations and correspondence with de Beauvoir were a primary influence on his development, and that her independent approach to the issues which concerned them both corrected some of the deficiencies in Sartre's thought. Her emphasis on the need to think of moral choices as always made in concrete situations, for instance, expressed above all in her masterly essay *An Ethics of Ambiguity* (1947), attempted to achieve a genuinely coherent ethics in a way which is not found in those existentialist writings of Sartre which were published in his lifetime (though it has similarities to the thinking in his posthumously published *Notebooks for an Ethics*, mentioned above). This emphasis also enabled her to escape from Sartre's characteristic sexism in dealing with relations between men and women, and so to apply her existentialism in laying the foundations for recent French feminism in her major study, *Le Deuxième Sexe* (Paris: Gallimard, 1949; English translation, *The Second Sex*, New York: Knopf, 1953), which will be more appropriately covered in a later chapter.

Of other characteristic figures of the 'existentialist' period, the most notable is the novelist, playwright, essayist, and journalist Albert Camus (1913–60). As a novelist, Camus had a talent which was probably as great as Sartre's, but he was far from Sartre's equal as a philosopher. Indeed, many would say that he was not a philosopher at all, if that means someone who seeks to go to the heart of the central problems of existence and to find an answer for them by means of rigorous argument. Rather, Camus was someone who could express philosophical ideas in elegant prose or in imaginative fiction. Probably the best of his philosophical essays is his book *Le Mythe de Sisyphe* (Paris: Gallimard, 1942; English translation, *The Myth of Sisyphus*, New York: Knopf, 1955) in which he reflects on the Greek myth about the mortal, Sisyphus, who was condemned by the gods for all eternity to roll a rock up to the top of a slope, only for the rock to roll back again to the bottom, so that the whole process had to be repeated. The myth seems to Camus to be an image for the human situation: we too are involved in meaningless pursuits, and our lives as a whole are simply a collection of such empty routines. Our existence, and that of the universe, have absolutely no objective meaning, but we cannot avoid seeking for such a meaning, this quest for meaning is inevitably frustrated, and it is then that we become aware of the absurdity of existence.

Since we are uncomfortable with absurdity, we may seek to avoid the feeling by imposing an allegedly objective meaning on things, whether in the form of religion, which cultivates the illusion that the universe is the product of a divine plan, or in the form of some secular ideology such as Marxism, which similarly cherishes the fantasy that human history has a direction. Such beliefs are not only 'inauthentic' or illusory, but are morally dangerous, since religious or political fanaticism leads people to believe that they are mere tools in the hands of a higher force, and so to forget all the normal restraints of human decency. To live authentically, for Camus, was rather to accept the absurdity and indifference of the universe, and to affirm all the more strongly the values and pleasures of humanity itself—to rebel in the name of humanity against the objective meaninglessness of existence.

Camus's existentialist humanism was thus more private, more moral, and less politically radical than Sartre's came to be. To Sartre himself, in fact, it seemed that Camus was implicitly siding with the Western side in the Cold War, endorsing the values of capitalism and colonialism: this was indeed the main cause of the rift in their personal relationship in the early 1950s. In many ways, however, Camus remained closer to the original spirit of Sartre's own thought, while Sartre himself had moved on in the ways already outlined to the position to be discussed in Chapter 6. Before coming on to that later position, however, we should first explore, in the next chapter, the views of the other leading exponent of existential phenomenology, Maurice Merleau-Ponty.

CHAPTER FIVE

Phenomenology and Existentialism: 2. Merleau-Ponty

1. Life and Works

The name of Maurice Merleau-Ponty is certainly not as well known outside the world of academic philosophy as that of Sartre, even in France. Although he wrote widely, and often journalistically, on a range of subjects of general interest—the cinema, literature, visual arts, psychology, and above all politics—he did not, like Sartre, produce novels or plays which might have brought his name to the attention of the wider educated public. As a philosopher in the technical sense, however, he is at least as important as Sartre and has probably had a longer-lasting and more substantial influence. In his work, he managed to produce a version of existential phenomenology which avoids most of the problems encountered by Sartre, and which is capable of development into the types of philosophy which became fashionable after his premature death.

Maurice Merleau-Ponty was born in 1908 in Rochefort-sur-Mer, the son of an army officer. His father died when he was still very young, and he, together with his brother and sister, was brought up by his mother: he was later to describe his childhood to Sartre as 'incomparably happy'. He went to school at the Lycée Louis-le-Grand and in 1926 entered the École Normale Supérieure, where he became friendly with Sartre and Simone de Beauvoir. He was still at that time, according to de Beauvoir, a practising Catholic. It was during that time that he first became acquainted with phenomenology, through attending a series of lectures on Husserl, Scheler, and Heidegger given by Georges Gurvitch: in 1929 he heard the lectures given by Husserl himself at the Sorbonne (later to be published as the *Cartesian Meditations*). In 1930, he received his *agrégation* in philosophy, and did his year of compulsory military service. After that, he mostly followed a conventional academic career, apart from a brief period of service as an officer in the French Army in the first year of the Second World War.

He taught first at a *lycée* in Beauvais, after which he did a year's research on perception, funded by the Caisse de la Recherche Scientifique, and then went back to teaching, at the *lycée* in Chartres. In 1935, he returned to the École Normale Supérieure as a junior teacher, staying there until the outbreak of war and his period of military service. During this time, he attended the lectures on Hegel given by Alexandre Kojève in Paris (see the next chapter) and studied the writings of Marx (broadly speaking, he was on the left of French politics, though he never became a Communist). He was also deepening his knowledge and understanding of Husserl's phenomenology, and was intrigued by what he read of Husserl's posthumously published work *The Crisis of European Sciences and Transcendental Phenomenology*. It was this which inspired him, in 1939, to visit the newly opened Husserl Archive at Louvain, where he read extensively in Husserl's unpublished manuscripts—a decisive moment in his own intellectual development.

When war broke out, he spent a year as a second lieutenant in the French Army. After being demobilized he taught again in Paris for the rest of the war, first at the Lycée Carnot and later at the Lycée Condorcet, and played some part in the Resistance. His first major work, *La Structure du comportement*, was published in Paris in 1942 by Presses Universitaires de France (English translation, *The Structure of Behaviour*, published in London by Methuen, 1965). His most important book, *Phénoménologie de la perception* was published in Paris in 1945 (English translation, *Phenomenology of Perception*, published in London by Routledge & Kegan Paul 1962). After the Liberation, Merleau-Ponty took up a post at the University of Lyons (where he became a professor in 1948) and also became a co-founder with Sartre of one of the leading post-war French intellectual periodicals, *Les Temps modernes*, of which he was both political editor and editor-in-chief.

In 1949, he was appointed to the Chair of Child Psychology and Pedagogy at the Sorbonne, and in 1952 to the Chair of

Philosophy at the Collège de France which had previously been occupied by Bergson: in Chapter 1 I quoted part of the tribute to Bergson in Merleau-Ponty's inaugural lecture at the Collège de France, published in 1953 as *Éloge de la philosophie* (English translation, *In Praise of Philosophy*, Evanston, Ill.: Northwestern University Press, 1963)). At this time relations with Sartre had become strained, largely because of disagreements over their attitude to Communism, and the dispute culminated in Merleau-Ponty's resignation as an editor of *Les Temps modernes* in 1952. (There was a reconciliation between the two men in the later 1950s, and Sartre wrote a very generous obituary of Merleau-Ponty when he died). Merleau-Ponty continued to teach at the Collège de France and to write on philosophy and other topics until his untimely death from a stroke at the age of 53 in 1961.

2. Phenomenological Method

The two central features of Merleau-Ponty's thought in all the major works published during his lifetime are his attachment to his interpretation of the phenomenological method and his doctrine of the primacy of perception. He had been impressed by Husserl's phenomenology, as already stated, since his undergraduate studies. Another early influence on his thinking, also associated with phenomenology, was Marcel. One of his first publications was a review of Marcel's *Être et avoir*, which appeared in the Catholic periodical *La Vie intellectuelle* in October 1936, in the course of which he says, 'It becomes more and more apparent that the analyses of the human body and the "thou" were the first attempts at a new general method, the first examples of a new kind of knowledge . . . phenomenology.' Although Marcel greatly influenced Merleau-Ponty's thinking, however, and seems to have been one major source of Merleau-Ponty's emphasis on our essential embodiment, it was Husserl above all who was his philosophical master. He was particularly excited, as already mentioned, by his reading of the writings of Husserl's later period in Louvain in 1939.

In the preface to what is undoubtedly his major work, *Phenomenology of Perception*, he sets out his interpretation of the direction which phenomenology was taking in Husserl's later thought (whether or not he is correct in his reading of Husserl is of secondary importance in comparison with the light which this preface sheds on his own approach to philosophy). According to Merleau-Ponty, Husserl's later philosophy turned aside from the idealistic byways into which phenomenology had been wandering in order to return to the concreteness of its original inspiration. Phenomenology was to be, as originally intended, a purely *descriptive* philosophy, to describe the world as we experienced it rather than to construct elaborate theories in order to explain it. But 'the world as we experience it' was to be seen, not as a world of inner consciousness, as on some interpretations of phenomenology, but as the 'life-world' (*Lebenswelt*), the pre-scientific and pre-philosophical but fully external world in which we act and have our being.

Merleau-Ponty asks what phenomenology is, and gives his own answer:

Phenomenology is . . . a philosophy which puts essences back into existence, and does not expect to arrive at an understanding of man and the world from any starting point other than that of their 'facticity'. It tries to give a direct description of our experience as it is, without taking account of its psychological origin and the causal explanations which the scientist, the historian or the sociologist may be able to provide.[1]

For Merleau-Ponty, therefore, to do philosophy in the phenomenological style, as he sought to do, was to set aside all assumptions derived from science or philosophy and to go back to the roots of all such theorizing in our ordinary experience. He compares the relationship between the theoretical accounts we may give of our experience and the experience itself to that between geography and 'the countryside in which we have learnt beforehand what a forest, a prairie or a river is'.[2] And our experience was of a world which was external to our consciousness of it: like Sartre, he interpreted the principle of the intentionality of consciousness to mean that consciousness is always already 'in the world'—that consciousness could not exist unless there were independent objects to be conscious of.

The world is not an object such that I have in my possession the law of its making; it is the natural setting of, and field for, all my thoughts and all my explicit perceptions. Truth does not 'inhabit' only 'the inner man', or more accurately, there is no inner man, man is in the world, and only in the world does he know himself.[3]

The echoes of Sartre's attack on Proustian 'fondlings of our inner selves' in his 'Intentionality' essay (see above, Ch. 4) are unmistakable: but, as we shall see, Merleau-Ponty was able to do greater justice to the notion that our being is 'in the world' than Sartre was in his existentialist phase.

3. The Primacy of Perception

If phenomenology consists in forgetting the theoretical construc- tions of science and replacing ourselves in the world as we actually experience it, then we can see why a phenomenological philosopher such as Merleau-Ponty should give the primacy to perception in his account of our relation to the world. For it is in perception above all that we are in direct and pre-theoretical contact with the world. A *phenomenology* of perception would thus set aside those scientific theories which seek to give a causal explanation of the way we perceive, and concentrate instead on recapturing what perceptual experience is actually like. Scientific theorizing about perception takes for granted certain presuppositions of the scientific view of the world. It sees the world as made up of discrete objects, related to each other in space and time, of which our own body is one. Perception is then the result of the causal action of one of these objects and its properties on our body, so that it seems to follow that it consists in having equally discrete 'sensations' corresponding to particular properties of the object. This scien- tific view of perception is taken up by those philosophical theories of perception (the various versions of empiricism) which interpret perception as the having of atomistic sensations (or 'sense-data' as they are more often called in Anglo- Saxon philosophy). Each of these sensations is also held to be fully determinate in character, just like the objects which cause them.

Other non-phenomenological philosophers, whom Merleau-Ponty calls 'intellectualists' (Kant would be an example) see that this empiricist account is unsatisfactory, though they share its basic assumption that sensory experience consists of atomistic data. It is unsatisfactory, in their eyes, because it fails to account for the unity of our experience—for instance the fact that we see objects as located in a single space and time. To account for that, the intellectualists argue, we have to bring in the mind or intellect (hence their name), which imposes a unity on the buzzing, blooming confusion which enters our consciousness through our senses.

Phenomenological attention to what perception is actually like, however, should bring to light the underlying assumptions which are shared both by empiricists and intellectualists. For the world as we actually perceive it does not consist of a collection of discrete, atomistic, and fully determinate sense-data, which acquire unity only because it is imposed on them by our own minds. Rather, we perceive the world as already structured and unified: the way in which we perceive a quality, for example, is affected by the sort of background against which we perceive it, or the context in which we perceive it. Perception is in this way 'meaningful' for us—by which Merleau-Ponty does not intend any kind of cosmic significance, only the sense of 'meaning' in which a part of a painting may be said to have a meaning in relation to the whole composition. The meaningfulness of perception and its unity are thus interconnected. And the unity which makes the world which we perceive a *world* is neither imposed on it by our minds nor something which is totally independent of the fact that it is *our* world, the world which we inhabit and perceive.

Another example which Merleau-Ponty uses is that of a three-dimensional object, such as a tomato. What we see of such an object is only one side of it, and only its surface, but the very way in which we see these aspects of the object implies that there is more, that it can be perceived from an infinite variety of possible angles, and that it has an inside as well as an outside. Physical objects, as we actually experience them, and the physical universe as we actually experience it, are *inexhaustible*: our way of experiencing them implies that there is always more to discover, always another way in principle in which they can be perceived. A phenomenology of perception thus reveals ourselves to ourselves as being in the world, looking on it, not from some external point, but from within, with the perspective which we get from the particular point at which we are. From this perspective, we see the world, not in a detached or disinterested way, but as having meaning for us because of its relation to us, and yet at the same time stretching out indefinitely from us and so infinitely transcending any meanings which we may find in it. Thus, Merleau-Ponty seeks both to rehumanize the world, after its reduction by science to an impersonal, objective system, and at the same time to deflate human pretensions by showing human beings as engaged in a never-to-be-completed project of trying to make sense of the world in which they are placed.

This account of perception thus makes it clear in what way our being, as human subjects, is essentially 'being-in-the-world'. We are in the world, not simply in the way in which inanimate objects are—located in space and time and subject to causal action by other objects—but in that there is a two-way relation between us and our situation. Even perception is not the merely passive receptivity described in traditional philosophy and psychology: our perception of objects cannot be separated from our active dealings with those same objects, or in general from our active participation in the world (a view which is not dissimilar to Bergson's—see Ch. 2). We see objects as having a meaning for us because they are related to our actions, and so to our bodies' capacities for action. At the same time, they can have these relations to our actions only because of properties which they have in themselves. The world that we perceive is thus neither purely 'objective'—completely independent in its character of our perception of it—nor purely 'subjective'—given its character by our minds. We who perceive it are, equally, not disembodied pure egos, as Descartes would have it, but consciousnesses which are necessarily involved in the external world, and so essentially embodied. But then our own bodies are not simply objects for us, but part of our very subjectivity, since it is in virtue of our embodiment (in virtue of having sense-organs and the capacity to act on the world) that our consciousness or subjectivity is able to open out on to the world and so to exist as a consciousness.

4. The body as subject

The notion of the 'body-subject', of the body itself as on the subject-side of experience rather than the object-side, is central to Merleau-Ponty's account of the human mode of existence, and is plainly influenced by Marcel's concept of the self as essentially embodied. It follows directly from his analysis of perception and is an aspect of the view which he shares with both Heidegger and Sartre that our being is 'being-in-the-world'. There is, however, an important difference between Merleau-Ponty and Sartre. Sartre, as discussed in the previous chapter, draws the conclusion from the intentionality of consciousness that consciousness has no content, is a 'nothingness', which implies a sharp distinction between consciousness and body, subject and object. Merleau-Ponty, on the other hand, gives a more consistent account of being-in-the-world which always makes it clear that consciousness or subjectivity is both distinct from objects and essentially related to them. As a conscious being, I am both distinguishable from the situation in which I happen to find myself (as is shown by my ability, by taking thought, to change that situation) and yet essentially involved in it, since my consciousness is consciousness *of that situation* rather than any other (so that even to change it requires me first to recognize what my situation is and in what way it needs to be changed).

Treating our body as part of our subjectivity in this way also implies that not all aspects of our subjectivity—not all ways, for instance, in which we may be purposive—need necessarily be fully 'conscious' in the sense of being objects of explicit aware-ness. For our bodies may have a purposive relationship to objects even if we do not cherish any explicit intentions for those objects. Reflex or instinctual actions, for instance, may be purposive but not consciously so: the baby who instinctively seeks out his mother's breast to suckle is acting purposively, but is not explicitly conscious of what his purpose is. The notion of the body-subject thus enabled Merleau-Ponty to resolve a number of difficulties which confronted both Cartesian dualism and traditional behaviourism.

For example, the Freudian concept of the unconscious mind seemed to Sartre, whose views about subjectivity tended, however unhappy he felt about it, towards a version of Cartesian dualism, to be inherently self-contradictory: if mind is by definition conscious, then there logically cannot be an *un*conscious mind. Merleau-Ponty, however, faces no such problem, since he does not equate subjectivity with consciousness. 'Repression', in the Freudian sense, is for him a kind of imprisonment in our own past thoughts and desires, made possible by the fact that we are embodied beings, so that those past thoughts and desires can continue to exist in the purposive behaviour in which our bodies engage without the participation of our conscious minds.[4]

Or again, there is much discussion, both in *The Structure of Behaviour* and in *Phenomenology of Perception*, of a number of puzzling psycho-physiological phenomena, such as the 'phantom limb' and the condition known as 'anosognosia'. The phantom limb phenomenon is the experience of still seeming to have sensation from an amputated limb; anosognosia is denial by a patient that a paralysed limb still belongs to his or her body (in the face of the clear perception that it is still attached). Both phenomena seem very hard to account for either on a Cartesian dualist or on a purely materialist account. Each of these opposing views shares the assumption that we can speak of something's being 'meaningful' only in relation to a *consciousness*. The difference is that the Cartesian, by postulating two substances, a 'mental substance' which is defined in terms of consciousness and a 'material substance' which excludes consciousness, at least makes limited room for us to speak of meaning; whereas the materialist, by retaining only the 'material substance' from Descartes's dualism, has to try to get by without using the notion of meaning at all.

The problem for the materialist is thus to account for the seeming emotional meaning of these phenomena for the individuals concerned—the desire in the one case to restore the bodily integrity which has been destroyed by amputation and in the other to detach oneself from the paralysis and the consequent limitations on one's activity. On the assumption that meaning involves a relation to consciousness, whose existence as such the materialist denies, this essential aspect of these phenomena seems inexplicable. For the Cartesian, according to whom all thought and emotion are necessarily conscious, the problem is rather to explain the apparent unconsciousness of the emotional meaning in these cases. Merleau-Ponty's doctrine of the body-subject, however, allows these phenomena to have an emotional meaning which is nevertheless unconscious.

5. Ambiguity and Historicity

'Being-in-the-world' thus implies that the human situation is essentially *ambiguous*.[5] (We saw in the last chapter how Sartre's failure to give an adequate account of being-in-the-world undermined *his* account of ambiguity.) That is, we are neither totally detached subjects, pure egos outside space, nor are we simply one kind of object among others. Merleau-Ponty himself expresses it almost poetically by saying: 'Man taken as a concrete being is not a psyche joined to an organism, but the movement to and fro of an existence which at one time allows itself to take corporeal form and at others moves towards personal acts.'[6] The historicity of human existence is therefore not something merely contingent and added-on, but something which is necessary to the kinds of beings we are. To be in the world is to be at some particular place and time in the world, to belong to a particular phase in human history, and indeed in the history of a particular society or culture. It is to be unable to step outside history and to see the truth from some kind of transcendent 'God's eye view'.

That might seem to imply a form of historical determinism, according to which our thoughts and actions are the mere outcomes of the particular past which we have inherited. But such a view would deny the ambiguity of human existence: it is no more true to say that the situation in which we find ourselves is imposed on us by a past which is external to us than that we freely create our own situations by our own choice. Rather, there is a complex dialectic. Our present situation is of course partly constituted by past actions—our own and those of others—which, as past, we can no longer do anything about. But it is also constituted by the significance which we see in the products of past action and which we see in the past itself. That significance itself, however, is necessarily seen in terms of a language and concepts which have themselves been inherited from the past, since we have no language or concepts except those which we have inherited. But it is a characteristic of language and concepts that they are operative for us only to the extent that we take them up for ourselves, and this creates the possibility of developing those concepts in new directions. We *transcend* our situation, in that we can always go beyond it: but we do not, in so doing, *negate* it, if that means that where we arrive at has no connection with where we started from.

So we create our own situation, but only subject to constraints imposed by the past. We might recall Marx's famous dictum (from *The Eighteenth Brumaire of Louis Bonaparte*) that 'Men make their own history, but they do not make it just as they please; they do not make it under circumstances chosen by themselves, but under circumstances directly encountered, given and transmitted from the past.'[7] We confront our present situations, whether individual or collective, as beings who already have a certain identity, derived from the past situations we have confronted and the ways in which we have dealt with them. It is this existing identity which supplies us with our way of seeing our present situation, and our reasons for responding to it in one way or another. None of this, however, removes from us the need to make choices or the possibility of making them. Our past does not furnish us with only one way of responding to our present, only with the alternatives between which we have to choose.

6. Identity, Freedom, and the Other

Merleau-Ponty can in this way repudiate determinism as vigorously as Sartre does, but without the temptation to fall into the trap constituted by Sartre's doctrine of consciousness as a 'nothingness', of treating human free choice as if it could or did take place in a void, outside any specific situation. If *all* our actions were equally free, Merleau-Ponty argues, then that would deprive the word 'free' of any real meaning.[8] The word 'free' gets its meaning by a contrast with something which is not free, so that if everything is free, then in an important sense nothing is free. It is our being in a certain specific situation which creates the constraints on our freedom which make it possible to distinguish between different degrees of freedom in our actions, and at the limit to say that some of the things we do are not free at all. Without the possibility of such a contrast, indeed, there would not even be any meaning to attach to the concept of 'action', since an action in the full sense is by definition free. In this way, the very possibility of meaningful concepts of action and freedom implies that the self has some content, some definite individualizing identity.

Sartre's concept of the self as a 'nothingness', as was argued in the last chapter, entailed a thoroughgoing individualism, a view which implied that real communication between different selves was impossible and so that the essence of our relations with others was conflict. Merleau-Ponty's much richer concept of the self, as having a definite identity derived from our relations to our situation, is plainly not inherently individualistic in this way. This is not to say, however, that Merleau-Ponty simply dismisses the problem of the self and its relation to others—the problem of solipsism. In some ways, he accepts, solipsism is not just a consequence of certain misguided philosophical theories, but a problem which arises from the very nature of human experience, from the distinction between myself and the other. We can and do communicate with each other: but even to talk of 'communication' is to recognize a distinction between selves. If I were not a different self from you, then I could not be said to communicate with you, so that the notion of communication both implies a gap between selves and the possibility of to some extent bridging that gap. If there is a gap between selves, however, then there is a genuine 'problem of other minds', as recognized in the philosophical tradition since Descartes. If my mind is distinct from yours, and I am conscious only of my own mind, then how can I be sure what is in your mind?

Although Merleau-Ponty recognizes this as a genuine problem, and one which gives rise to the possibility and often the actuality of conflict and competition between human beings, he nevertheless denies that this possibility represents the *essence* of our relations with others. Feelings and thoughts, whether our own or other people's, are not simply objects of knowledge, about which we may, in the case of other people, have insufficient evidence. Feelings and thoughts are things which necessarily find expression, and so can be communicated to others. At the simplest level, the expression of feelings in particular takes the form of gestures, facial expressions, 'body-language', etc.; at a more sophisticated level, the expression, of thought above all, is verbalized in language. There is a sense in which, when we recognize these expressions in another, we are in direct contact with the other's thoughts, feelings, and so on.

Merleau-Ponty uses this point to make an interesting criticism of the 'argument from analogy'. Philosophers in the tradition of Cartesian dualism, seeing that dualism creates a problem of other minds, sometimes attempt to overcome that problem by proposing that we infer the contents of another person's mind by means of analogical reasoning. I might, for example, reason like this: 'When I feel pleased with life, I smile; he is smiling, so I infer that he is feeling pleased with life.' The analogy between my facial expression when I am feeling this way and his facial expression now is supposed to be what justifies me in inferring how he is feeling now. But this, Merleau-Ponty argues, gets things the wrong way round: we first understand the expressions of others, and then understand the point of our own. He gives the example of a baby of fifteen months, who has not yet even looked at its own face in a mirror, but immediately opens its mouth as if to bite when I playfully take its finger in my mouth and pretend to bite it. ' "Biting" ', Merleau-Ponty says, 'has immediately, for it, an intersubjective significance.'[9] In this case, the meaning of a particular expression in another is immediately grasped, without any inference from one's own case: indeed, the baby understands its own expressions only through having first understood those same expressions in the other person.

7. The Individual and the Social

This fact about human thought and feeling makes human beings essentially social rather than essentially isolated, as Sartrean individualism maintains. We are social beings because we necessarily communicate our thoughts and feelings to each other by means of signs of different sorts. Some of these signs are more 'natural' than others: for example, basic facial expressions and gestures. They are relatively natural in the sense that they appear to have a fairly direct connection with our biological constitution. But, Merleau-Ponty contends, no sign is *fully* or *simply* natural: even within the limits set by our biological constitution there is room for divergence between the gestures which belong to one culture and those of another—the 'natural' expressions of grief, for instance, may vary from one society to another. And at the level of more complex thoughts and feelings, the cultural variation becomes even greater. To speak of this variation as merely 'conventional', however, is, Merleau-Ponty argues, misleading, since it implies that the variation is only in a superficial sign, rather than in the feeling or concept signified. It is not just the *word* for 'love', for instance, which varies from culture to culture, it is love *itself*: the feeling is differently expressed because it is a different feeling.

What ultimately determines the meanings of our signs, therefore, for Merleau-Ponty, is the culture of the society to which we belong, not anything purely natural or biological. Conversely, what we mean by a 'culture' is the sum of the meanings of the signs used in a particular society. A culture, and its associated language, exist in time: the meanings of the signs in the language develop and change in the interaction of that culture with its situation. A culture, in other words, has a *history*, and thus the individuals belonging to it necessarily exist in a situation which is in part historical. For the character of the situation which any individual is in at any given time is in part determined by the meanings which he or she attributes to the objects in the situation, and these meanings are constituted by the culture to which the individual belongs, in the particular historical phase of its existence which it presently occupies. In this sense, again, an individual's existence is necessarily in a particular place and time, that is, in history: to understand our situation, we need to understand the way in which it has come to be historically, and conversely we can understand our society's historical past as leading up to our present situation.

In 1799, Merleau-Ponty argues,[10] the French Revolution had reached a stage when it was possible neither to take it further nor to put the clock back. This was the historical situation which confronted Bonaparte—the meaning which in a sense history 'offered' him. But he had nevertheless to 'take up' that significance, 'which was merely a precarious possibility threatened by the contingency of history'. There was still more than one alternative way of seeing that historical situation, and so more than one choice available to him. 'It may well happen that now having taken command of history, he leads it, for a time at least, far beyond what seemed to comprise its significance, and involves it in a fresh dialectic, as when Bonaparte, from being Consul, made himself Emperor and conqueror.'[11]

As this quotation shows, our ambiguous relation to our situation results from the fact that we are essentially active and purposive beings. Because of that, we are in a situation, in a world, in a different way from that in which inanimate objects are. We *transcend*, or go beyond our situation as it is 'given' to us. That transcendence, however, does not consist in being detached from our situation or from time. We cannot step outside time, and this has a bearing even on philosophy itself. The traditional notion of philosophy saw the philosopher as rising above the perspective of his or her own time to perceive truths non-perspectivally, so that the truths were 'eternal' or timeless. If we cannot escape from time, however, then neither can we escape from the perspective of our own time. Even the philosopher can have no access to eternal truths: the standards of rationality by which philosophers judge the beliefs and institutions of their own time must not be timeless, but themselves belong to our own time and be formed by the history which has led to our present situation.

8. Philosophy and Politics

This notion, derived from Kojève's interpretation of Hegel (see above and Ch. 6), clearly has political implications. What is meant by the fully rational, fully human, society will be determined, if it is correct, not by some timeless criteria of rationality and humanity existing outside history, but by the development of history itself. There is no such thing as '*the* meaning of history', only the meaning of history, or some particular fragment of history, *for us*, the meaning which we discover by acting in our particular situation. This meaning which we find in history will not be purely arbitrary: in order to act at all, we need to discover some intelligible connection between events, as those events are seen from our particular perspective. But we have to operate within our particular perspective: there is no ultimate 'end of history' which some élite vanguard has special insight into, and towards which our activity has to be directed. It is easy to see how this philosophy of history could come into conflict with the vision of history as having an ultimate purpose, discoverable by 'scientific socialism', which was implicit in the Stalinist view prevalent in contemporary Communism, and so could lead Merleau-Ponty away from the sort of revolutionary ideology proclaimed by the French Party. (The dispute with Sartre arose because, although Sartre shared much of this scepticism about an end of history, he nevertheless felt it politically necessary, in the circumstances of the Cold War, to moderate any criticism of the Communists.)

Merleau-Ponty's own political views, however, cannot merely be labelled 'anti-Communist': they are far too complex to be given any such simple label. The three political thinkers who had most influence on his position were Max Weber, Machiavelli, and Marx (though his Marxism was of the 'humanist' variety to be discussed in the following chapter). From Weber and Machiavelli, he took over the view that politics, in present society at least, was essentially about power, and so about violence. Following Marx, he saw people in existing society as divided into oppressors and oppressed, with the oppressors using the power which they held to subject the oppressed.

Human beings find themselves in a situation which they did not choose, shaped by natural and historical factors. We do not choose when and where we are born, whether we are born into the oppressed class or that of the oppressors, whether we are men or women, white or black: these aspects of our situation impose constraints on what we can choose, but they do not remove from us the power of choice itself. As active beings, we necessarily, as suggested earlier, transcend our situation to give meaning to it. This very power of choice is constrained for the oppressed by their social situation, but at the same time offers the possibility of envisaging a different social situation in which they would not be so constrained. There is and can be no mechanical necessity that the oppressed will become aware of their situation in this way or desire to change it. It seems clear to Merleau-Ponty, however, that they ought to: that oppression ought to be removed, so that human beings could realize their possibility of true community with each other, in which each recognized each other's freedom and no one group of human beings exercised domination over any other.

9. Art and Meaning

The concept of the ambiguity of human existence thus runs through all of Merleau-Ponty's thinking, on topics ranging from perception and mind–body relations to the ultimate aims of political activity. His vision is of human beings finding themselves in a pre-existing situation, whose meaning and structure are neither objectively there, waiting to be discovered, nor simply imposed on objects by our consciousness, but emerge out of the interaction between our purposes and the external world. The rationality and order of the world, likewise, were seen neither as eternal principles discoverable by the philosopher's intellectual intuition nor as a merely subjective organization of things, reflecting only our human needs.

The fact that our being is 'being-in-the-world' must be taken seriously: we are neither disembodied consciousnesses, loosely attached to matter via our own bodies, nor mere physical objects like any other, but human beings who are embodied, who move around the world and have purposes in the world. The root source of Sartre's problems, with solipsism, with our relations with others, with our relation to our own bodies, with human historicity, lay, for Merleau-Ponty, in Sartre's withdrawal from the concept of the human being as embodied and in the world to the more restrictive (and more Cartesian) conception of consciousness as a nothingness, detachable from the situation in which it finds itself.

Having developed this view, Merleau-Ponty came to realize its applicability in many fields outside pure philosophy—not just in politics and psychology, but even in thinking about painting, literature, and the cinema. He wrote about these applications in a number of articles, in *Les Temps modernes* and other periodicals, some of which are brought together in his collections *Signs* and *Sense and Non-Sense*.[12] Cézanne, for instance, is described (in the article 'Cézanne's Doubt'[13]) as exercising his creative freedom in his paintings in the way he reacted to things: 'The meaning Cézanne gave to objects and faces in his paintings presented itself to him in the world as it appeared to him. Cézanne simply released this meaning: it was the objects and the faces themselves as he saw them which demanded to be painted, and Cézanne simply expressed what they *wanted* to say.' In this way, Cézanne's painting becomes a kind of phenomenology, a discovery of meanings in objects which themselves exist only in relation to us.

Similarly, literature in the modern age becomes 'metaphysical', not in the sense of the old rationalism 'convinced it could make the world and human life understood by an arrangement of concepts',[14] but in that it reveals the ambiguity of our relations with the other person, with our bodies, with values, and with history (Simone de Beauvoir's novel *L'Invitée* and Sartre's novels of the 1930s and the post-war period are cited as examples). Finally, in 'The Film and the New Psychology',[15] he interprets film as the representation of the coming-to-be of meaning and order, which he sees as happening in the real (non-cinematic) world as the result of human activity and attempts at rational understanding. In these ways, although Merleau-Ponty himself painted no pictures, wrote no novels and directed no films, he was able to illuminate all these forms of art by means of his general account of the human mode of being.

10. The Ontological Turn

His account of human existence as 'ambiguous', of human subjectivity as essentially embodied, and so not to be identified simply with the clear and distinct deliverances of a Cartesian consciousness, of principles of rationality as emerging indistinctly from our dealings with the world and with each other, helped to transform both French philosophy and French intellectual life generally. Merleau-Ponty is sometimes denigrated by more recent French thinkers because he is said to be unable to liberate himself from traditional humanism. In fact, however, although he is certainly a 'humanist' in the sense of seeking a more humane and rational world for human beings to live in, his philosophy marks, more than that of Bergson, Marcel, or Sartre, the beginning of the end of French *philosophical* humanism and rationalism. Bergson and Marcel both, in their different ways, retain the idea of transcendent values which reveal themselves to human beings; Sartre, though he rejects that idea, still has an essentially Cartesian picture of the human subject as identified with a consciousness which, although contingent, is still totally detached from the messy world of existence. The concept of human subjectivity as ambiguous, found in Merleau-Ponty, is the beginning of that 'decentring' of the subject in structuralist and post-structuralist thought, to be considered in later chapters.

In the last years of his life, Merleau-Ponty's thought, as represented in his posthumously published works *The Visible and the Invisible* and *The Prose of the World*, was developing even more clearly in that direction. Heidegger had always been an important influence on his thinking, (as in his key notion of human being as 'being-in-the-world', which was directly derived from Heidegger), but in the earlier works Husserlian phenomenology was dominant. In these last works, a Heideggerian concern with ontology, with the study of Being as such, moves much more to centre-stage. At the same time, there is an

increased emphasis on language, again foreshadowing the linguistic turn of subsequent French philosophy.

In 1952, when he was presenting his candidacy for the Chair
at the Collège de France, Merleau-Ponty wrote a prospectus of
the work which he intended to do in the following years.[16] In
this, he announces that his works in preparation 'aim to show
how communication with others, and thought, take up and go
beyond the realm of perception which initiated us to the truth'.[17]
Language rescues thought from the transitory, but it is 'never the
mere clothing of a thought which otherwise possesses itself in full
clarity'.[18] Literary uses of language in particular are not the mere
expression of the writer's thought, as if thoughts could be
identified independently of the words in which they are expressed. Rather, language, even prose, has a certain autonomy,
an ability to capture 'a meaning which until then had never been
objectified'.[19] In his forthcoming work, Merleau-Ponty announces, he intends, in the spirit of Hegel's remark that the
Roman state was the 'prose of the world', to extend this concept
of prose outside the realm of language proper into wider spheres
of human relations and even 'to a reflection on this Logos which
gives us the task of vocalizing a hitherto mute world'.[20] To
achieve this, he concludes, would amount to constructing a
metaphysics.

11. Language and Metaphysics

The programme announced in the prospectus has two parts—a
reflection on language and its relation to the world, and a
discussion of our relation to Being in general—and the first is
intended to lead on to the second. It is clear that Merleau-Ponty
was working on the manuscript of his proposed *Introduction to
the Prose of the World* at the time when he was preparing this
prospectus, and that at some later date (it is not certain exactly
when) he abandoned this text. The completed portion of it was
found among his papers after his death, and was published as *La
Prose du monde* in Paris by Gallimard in 1969.[21] The work seems
to have originated as Merleau-Ponty's answer to Sartre's *What
is Literature?*, but whatever its origins it is much wider in scope.

It is a meditation on language and expression in general, taking up the discussion in *Phenomenology of Perception* of the relation between embodiment and expressivity. Already in that earlier work Merleau-Ponty had argued that the 'lived' body, the body through which we experience and act upon the world, is intrinsically expressive, and it is this which gives rise to speech— 'thought tends towards expression as towards its completion'.[22]

Speech, the direct expression of our thoughts, however, becomes institutionalized as language, the rule-governed structure which linguistics studies. Institutionalized language is one step removed from lived human experience, and so from human creativity: it generates the illusion of a relation of one-to-one correspondence between words and what they signify. Language in this sense is something which we learn, and the learning consists in following the rules correlating particular linguistic expressions with particular objects. The world then becomes that set of objects which are referred to in the language we use: we ourselves, who use the language, drop out of sight. Traditional philosophical thinking about language and its relation to the world bases itself on this model of language and consequently sees all languages as essentially the same, no matter what the cultural differences between the human beings who use them may be: such differences become simply superficial clothing, concealing the underlying essential form. (Those who are familiar with analytic philosophy may recognize this as similar to the view of language found in Frege and the early Wittgenstein.)

Language as we actually experience it, however, is not like this at all: we do not use it simply to reflect an objective reality, but to express our own involvement with reality. It grows out of that involvement: individual expressions get their meaning, not from referring to independent objects, but from their relation to other expressions in the language. 'The expressive power of a sign derives from its part in a system and its coexistence with other signs'.[23] The use of language in literature is closer to this use in speech than to the purely fact-stating language to which science aspires. Poets and even prose-writers use words creatively: they have to start from the established meanings of words in institutionalized language, but they can make use of these meanings to communicate something radically new to their audience, to change our ways of seeing the world, or (more correctly) to change our involvement with our world, and with each other, through language. In this way, creative language builds on an inherited tradition, even in adding new contributions to that tradition (Merleau-Ponty compares this to the way in which painters identify themselves with a certain tradition and produce what is new by developing what is already inherent in the tradition).

The link here between reflections on language and metaphysical considerations about our relation to our world is obvious. At the time of his death, Merleau-Ponty was working on a more explicitly metaphysical manuscript, which was discovered after his death. The unfinished text and working notes were published posthumously as *Le Visible et l'invisible* (*The Visible and the Invisible*),[24] edited by Claude Lefort. The text constitutes only about 160 pages in the English translation, followed by just over 100 pages of 'Working Notes'. Much of that is taken up by methodological considerations and critical discussion of other philosophers such as Bergson and Sartre, but there is also to be found, in a frustratingly incomplete form, Merleau-Ponty's own substantial contribution. Because he was still working on it, this contribution remains in many places obscure and is at best a matter of tantalizing suggestions rather than of finished thoughts, but even so it reveals how Merleau-Ponty could have taken the ideas of his earlier works in new and provocative directions.

Perhaps the best place to start is with the familiar notion of human experience as ambiguous, of our subjectivity as essentially embodied. Given that, then our own bodies have an ambiguous status—they are both themselves objects of our perception, part of what is 'visible' to us, part of the world, and also subjects, the means by which we perceive and act upon the world (and in that sense 'invisible'). Because we are embodied perceivers, the world which we perceive is neither totally distinct from us nor a mere part of us: we and our world are distinct aspects of the same Being, part of it and yet apart from it. 'We say therefore that our body is a being of two leaves, from one side a thing among things and otherwise what sees them and touches them.'[25] Because of its ambiguous status, however, a body is not a 'thing among things' in quite the same way as the objects it enables us to perceive: as a subject, it has its 'invisible' as well as its 'visible' aspect. Our 'carnal being' however is ultimately not separable from Being as a whole (and this inseparability of our being is what Merleau-Ponty designates as 'flesh'). Our dual position as subjects and objects both 'inaugurates . . . facticity, what makes the fact be a fact' and is 'what makes the facts have meaning, makes the fragmentary facts dispose themselves about "something" '.[26]

If our being is inseparable from Being as a whole, then the task of philosophy becomes, not to describe or explain an independent reality, but to let Being speak for itself. A final quotation from *The Visible and the Invisible* will round off this discussion of Merleau-Ponty's philosophy by showing how his uncompleted final work was developing his earlier themes in ways which were to be taken further by the philosophers to be considered in later chapters:

The philosopher speaks, but this is a weakness in him, and an inexplicable weakness: he should keep silent, coincide in silence, and rejoin in Being a philosophy that is there ready-made. But yet everything comes to pass as though he wished to put into words a certain silence he hearkens to within himself . . . . One has to believe, then, that language is not simply the contrary of the truth, of coincidence, that there is or could be a language of coincidence, a manner of making the things themselves speak—and this is what he seeks. It would be a language of which he would not be the organizer, words he would not assemble, that would combine through him by virtue of a natural intertwining of their meaning, through the occult trading of the metaphor—where what counts is no longer the manifest meaning of each word and of each image, but the lateral relations, the kinships that are implicated in their transfers and their exchanges.[27]

CHAPTER SIX

Three French Marxists

1. Marxism and the French Left

At least since the Revolution of 1789, French intellectuals have usually seen themselves as in opposition to the bourgeoisie. In some cases this has amounted to little more than a general distaste for bourgeois conventionality, but it has often gone beyond that into the domain of political activity. Sometimes this political activity has taken a right-wing form—support for royalism, for ultramontane Catholicism, or in more recent times for some variety of fascism. But many politically anti-bourgeois intellectuals in France have seen themselves as on the left, as radicals, socialists, or communists. In literature, this political radicalism has found expression, for instance, in the great polemical novels of Émile Zola, or, more recently, in André Malraux's novels of the 1930s, *L'Espoir* (*Days of Hope*) and *La Condition humaine* (*Man's Estate*).

To a much greater extent than the Left in the English-speaking world, the French Left has sought a philosophical basis for its politics. There is a strong tradition of native French radical thought—Fourier, Saint-Simon, Sorel, and so on: but for much of the present century, the major current of philosophical thinking on the French Left has been Marxism. Many intellectuals have (until very recently) joined the French Communist Party (PCF); others have found the Party's uncritical support for the Soviet Union and its crimes intolerable, but have still found in some version of Marxism the most satisfactory philosophical underpinning for their political beliefs and values.

The debate between 'orthodox' (pro-PCF) Marxists and the supporters of deviant versions of Marxism, with its repercussions on the wider intellectual culture, is the theme of the present chapter. However much they shared the political and social aims of the PCF, it was not easy for sophisticated French intellectuals to stomach the Party's official ideology, which was simply copied from the crude, mechanistic, and dogmatic 'Marxism' promulgated in the USSR. and owing more to Engels, Lenin, and Stalin than to Karl Marx himself. On this version, Marxism was 'scientific socialism', a scientific theory of the laws of social development, according to which the ultimate determinant of human social activity and arrangements was the economic system of society (the 'relations of production'), which in turn mechanically reflected the stage of development of the 'means of production', the technology by which a society produced the goods which it needed. Human thought (philosophical, religious, artistic, legal, etc.) was seen as a mere epiphenomenon of this economic system, a more or less illusory reflection in men's brains of what was really going on, which could therefore have no independent influence ('in the last analysis', as Engels put it) on the course of events. The laws of scientific socialism made it possible to predict the ultimate collapse of the capitalist system under the weight of its own internal contradictions and its replacement, first, by the 'dictatorship of the proletariat' (as in the Soviet Union) and ultimately by full communism.

The conception of 'science' in this account was thoroughly positivistic: that is, it assumed that the attempt to gain rational understanding of human society must proceed along the lines of the mechanistic explanations of classical physics. But this assumption can be questioned. Classical physics, after all, deals with a world of inanimate objects, or of objects (including human bodies) considered as inanimate: inanimate objects have no thoughts about their own situation, and so such thoughts can play no part in explaining their behaviour. Human societies, however, are made up of human beings, who do have thoughts about their own situation, and it is at least plausible to suggest that such thoughts need to be taken into account if we are to understand what people do, the institutions which they create, and so on. Thoughts have a history in a sense in which the movements of inanimate objects do not: my present thoughts about my present situation (and so the character of the situation itself) are influenced by what I know and what I think about my own past. To understand the present state of society can thus be argued to involve, not the application of timeless general 'laws of social development', but a historical grasp of the particular way in which it has emerged from what came before. Furthermore, to understand one's own society is itself a social act, and so may be a contribution towards changing the character of that society.

What Soviet Marxism left out, according to this critique, was simply the humanity of human beings. But to leave that out, it could be, and was, argued, is to make it impossible to understand why the creation of socialism should be desirable, and maybe even to see how it could be achieved. Why should anyone think, after all, that a proletariat which had been oppressed by capitalism to the extent which the Soviet Marxists claimed should be capable of getting together the forces required, not simply for an outburst of sheer destructive rage, but for the creation of a new kind of society in which the oppression of one human being by another was ended once and for all? As long as only the mature works of Marx were known, it was possible to think that the choice was either to be a Marxist and accept these intellectual problems or to cease to be a revolutionary socialist altogether and embrace some version of liberal or social-democratic humanism. The later writings of Marx after all contained many passages which could only plausibly be interpreted in the 'Soviet' way. The publication, from 1927 onwards, of French translations of the writings of Marx's youth, however, suggested that Marxism itself could be reinterpreted as a form of 'humanism'.

2. Hegelianized Marxism

The early Marx was still very much under the influence of Hegel's philosophy, and the rediscovery of Marx's early writings in France went along with a new interest among French philosophers in Hegel. Hegelian concepts seemed to offer the possibility of reformulating Marxism as a species of humanism. The most powerful single influence in introducing Hegel's philosophy, and a Hegelianized Marxism, into France was a Russian émigré called Alexandre Kojève, who lectured on Hegel's

Phenomenology of Spirit at the École Pratique des Hautes Études in Paris from 1933 to 1939. These lectures attracted the attention of a number of the leading younger intellectuals of the time, including Merleau-Ponty (as mentioned in the preceding chapter), Raymond Aron, Raymond Queneau, Georges Bataille, Jacques Lacan, and (it is said, though there seems to be no evidence for this) Sartre. We have already seen in Chapter 5 some sign of the effect of these lectures on Merleau-Ponty's thinking, but their influence was much wider than that, especially when they were published in book form after the Second World War.[1] By that time, the change in the political atmosphere after the experiences of the Resistance had made intellectuals much more receptive to the ideas of a humanistic and Hegelianized Marxism. It was not only Kojève's interpretation of Hegel which benefited from this mood, but also that of Jean Hyppolite, as well as such non-French Marxists as the Hungarian Georg Lukacs and the Italian theorist Antonio Gramsci.

Kojève's intepretation of Hegel's *Phenomenology* struck a chord with left-leaning but non-Stalinist French intellectuals because it seemed to open up the possibility of a way of thinking about society and social action which avoided both a pessimistic conservatism and a vague liberal idealism which took no account of historical realities. Such a way of thinking could well be taken to be true to the spirit of Marxism, but it did not correspond to the official Party account of Marxist theory. For the peculiarity of that official account was that it took over, as was said earlier, precisely that Enlightenment view of 'science' and 'rationality', derived from what was called in Chapter 1 the 'Galilean' element in Descartes, which underlay both conservatism and liberal idealism. According to the Enlightenment view, rational social action was action to achieve rational social goals using means derived from a 'scientific' understanding of society. Scientific understanding of society meant, as we have seen, explaining the particular phenomena of society in terms of timeless, universal laws, modelled on the timeless universal laws of classical physics. And rational social goals were equally timeless and universal, discernible independently of the particular historical or cultural position which one occupied. There was thus a gap between reason and history: history was not rationally intelligible, and could not count as a genuine 'science', but only at best, as Descartes had described it, as a source of uplifting stories.[2]

It is easy to see how this view of rational social action could lead either to conservatism or to liberal utopianism. The concept of a fully rational or fully human society, on this view, is necessarily removed from the messy reality of actual historical societies. Either, therefore, one is impressed by the gap between existing society and the ideal, and becomes a despairing conservative; or one rejects such despair and seeks to close the gap. In the latter case, however, because one's ideals bear no relation to what actually exists, one cannot realize them by building on what is already present in existing society: the attempt to achieve the ideal has to be the work of an enlightened élite, manipulating the unenlightened masses in the name of goals which they alone are equipped to discern. Either the attempt at manipulation fails completely, in which case one returns to conservative despair, or, even worse, it succeeds in one sense, but only at the cost of entrenching the progressive élite in power.

3. Alexandre Kojève

The distortions of Stalinism could in some such way be linked directly to the positivist interpretation of Marxism. Marxism itself, however, could be seen, especially after the rediscovery of the early Marx, as an essentially anti-élitist, democratic doctrine, and this provided the impetus for the search for an alternative non-positivistic interpretation such as Kojève's account of Hegel suggested. Kojève's Hegel *historicized* reason, and so made possible a rational view of history. The *Phenomenology of Spirit* was taken as the key Hegelian text for this purpose, since in it Hegel offered a vision of reason as gradually emerging from human experience, and (as Kojève saw it at least) of human beings progressively achieving their own humanity. On this view, to be human was not a mere biological or otherwise natural fact about the members of our species, but rather an achievement, to be progressively realized; and the way in which it was realized according to Hegel pointed forward, on Kojève's reading, to the Marxist account of human history as the history of class conflict.

The starting-point of Hegel's analysis, according to Kojève, was that man is self-consciousness:[3] that is, that to be fully human is to be conscious of oneself as a human being. To be self-conscious in that sense is, however, an achievement, and the important thing is to grasp the conditions which need to be fulfilled to make that achievement possible. At its most basic level, consciousness is simply 'animal'—directed towards and completely absorbed in its objects. This is the sort of consciousness which we have when we are simply 'knowing subjects', when our relationship to the world is only that of knowers: to have a knowing or purely cognitive relation to objects is to be completely absorbed in what is known, with no sense of ourselves as having a subjective existence. (This, of course, is the conception of the human subject found in classical philosophy, in which the theory of knowledge was central). To have the possibility of a sense of ourselves as subjects, we need to go beyond a merely cognitive relation to things and to introduce the element of desire. 'Desire is what transforms Being, revealed to itself by itself in (true) knowledge, into an "object" revealed to a "subject" by a subject different from the object and "opposed" to it.'[4]

It is worth reflecting on this sentence. We become aware of ourselves as 'subjects', and of the world which we encounter as made up of 'objects', distinct from ourselves, Kojève is saying, only through desire. To 'know' is simply to be aware of the world (of 'Being'), without being aware of ourselves and so without being aware of any gap between ourselves and the objective world. But to desire something is to be aware of it as different from oneself, as recalcitrant to one's wishes, and so as an 'object' distinct from oneself as a 'subject'. It is because we have desires, therefore, that we can become aware of 'subject-object' relations. We have such desires, however, as part of our animal existence: there is nothing specifically human about having desires as such, and so our self-consciousness simply as desiring beings is not yet a consciousness of ourselves as human. As Kojève puts it, animal desire is the *necessary*, but not yet the *sufficient*, condition of self-consciousness.

The further element which was needed for true human self-consciousness was, according to Kojève's reading of Hegel, that the object of desire should itself be another non-natural desire. For desire defines itself by negating its object, so that what kind of desire it is, and so what kind of a desiring self one is conscious of, will depend on what kind of object it negates. To be fully human, therefore, requires one to be a member of a society of other human beings, such that each of these members of society desires each other's desire *as the desire of another human being*. But what is meant by the desire of another's desire? It means, as Kojève interprets it, the desire to have one's value as a human being recognized by another human being: it is the desire for *recognition*, and human society thus exists because of the human need for recognition by others. Human society differs from a herd of non-human animals, which simply involves collaboration in the satisfaction of animal desires (e.g. hunting for food in packs rather than individually).

But there is another crucial respect in which fully human desire differs from the merely animal sort. All animal desires are in the end variations on the desire to preserve one's own animal life. If human desire is to be distinguished from them, it must be by overcoming this animal desire for self-preservation: it must involve a willingness to risk one's biological existence in order to secure one's dignity as a human being. To be truly human, therefore, is to prefer recognition of one's humanity by other human beings to simple biological survival. And since this logically implies that those other human beings must be willing to risk their lives in order to be recognized by oneself, it follows, Kojève argues, that the origin of self-consciousness must lie in a fight to the death for recognition.[5]

It is at this point that Kojève introduces Hegel's discussion of the Master–Slave relationship, which is crucial to his interpretation of Hegel's *Phenomenology*. For, if we become human through a fight to the death with another human being for recognition as an autonomous individual, then humanity can continue to exist only if that fight is not taken to the point of the death of either combatant. We can be self-conscious, and recognized as human, only if both we ourselves and the other person continue to live in a biological sense. If either is dead, he or she cannot recognize the other's human status. The only satisfactory outcome of the 'fight to the death', therefore, must be that neither should in fact die, but that one should triumph in a way which falls short of killing the other. The victor will be the one who is prepared to risk his life, the vanquished the one who is not, and so submits to the victor as the latter's *slave*.

In other words, in his nascent state, man is never simply man. He is always, necessarily, and essentially, either Master or Slave. If the human reality can come into being only as a social reality, society is human—at least in its origin—only on the basis of its implying an element of Mastery and an element of Slavery, of 'autonomous' existences and 'dependent' existences.[6]

The history of human society must therefore be the story of the struggle between these two essential elements, the rulers and the ruled, the oppressors and the oppressed: in other words, as Marx and Engels famously put it in the 'Communist Manifesto', 'the history of all hitherto existing societies is the history of class-struggles'. The difference, in the case of Marx, was that he gave historical flesh to this abstract schema of 'Master' and 'Slave' by specifying different sorts of rulers and ruled at different stages in history, and by showing how the character of the struggle, and its outcome, differed according to the changes in the character of the combatants.

Kojève, however, does stress the connection between Hegel's metaphysical analysis of the conditions for humanity and Marx's account of the actual course of human history—a connection which is made by the concept of *labour*. For man to be truly man, Kojève argues, he must impose his own idea of himself on the world, both natural and human. He must be recognized as human by other human beings, as we have just seen; but he must also be 'recognized', as it were, by nature in the sense of imposing his own idea of himself on to nature, transforming the natural world into a world in his own image. Thus, the fight to the death by human beings for mutual recognition will also be a fight to the death between them for the triumph of their particular aim of transforming nature. When it ends with one becoming Master and the other Slave, that will also mean that the Master will force the Slave to transform the world in accordance with his (the Master's) ideas.

The division of human society into Masters and Slaves will thus not be simply a division in terms of social status: it will also be a distinction in economic power. The Master will make use of the Slave's labour in order to achieve his (the Master's) ends in transforming nature and making it more 'human'. Herein, however, lie the seeds of the Master's downfall (and here we can see another Marxist theme). The Master necessarily has only a 'mediated' relation to things. He does not himself transform nature, but has the Slave do it for him. The Master simply *consumes* things, that is, reduces them to nothing. The Slave, on the other hand, has a direct relationship to things: he transforms them by his own labour. The Master gets his recognition therefore only from another consciousness (that of the Slave), and is in that sense dependent for his humanity on the Slave. The Slave, however, by transforming nature by his own labour, gets recognition of his own humanity directly from nature, and is not in that sense equally dependent on the Master. There is thus a curious reversal of role: the Master's self-consciousness becomes dependent, less than autonomous, and so less than fully human. The Slave, on the other hand, becomes truly autonomous through his labour, and in that sense overcomes his slavery, his dependency. 'If idle Mastery is an impasse, laborious Slavery, in contrast, is the source of all human, social, historical progress. History is the history of the working Slave.'[7]

It is not hard to see here again, in abstract outline, Marx's account of human history as a succession of conflicts between those who own the means of production and those who operate them on the owners' behalf. In these conflicts, the operators (the 'working Slave') are the ones who impose a human stamp on non-human nature and in so doing develop the means of production to a new level; in so doing, they also develop themselves to a level where they in turn can take power, become 'Masters', whereupon the whole cycle starts again. This, for the Marxist, represents 'human, social, historical progress', in that, with each such revolution, human mastery over nature is increased.

It is perhaps now clear why Kojève's reading of Hegel had such an appeal for those who hankered for a more humanistic and less mechanistic Marxism. For it seemed to show how it was possible to present a Marxist account of human history as a story of class struggles in which at each stage the oppressed, or labouring, class represented progress, while retaining the view of human beings as autonomous subjects, distinct both from non-human animals and even more from mere inanimate objects. Such a view thus made it at least conceivable, in a way that mechanistic Marxism could not, that the final class struggle, in which we were now engaged, might result, not in the mere replacement of one ruling class by another, but in the creation of a truly human society, in which human beings were no longer divided into Masters and Slaves but could truly recognize each other's humanity on an equal footing, and collaborate in transforming nature. If human beings were naturally destined to live in society, if even their individual identities depended, as Kojève's interpretation of Hegel implied, on mutual recognition by others, then it was not necessary to accept the conservative pessimism which declared that human beings could never be fully socialized but were doomed to remain individuals in conflict with each other. On the other hand, if a fully human society of co-operation and mutual recognition was not just a vague ideal but rooted in the real nature of human beings, then realistic action to create such a society was possible: we did not need to depend, like the liberals, on mere preaching or appeals to people's 'better nature'.

Kojève was sometimes criticized for passing off his own views as an interpretation of Hegel (Jean Hyppolite was widely regarded as much less guilty in this regard); but this sort of criticism is strictly irrelevant to an assessment of his views in themselves, rather than as a contribution to the history of philosophy. A more significant objection is that Kojève's narrative of human history can be seen as an illegitimate combination of a priori metaphysics and a selective account of contingent historical facts. In this combination, according to the objection, the metaphysics determines the selection of the facts, while the factual connections in turn are given a spurious necessity by the

metaphysics. For instance, the selection of Master–Slave conflicts as specially significant to the development of human history
can be seen as determined more by the need to justify the
Marxist conception of class-struggle as essential to historical
progress than by a dispassionate reading of the historical facts
themselves. At the same time, it does not appear to be a matter
of *logical* necesssity that the human need for recognition should
result in a struggle to the death for mastery, even if it may be
factually true that 'the history of all hitherto existing societies is
the history of class-struggles'.

It is only when metaphysics and the facts of history are
combined in this way that it becomes plausible to suggest that
the character of human history points necessarily towards an
eventual fully human society. Furthermore, there is, to say the
least, a tension between the humanistic socialist concept of a
fully human society implicit in Kojève's reading of history, in
which recognition of the rights of each would imply recognition
of the rights of all others, and the vision of human society as
founded in the Master–Slave conflict. If such conflict is part of
the essence of human society, after all, then how can it be
possible to have a human society which is free of such conflict
and in which human relations are based instead on mutual
respect? If class-struggle were a merely contingent phase of
human history, then it could conceivably be superseded, but if
the whole character of human consciousness, which gives rise to
society in the first place, makes a fight to the death logically
necessary, then such conflicts are necessarily unavoidable.

It cannot be simply an accident that Marx's own vision of
human history moved progressively away from such Hegelian
metaphysics towards what at least purports to be a concrete
account of how human society has as a matter of fact developed
to its present stage, and how it will be further transformed in the
future. Considered purely as a general philosophical account of
humanity and of human identity, there is much of value in the
earlier part of Kojève's discussion—the idea that self-consciousness depends on desire and action, rather than contemplative
knowledge, for instance, is original and worthy of further
development. Similarly, the notion of the essential relation

between my consciousness of myself and my consciousness of others' being conscious of me is an important corrective to the egocentricity of Cartesian accounts of self-consciousness. But as an attempt at a humanist, Hegelianized Marxism, Kojève's account fails (as perhaps do all attempts at humanizing Marxism): its concepts seem too abstract to provide us with any explanation, or even a basis for an explanation, of the origins of class conflict in society, let alone with an explanation for the way in which the nature of classes and class conflict change as human technological capacity changes. The latter explanation is what Marxism seeks to provide (whether successfully or not is irrelevant from the present point of view), and in that task it can receive no real help from Kojève's peculiarly unhistorical analyses.

4. Sartre's Move to Marxism

If a philosophical basis for a humanistic Marxism were to be found, therefore, it would have to be elsewhere. We have seen something in the preceding chapter of Merleau-Ponty's humanistic politics (which, though left-leaning, were not *specifically* Marxist). In this chapter, however, I prefer to concentrate on one other attempt to integrate Marxism and a belief in human liberation, namely, the later thought of Sartre. In Chapter 4, I argued that Sartre's version of existential phenomenology was inescapably individualistic, and thus incompatible with the kind of socialist politics to which Sartre was drawn as a result of his experiences in the Resistance and in the radical atmosphere of post-war France and of his reflections on the Cold War. Furthermore, by making the human subject a 'nothingness', he created a gap between subjects and the particular historical situation in which they found themselves. Such a completely unhistorical view of human existence was poles apart from Marx's historical materialism, which was the accepted philosophical basis for the socialist movement in France. It would have been natural for him therefore simply to abandon existentialism and to become a full-blown Marxist. His own independence of mind, however, together with his awareness of the evils of Stalinism in the Soviet

Union and in the Eastern European Communist states, made it difficult, if not impossible, for him to give unreserved allegiance to the PCF and to Marxism. This vacillating support for the Communists made him a frequent target for their attacks.

Marxism was fundamentally correct, Sartre came to believe, but it needed to be tempered by existentialism if it were not to degenerate into the mechanical and ultimately anti-human doctrine propagated in the Eastern bloc. The culmination of this line of thought was the major philosophical work of his later period, the *Critique de la raison dialectique* (*Critique of Dialectical Reason*).[8] This had been preceded a few years earlier by a much shorter essay outlining the main themes of the *Critique*, the *Question de méthode* (*The Problem of Method*).[9] In these two works, Sartre set out his new vision of the relation between Marxism and existentialism—the precise way in which the existentialist stress on human subjectivity could correct the distortions which had grown up in Marxist theory and practice.

Marxism (by which he meant primarily historical materialism) was the fundamental truth of the epoch in which we are now living, and would not be superseded until that epoch had passed. He distinguished, however, between *historical* materialism and *metaphysical* forms of materialism. Historical materialism is primarily an attitude, a view of human existence which rejects any role for any transcendental or spiritual reality, which sees human beings as engaged in concrete ways with the visible and tangible world. From this point of view, 'matter' is simply a human concept, a human way of thinking about the world with which we are involved in our practice. For metaphysical materialism, however, 'matter' is treated as something more than that, as the ultimate stuff of which all reality is composed. Metaphysical materialism, in effect, takes the scientific concept of 'matter' and gives it an all-embracing significance. In that sense, metaphysical materialism is a world-view which is derived from natural science and which treats scientific ways of thinking as the key to all understanding.

Metaphysical materialism thus implies that human beings are simply one kind of natural object amongst others; their behaviour is to be explained by the same laws as that of any other kind of object. The 'dialectical materialism' of the Stalinists (originated by Engels rather than Marx himself) is one form of metaphysical materialism, which attempts to apply the 'dialectical laws', which have some meaning in relation to human history, to the whole of nature, and thereby to reduce human history itself to another natural phenomenon. In so doing, however, dialectical materialism in Sartre's opinion distorts the original point of historical materialism, since it fails to do justice to the historical character of human existence.

Human beings have a history because they are *not* merely natural objects. We discover this in practice, in that our action on the world and interaction with it involves consciousness, intentions, and meaning. Unlike natural objects, we have subjectivity: we live our experience from the inside, so that human behaviour is understandable in a different way from the behaviour of objects. The behaviour of objects (such as the motion of a lump of matter from one place to another) can be *causally explained*, in terms of general laws of nature of the form 'When A happens, B will happen'. Human behaviour, on the other hand, can be *understood* 'from the inside', because it is an expression of what is on the inside. Someone acts to achieve a certain purpose: their behaviour can be understood by others provided that they can see that that is what they would have done if they had wished to achieve that purpose. We have a history because the purposes, intentions, etc. which we now express by our actions necessarily relate to our thoughts about the past.

Dialectical materialism, or 'scientific socialism', thus cannot account for the fact that human beings have a history, and that that history needs to be taken into account in understanding the present actions of human beings. It takes the 'historical' out of 'historical materialism' and thereby dehumanizes human beings: in so doing, it degenerates into a mechanistic pseudo-science of human development rather than a guide to understanding that development. In this context, it is easy to see how it could be suggested that existentialism, with its emphasis on subjectivity, could help to revitalize Marxism by restoring its original character as a *historical* vision of human existence. Existentialism itself, however, is, as has already been suggested, fundamentally ahistorical. Existentialism needs the materialist element in historical materialism, the notion of human consciousness as involved, through action, with its own physical milieu, in order to have a historical dimension. But of course, if human consciousness is as closely involved with its physical milieu as that, it can no longer be regarded as a mere 'nothingness', totally transcending its situation: it must be defined in part at least by the situation in which it finds itself.

Marxism needs existentialism, but not as much as existentialism needs Marxism. Marxism is the fundamental truth of our epoch, and needs existentialism only in order to be restored to its original inspiration, to avoid degenerating. Existentialism needs Marxist materialism (properly understood), however, in order to achieve some contact with the truth. Hence, for Sartre in the *Critique*, the relation of Marxism and existentialism is unequal: Marxism is *the* defining philosophy of our time, and existentialism has only a marginal function of helping to keep that defining philosophy on the right track. (Marginal though that function is, it may in practice be vitally important. The need to keep Marxism on a humanistic track becomes a moral necessity when the dehumanized theories of Stalinism lead to inhuman ways of treating the citizens of Communist-ruled countries.)

The attempt to fuse Marxism with existentialism is thus rather one-sided: the outcome is meant to be, basically, a Marxist theory which existentialism enables to be true to itself, without degenerating into the kind of mechanistic metaphysics which betrays the essential spirit of *historical* materialism. A truly historical materialism, Sartre argues, must be 'dialectical', but it must not be like the 'dialectical materialism' or 'diamat' preached by Soviet ideologues. 'Diamat' was in fact anti-historical, since it required the Marxist theorist to adopt a position *outside* history, from which the 'dialectical laws' of history could be discerned in the manner in which, in nineteenth-century conceptions of natural science, the laws of nature were supposed to be discovered by the scientist. A truly *historical* approach, however, involved the historian in being inside the history which he or she studied, and viewing history from that perspective.

A genuinely 'dialectical' approach, Sartre argues, is possible only for beings who are already dialectical, in the sense that 'man is "mediated" by things to the same extent as things are "mediated" by man'.[10] In other words, we are dialectical beings in the sense that we stand in what Merleau-Ponty would call an 'ambiguous' relation to our situation. We act freely, and modify the situation therefore by our free choices: but the choices that are available to us are not unlimited, since our real choices are constrained by the situation which we have inherited from the past. Sartre quotes the passage from Marx already cited in the previous chapter, in which Marx says 'Human beings make their own history, but they do not make it just as they please; they do not make it under circumstances chosen by themselves, but under circumstances directly encountered, given and transmitted from the past.' It is this interplay between human freedom and the necessity under which it operates which gives rise to history. The existentialism of *Being and Nothingness* played down the element of necessity; the scientistic version of Marxist materialism found in 'diamat' denies human freedom and so denies that men make their own history at all. Both, in their different ways, thus make it impossible to think in truly historical terms.

We are historical beings, in Sartre's view, because we are *active* beings: our relation to the world we inhabit is not a merely detached and contemplative one, but that of beings who in their activity (in their *praxis*, as Sartre calls it) conceive of ways of transcending their present situation towards a future, and of 'totalizing' the diverse elements of the present situation in the new situation which they aim to create by their action. We are active beings because we have *needs* which motivate us to intervene in our situations to change them: thus, for example, we have a need for food, which leads us to transform objects around us into things to eat. In eating (or in action generally) we are 'negating the negation': the hunger is a negation, a lack, which we negate by consuming food, and in gathering food, we are transforming our external situation, making it into something new which our future actions (and those of others) will have to take account of. '*The entire historical dialectic rests on individual* praxis *in so far as it is already dialectical*, that is to say, to the

extent that action is itself the negating transcendence of contradiction, the determination of a present totalisation in the name
of a future totality, and the real effective working of matter.'[11]

It is only if we see human beings as active and purposive in
this way, Sartre contends, that it makes sense to use such terms
as 'struggle' (as in 'class-struggle'). Mere objects could not be
said to 'struggle' with each other—when the shutter beats against
the wall, that interaction does not deserve the name of a
'struggle'.[12] Once we see human beings as agents, however, then
we can begin to make sense of human history in terms of such
concepts. We seek to act to satisfy our own individual need: but
we become aware in so doing that we must act in a situation
created by the past actions of others and ourselves—that we are
part of history. At the same time, our own involvement with the
world in the pursuit of the satisfaction of our own needs brings
us into contact with others, who are also involved with the world
in the same pursuit. Thus historical materialism implies that our
'being-in-the-world' is a being in the *social* world, that we cannot
separate ourselves as active beings from our relations with
others.

The details of Sartre's dialectical analysis of various historical
situations belong more to sociology than philosophy, but some
indication of his central concepts may help to illuminate his basic
philosophical approach. For instance, he introduces the notion
of 'scarcity', as a contingent but none the less seemingly inescapable condition of human existence: 'At the same time, it is
worth pointing out that this univocal relation of surrounding
materiality to individuals is expressed *in our History* in a particular and contingent form since the whole of human development,
at least up to now, has been a bitter struggle against *scarcity*.'[13]
The need to struggle against scarcity has made human relations
essentially competitive and antagonistic, though the antagonism
is usually between groups rather than between individuals, and
has occasionally been replaced temporarily by solidarity in the
face of a common external enemy. In significant contrast to his
position in *Being and Nothingness*, his view here is that conflict
between human beings is a merely *contingent*, no longer an
essential, feature of human existence. It is logically conceivable,

though Sartre seems to have been uncertain about how possible it might be in practice, that scarcity could be eliminated, and in that circumstance genuinely free and reciprocal relations between human beings would be possible. Unless and until that happens, however, human history is depicted as driven by the antagonisms resulting from scarcity, interrupted by occasional short-lived and unstable periods of human solidarity.

The new-found historical materialist approach, in which human behaviour is to be understood in terms of a dialectical relation with our concrete environment, is manifested in Sartre, not so much in his political activity (active though he was in Maoist and similar groupings in the 1960s and 1970s) as in his monumental work on Flaubert, *L'Idiot de la famille* (*The Family Idiot*).[14] This biography of a very bourgeois writer, dismissed by many of Sartre's Maoist friends as an abdication from political activity, was fundamentally an application of the historical materialist method, making the writer's life and work intelligible by seeing him in dialectical relationship with his material and historical environment. His use of the method to write a biography of an individual was itself an expression of his essential belief that history was made by individual human beings and could be understood only in the light of their projects.

There is, however, an inescapable problem in Sartre's attempt to reconcile existentialism and Marxism in this way. Marxism is a vision of human history as a whole, as tending towards an ultimate consummation in a communist society, in which the humanity of human beings would at last be fully realized. It can offer this vision only by assuming a standpoint *outside* history, since only from that point of view can history be regarded as a whole. But this means, first, that Marxists must deny that the actions and choices of individual human beings are ultimately determinant in history: they figure only as elements in the broad sweep of forces which move history as a whole, and are themselves determined by those forces. Secondly, it implies that the 'fully human society' will be the complete realization of an essential humanity which has all along been implicit in human history and which is therefore not to be identified with any of the particular historical manifestations of humanity to be found at different periods. A 'Marxist humanism', in other words, is a belief in an abstract and unhistorical essence of human beings as such.

If so, then existentialism in any sense cannot even have a peripheral relationship to Marxism, since it is incompatible with it. For the existentialist, the concrete choices of actual human individuals must be what finally determines what happens in human life; it is impossible for us to step outside our concrete historical situation and view human history as a whole; and no meaning can be given to any conception of an 'essence' of humanity, and so to that of a 'fully human society' to be realized at the 'end of history'. Sartre can, consistently with his general position, be 'Marxist' in the sense that he can apply Marxist concepts to understanding our dialectical relationship with our material situation, and so to understanding the course of human history in the past and in the present. But he cannot be 'Marxist' in the sense of offering a goal for human history as a whole, to be achieved by revolutionary action. He can be 'humanist' in the sense of his lecture *Existentialism and Humanism* (see Ch. 4)— that is, can believe in the need for individual human beings to make free choices. But he cannot be 'humanist' in the sense of believing in an abstract humanity working towards the fulfilment of its own essential nature. In this sense, Sartre's project in *Critique of Dialectical Reason*, for all the value of its detailed insights, is ultimately a failure.

5. Louis Althusser

By the time Sartre published his reflections on Marxism at the end of the 1950s, however, the intellectual climate in France was already beginning to change. The fashionable school of thought was 'structuralism' (see the following chapter), and structuralism was in many ways a reaction against the post-war belief in 'humanism'. Amongst interpreters of Marx, this new mood was expressed most notably by Louis Althusser. Born in Algeria in 1918, Althusser studied philosophy at the École Normale Supérieure, where he later taught (one of his students was Michel Foucault, to be considered in Chapter 7). He joined the French

Communist Party in 1948, and remained loyal to the Party through the traumas of the Hungarian uprising of 1956, the crushing of the 'Prague Spring' in 1968 and the events of May 1968 in France, in which the PCF adopted an essentially anti-revolutionary stance. Towards the end of his life, Althusser underwent a mental crisis: in 1980, he killed his wife, and was confined in a mental hospital, where he died in 1990. By the time of his mental collapse, however, Althusser had already completed the work for which he is most well-known, in offering an antihumanist reading of Marx and Marxism.

Althusser saw himself as primarily a commentator on Marx, rather than as an original philosopher offering a revisionist version of Marxism. Indeed, Althusser denied that Marxism was 'philosophy' at all: rather, it was a science of history. Philosophy aspires to transcend class and other divisions between different types of human beings in order to arrive at a universal human 'subject'. In fact, however, Althusser argued, philosophers always represent the viewpoint of a particular class. 'Philosophers are intellectuals and therefore petty bourgeois, subject as a mass to bourgeois and petty bourgeois ideology'.[15] He was prepared to accept that Marxism was a form of humanism, but he wanted to emphasise that this could only mean a 'class humanism' or 'proletarian humanism'.[16] The kind of humanism to which Althusser objected was precisely that which came from those who wanted to turn Marx into a philosopher. The notion of a universal humanity, or transcendental human subject which characterized this philosophical humanism seemed to him to be based on a failure to recognize distinctions between social classes, and so on an essentially individualistic view of humanity.

Such a concept was too abstract and general to be of any scientific value. Moreover its acceptance would undermine the class struggle, in that it implied that human history was made, not by real concrete human beings acting in pursuit of their material interests in particular contexts, but by a timeless 'human subject', expressing a freedom which was independent of the situations in which it was exercised. Human beings had to be understood, on Althusser's view, not as such abstract subjects, individuals considered in isolation from society, but as material beings determined by their particular historical, which meant *class*, situation. The aim of political activity was not to emancipate 'humanity', but to emancipate the particular class of human beings which was oppressed in contemporary (capitalist) society, namely, the proletariat.

The reaction against humanist Marxism was in this way a rejection of philosophy itself as traditionally conceived, which in this respect makes Althusser typical of the 'structuralist' and 'post-structuralist' thinkers whom we shall be considering in the remaining chapters of this book. The humanism which was rejected was not, as the word usually suggests to Anglo-Saxon ears, an anti-religious secularism (with which undoubtedly Althusser would have sympathized). Nor was it exactly a moral belief in the importance of human beings. Rather, it was, as stated earlier, the belief which has been central to the whole Western tradition in philosophy—that it is possible and necessary to isolate a transcendental subject, who cannot be identified with the point of view of any concrete, historically and socially defined individual or group but who represents what is common and essential to human beings as such.

This pure subject will then recognize universal principles of reason and universal moral values, valid for all human beings, and will be the subject of knowledge of the world. The 'humanist' interpretation of Marxism would regard this universal humanity as the maker of history, and the goal of history as the realization of universal human values. The very universality of these values, however, rests on an appeal to individuals as such, independent of their particular situation in a particular society. Against this, Althusser, from the viewpoint of Marxist 'science', wanted to see truth and values as class-bound, and classes as the makers of history in ways explainable by the laws of that science. Individuals would then feature only as members of a particular class.

The humanist interpretation of Marxism was based, as suggested earlier, on a particular reading of Marx's own writings, in which his earlier, youthful, more 'humanistic' and more philosophical works were seen as part of a continuous development with his later, more mature works, such as *Capital*. This reading implied, of course, an interpretation of the later writings which made them consistent with the earlier. Much of Althusser's intellectual activity consisted in a scholarly attempt to show that there was in fact a radical break between Marx's earlier and later writings, so that the later works, which represented genuine, mature, 'scientific' Marxism, could not be interpreted as expressing the same cast of thought as the more youthful writings. Leninism was thus, he concluded, both truer to Marx's real, mature intentions and a more adequate basis for the explanation of the current political situation.

Real Marxism then was, in Althusser's opinion, a scientific theory. Marx came to maturity when he learned (at the time of writing *The German Ideology*) to reject both the conceptions of classical German philosophy and those of the British economists. (Notice here how Althusser's antihumanism rests on a rejection of Hegelian Marxism, just as the humanists emphasized Marx's Hegelian inheritance.) The economists' view of society as constituted by individuals merely reflected the philosophical conception of a transcendental subject. For the economist's individual atoms were clearly seen as definable independently of their membership of a society (since it was their coming together which created the society in the first place), and so as much outside society and history as the universal subject of philosophy. Marx, by contrast, saw the individual as inseparable from his or her social context, so that the 'subject of history' is him- or herself produced by the workings of history.

Society, according to Althusser's Marx, is thus not composed of pre-social individuals, interacting with each other as such. Instead, it is made up of, and to be understood in terms of, what Althusser calls 'practices'. Individuals then exist only as place-holders within these practices, not as independent subjects in their own right. Their behaviour is to be explained, not in terms of their 'subjective' intentions and purposes, but in terms of the workings of the practices in which they are involved. Technical practices are defined by their ends: they involve certain means to achieve these ends. Theoretical practices produce knowledge which then provides means to the achievement of technical ends.[17]

This notion of a practice, though 'antihumanist' in a particular sense, is not intended to be an example of the kind of mechanistic materialism against which the humanist Marxists were reacting. To escape from the economists' idea that the ultimate human motivation is a pre-social economic self-interest is precisely not to make the vulgar Marxist distinction between economic 'base' and ideological 'superstructure'. Rather, a 'practice' embodies both the pursuit of economic ends and a set of ideas which give form to those ends. The particular 'relations of production' of capitalist society, for instance, in which the means of production are owned by capitalists and operated by workers, are unintelligible except in the context of a particular legal system, which is part of the 'superstructure'.

These practices which constitute a society can be inconsistent with each other, and then we get a 'contradiction' in the classical Marxist sense. Such contradictions could, Althusser argued, explain revolutionary social change. As one example, he takes Lenin's analysis of the reason why revolution happened in Russia in 1917 rather than anywhere else. It was not that the situation throughout Europe was not 'objectively revolutionary': the war of 1914–18 had exposed to full view the capitalist exploitation which had been going on for more than a century. This objectively revolutionary situation, however, became actual revolution only in Russia because all the contradictions then possible in a single state were present, in exacerbated and accumulated form, in Russia:

Contradictions of a regime of feudal exploitation at the dawn of the twentieth century. . . . Contradictions of large-scale capitalist and imperialist exploitation in the major cities and their suburbs, in the mining regions, oil-fields, etc. Contradictions of colonial exploitation and wars imposed on whole peoples. A gigantic contradiction between the stage of development of capitalist methods of production . . . and the medieval state of the countryside.[18]

This account of history, whatever else may be said about it, is certainly not an expression of 'vulgar materialism', of a crudely mechanistic theory which makes one kind of cause alone operative. Historical change, especially of a radical or revolutionary sort, is on this view 'overdetermined'. It might be doubted, however, for this very reason whether Althusser has not abandoned the historical materialism which he aims to defend. Althusser is aware of this objection and seeks to meet it. Society is indeed a 'whole' in which the various practices interact with each other on the basis of their relations within the whole. But this whole is also what Althusser calls a 'structure in dominance', a totality in which one element has a particular causal significance: this element is called the 'dominant instance'. If, as in capitalist society, the dominant instance is the economic practices of the society, then it remains true, as in classical Marxism, that 'in the last analysis' at least the structures of that society have to be understood in economic terms.

Althusser's claim that Marxism is a 'science', rather than a mere 'philosophy', is itself the statement of a philosophical position. It involves a particular philosophical view of the nature of science, and especially of social science. The causal role which Althusser attributes to 'practices', above all, implies an important distinction between the natural and the social sciences. For what constitutes a 'practice' cannot be defined without reference to the *ideas* and *intentions* of the people involved in the practice. Capitalist methods of production, for instance, which Althusser cites as an example of a practice in the quotation above, cannot be distinguished from other methods of production without reference to legal and moral ideas. Capitalism is distinguished from feudalism by, amongst other things, legal concepts of property ownership, the firm, and so on, and moral concepts of the proper relationship between employers and employees, the value of the pursuit of profit, and the like.

If practices in this sense play the crucial explanatory role in the Marxist science of history, then that makes Marxist explanation very different in character from explanation in a natural science such as physics. The concepts of the participants in a physical interaction play no role whatsoever in the explanation of that interaction, even when the participants are the kind of beings (human beings) who are capable of having concepts. If a human being falls to her death from the top of a cliff, then the explanation of the way in which her body falls will be the same whether she jumped intentionally, was pushed by someone else, or slipped accidentally. Her own conception of what was happening plays no causal role in the event considered purely as a physical episode, which is fully explained in terms of the law of gravity, as it would be if what had fallen was a sack of potatoes of the same mass. To say, as Althusser does, that practices are the key to understanding what happens in society is to say, by contrast, that human conceptions of what they are doing play a crucial causal role in social science.

Of course, the human conceptions in question need not be those which are consciously in the mind of any individual participant in the events to be explained, and there are certainly strong arguments for the view that concepts could not exist except in a *social* or collective context. Legal concepts, for instance, can exist only if a society has a legal system in which these concepts can get meaning. In this sense, Althusser is clearly right to say that his model of scientific explanation in society is incompatible with any individualistic idea that individuals, acting on their own or on the basis of their self-conscious thought, could transform society or even influence its structures. There is a sense in which his version of Marxism makes the driving force of social change into something which is over and above individual human beings and their conscious intentions and which makes use of individuals in pursuit of ends which they may not, as individuals, consciously share. But it is important to see that this 'something over and above' is not something *non-human*, but something which can be accounted for in terms of the collective activity of human beings.

In that sense, Althusser remains a 'humanist' (though not in the sense of that term which he criticizes). He is a 'humanist' in the sense that human beings still, for him, make their own history: it is just that they do not make it *consciously* or in terms of some common humanity which all human beings as such share with all other human beings. Rather, they make it in terms of concepts and values which they share with other people in the same situation as themselves. We can understand what they do, therefore, only by seeing them in their concrete social and historical situation, not by appealing to some universal rationality shared by all human beings at all times and in all places. As a programme for a science of history, a way of making sense of what has happened in the past and is happening now in society, there is a great deal to be said for this view. But, as an account of Marxism, it faces problems in showing the connection between theory and practice. It denies the possibility of a universal human subject: but the idea of a final, revolutionary transformation of society seems to require precisely that that possibility should be realized.

A scientific analysis of an existing society which is divided by classes, and in which one class oppresses another, can offer an explanation of the behaviour and even the desires of the oppressed class. On that basis, one could motivate the members of the oppressed class to act in order to achieve their desires: but to achieve their desires as a class would require their continued existence as that class, and so the perpetuation of a class-divided society, perhaps with a reversal of the relative positions of themselves and their former oppressors. Such a mere reversal of positions would not, however, be a revolutionary transformation of the kind which Marxism proposes, producing a classless society in which the oppression of human beings by other human beings would once and for all be ended. The possibility of a classless society implies the possibility of a universal human subject, not limited by the perspectives of a particular class. But how could the members of an oppressed class in present society even have the vision of such a possibility, let alone act to realize it, unless their own perspective was not completely limited by their class-position? In short, Marxism as a theory of revolutionary action seems to require the very universal 'humanism' which Althusser's Marxism, as a science of existing society, rejects.

It is not surprising, in the light of this, that Althusser's account of Marxism, for all its cultural appeal as an instrument for understanding history and sociology, had little or no practical political influence, since it could offer no rational basis for revolutionary political action. Perhaps partly because of this, the Communist Party to which Althusser gave his allegiance felt suspicion of him as a mere theoretician rather than a political activist (though their own, more mechanistic, version of

Marxism did not really provide any better basis for revolutionary activity). What is curious is that both Althusser's 'scientific' Marxism and its 'humanist' opponents seem to lead to similar results in practice. All such accounts seem much too 'theoretical' to have much relevance to real political activity. In France in the 1960s and 1970s, significantly, radical left-wing activity became irrationalist, degenerating into what was called 'Maoism' or other even more extreme forms of terrorist politics. Or, in other cases, such as that of Foucault, what might be described as 'structuralist politics', while retaining some of the rhetoric of Marxism, took up a critical attitude to existing society without any clear vision of what kind of society might be better.

On a more strictly philosophical level, however, as we shall see in the following chapter, the sort of anti-humanism represented by Althusser marks a turning-point. French philosophy up until that time, for all its criticisms of the mainstream of Western philosophy, was still much more recognizably in that mainstream than it became after the structuralist revolution. It is probably for that reason that those reared in the Anglo-Saxon philosophical tradition find it much easier to get to grips with the French philosophers of the first half of this century, however different their approach may be in detail, than with those who come later. Like all revolutions, of course, the structuralist revolution did not spring fully formed into existence, but was prepared for by what came before, and I hope to point out such anticipations at relevant points in subsequent chapters. It was, nevertheless, as we shall see, a genuine revolution.

CHAPTER SEVEN

Structuralism: Lacan and Foucault

1. Saussure and Structural Linguistics

As was suggested in the previous chapter, the late 1950s and the 1960s saw a radical change in the character and style of French philosophy, which could justifiably be described as a 'revolution'. The label usually associated with this revolution is 'structuralism', though the use of such terms carries the same danger of oversimplification and distortion as all labelling in philosophy. Structuralism itself is a relatively well-defined name for a particular approach to the human sciences, but the strictly *philosophical* developments associated with the rise of that approach in France are much harder to pin down precisely. Furthermore, as was also suggested in the last chapter, some of the ground for these philosophical developments had been prepared before the term 'structuralism' became fashionable, by the philosophers whose work has been considered in earlier chapters. Nevertheless, there were important connections between structuralism in the human sciences and the change in direction in philosophy, so that it is important to understand a little about structuralism before coming on to strictly philosophical developments.

At its heart, structuralism is a doctrine about language, though it can be applied to other aspects of human life to the extent that they can be understood on the analogy of language. The classical text of structural linguistics is the *Course in General Linguistics* of the Swiss linguist Ferdinand de Saussure, which was put together by two of his students in 1916, three years after his death, from notes taken on his lectures in Geneva. What was distinctive about Saussure's approach to language was his insistence on studying, not the historical processes of change in particular languages, but the underlying structures which are common to language as such. In some ways, his project could be compared to that of Wittgenstein in the *Tractatus*, of seeking for the 'essence' of language which underlies the diversity of actual linguistic forms. The difference is that Wittgenstein's quest was that of a logician, who looked for the a priori or necessary features of sentences which made them capable of being true or false, while Saussure approached language as an empirical linguist, whose views were informed by knowledge of the features of a variety of actual languages. This difference, as we shall see, extends to the character of the 'linguistic turn' which each of the two men's work gave to philosophy.

The persisting (though not necessarily unchanging) structures of language had to be studied, in Saussure's term, 'synchronically', that is, as coexisting in a kind of timeless present (as opposed to the 'diachronic', or historical, study of successive phases of language against which Saussure was reacting). This coexistence was not a matter of simply existing side-by-side without real connection, but of belonging to a *system*. Language formed a system because it was a social institution, a set of rules which necessarily operated in a society. Language was essentially a *social* possession, not something which belonged to isolated individuals as such. It was of course *used* by individuals, but that very use presupposed the prior existence of language as a collective possession. Saussure's term for language as a collectively owned system was *langue*, which he contrasted with *parole*, the use by individuals in particular situations of the linguistic structures which they share with others. (These words, in their Saussurean use, are not easily translated into English, and are probably best treated simply as technical terms.)

What is the system composed of? Saussure's answer was 'signs' (roughly equivalent to 'words'), which can be regarded on the one hand as sets of *sounds* (Saussure gave priority to *spoken* language) and on the other as having a *meaning*. These two aspects of the sign are not separable except in thought: the sign is a set of sounds (a 'signifier') with a meaning (a 'signified'). The 'signified' is not, however, to be identified with the word's *referent*, that is, with the object to which the word refers: rather, it is what Frege called the expression's 'sense', or, as we might say, the concept expressed by the sign. The signified of the English word 'sheep', to adapt an example from Saussure himself, is not the animal which grazes on the hillside and which is also referred to by the French word *mouton*, but the concept which English-speaking people have of that animal.

Signs are 'arbitrary', in that there is no necessary connection between a sign and its referent. Quite simply, different languages refer to the same things using different signs, which 'signify' differently, as, for instance, the English word 'sheep' and the French word '*mouton*' express subtly different concepts. And because each language is a system, what is signified by one term in a language cannot be separated from what is signified by other terms in the same language. Saussure, in other words, held what is often called a 'holistic' theory of meaning, in which no term has meaning in isolation, but only in the context of the language as a whole (this also clearly implies a holistic theory of reference, according to which what refers is not individual terms taken one by one, but the language as a whole). The arbitrariness of language, taken together with the holistic theory of meaning and reference, means that each language is a system which divides up the world differently.

On a holistic theory of meaning, the meaning of any individual term cannot be given except by considering its *differences* from other terms. The meaning of 'sheep', for instance, cannot be given except in terms of a system of contrasts—between 'sheep', 'horses', 'pigs', 'men', and so on. Indeed (and this is the point of Saussure's example which was adapted earlier), the English word 'sheep' has a different meaning from the French word '*mouton*', precisely because in English 'sheep' (the living animal) is distinguished from 'mutton' (the meat of that animal), whereas the French word does not differentiate between the animal and its meat. What a language is, then, is a *system of differences*, and the kinds of differences which a particular language embodies are plainly related to the particular way of carving up reality existing in the society which uses it.

2. Structuralism and Anthropology

It is easy to see how structuralism so characterized could have relevance, for example, to cultural anthropology. If a society and its culture can be seen as a kind of 'language' which can be understood as a system in the Saussurean fashion, then we have, as for instance Claude Lévi-Strauss saw, a potent instrument for making sense both of the differences and the similarities between cultures. The adoption of a structuralist approach, whether in linguistics or in anthropology, however, carries with it important philosophical implications. First, it undermines the view of language (and so of thought) as a transparent representation of an objective reality: it is not the nature of the world which determines the concepts which we can have of it, but the reverse. The structures of our language determine the kinds of distinction which we make between types of objects, the sorts of categorization of things which we use in our thought. If we do not see the world 'as it is in itself', in the way in which traditional realists thought we did, nor even according to a single a priori set of categories, as Kant thought, then this seems to undermine all metaphysical doctrines of the possibility of absolute knowledge. If there is any sense in which all human beings share the same categories (as Lévi-Strauss certainly thought they did), it is not something which follows necessarily from the very nature of human rationality, as in traditional philosophy, but simply something which arises because of the contingent structures of human language: the explanation of their universality would lie, presumably, in something equally contingent, such as the mode of functioning of the human brain.

Secondly, if the categories of thought used by an individual in making sense of the world are not those which are self-evident to him or her as a rational being, but need to be empirically discovered by examining the actual thought-patterns of human beings, then the concept of a transcendental subject which has been at the heart of most European philosophy since Descartes is called in question. (We had the first hints of this in discussing Althusser in the previous chapter). Descartes, in pursuing his method of doubt, was effectively isolating the pure rational core of each individual human being, that which was most essentially human because it was not associated with anything purely individual about us. In doubting the existence of anything external, Descartes was rejecting the identification of ourselves with our bodies, and so any association between the way we think and the way our brains are structured. The one proposition which survived doubt, 'I think, therefore I am', identified our selves with that which is most purely rational and necessarily universal—pure thought which is not the thought of anyone in particular.

If we cannot think without language, however, and if language is simply an empirical characteristic of human beings, then the investigation of our patterns of thought becomes a task for empirical anthropology rather than philosophy. In particular, the idea of a 'self' or 'subject' ceases to refer to a metaphysical absolute, existing outside time, space, and history, and becomes something constructed in language. It is not a self-transparent 'given' of our experience, but something which comes into existence as part of the structures of language as they function in our developing relationships with others in society. In this way, the rejection of the transparency of thought and of a priori structures of rationality and the downgrading of the 'subject' from a transcendental foundation to an empirical construction are mutually inseparable presuppositions of the adoption of a structuralist approach. Structuralism marked a revolution in philosophy because those who adopted it could no longer consistently think of the philosophical project in the same way. Philosophy could no longer take the high a priori road, ignoring the empirical conditions of human experience and reasoning to what *must be so* if human beings were to have the kind of experience they do. It had to treat human beings as simply empirical individuals in the world, whose own thoughts were not necessarily transparent to themselves, but whose behaviour and responses were shaped by underlying and largely unconscious structures of thought.

To repeat, this was not entirely new. Philosophers such as Sartre and Merleau-Ponty, influenced above all by Heidegger, had already cast doubt on the Cartesian subject. Heidegger's doctrine that the human mode of being was 'being-in-the-world', which both accepted, makes it impossible to conceive of the human subject as transcending the particular situation in which he or she finds him- or herself. (Even the need to use gendered pronouns in the preceding sentence makes plain the difference between this concept of human subjectivity and that of Descartes, which has no gender). As suggested in an earlier chapter, Sartre's concept of the self as a 'nothingness' is closer to the Cartesian view than is really consistent with the idea of 'being-in-the-world'; but Merleau-Ponty's insistence on the 'ambiguity' of human existence, and the embodiment of the self, is as far from the Cartesian concept of the self as fully 'present to itself' as is any of the accounts influenced by structuralism. Consistently with this, moreover, Merleau-Ponty rejects the idea that the universal principles of rationality are self-evident to us: the ambiguity of existence implies that we can only make a tentative approach to them from the perspective of a particular time in history. And in his later writings, as we have seen, Merleau-Ponty too took a 'linguistic turn' which was very similar to that taken by the structuralists.

Nevertheless, Merleau-Ponty seems still to have held that there *were* necessary principles of rationality, however dimly we might be able to perceive them from our historically limited point of view. The decisive further step taken by those influenced by structuralism was to reject the whole notion of necessary principles of human reason, or at the very least to leave such a notion outside their thinking. Whether they were right to do so is a question which can be answered only once we have looked at one or two examples of such philosophers and considered how this abandonment of necessity affected their thought.

3. Jacques Lacan: Philosophy and Psychoanalysis

There is clearly a natural affinity between the structuralist conception of our conscious thought as intelligible only against the background of structures of which we are not conscious and the Freudian theory of the importance of unconscious mental activity. Both are certainly equally opposed to the Cartesian view that all mental activity is by definition fully accessible to consciousness. The structuralist idea that the subject is not something given and transparent, but something constructed in language, moreover, fits well with the Freudian view of the ego as coming into being in the process of infantile development. We might expect, therefore, that structuralist concepts would have an appeal to psychoanalytically orientated thinkers seeking a general theoretical basis for psychoanalysis which was not couched, as Freud's was, in biological or mechanistic terms. In France, the most distinguished and interesting exponent of this combination of Freudianism and structuralism was Jacques Lacan.

Lacan was born in Paris in 1901. He trained as an orthodox psychiatrist, and in 1932 published a doctoral thesis on 'Paranoiac psychosis and its relationships with personality'. In the course of the 1930s, however, his thinking took an increasingly psychoanalytic direction, and he came more and more to the attention of the psychoanalytic world through his papers. Perhaps the best-known of these, and certainly one of the most characteristic of Lacan's approach to Freudianism, was his 1936 paper on 'The mirror stage as formative of the function of the I'. In the 1950s, Lacan's regular seminars on psychoanalytic issues in Paris attracted a wide range of intellectuals: many of these seminars have since been published, with some of the most important of them included in Lacan's work called simply *Écrits*.[1]

In these papers, Lacan develops an interpretation of Freudian theory which is markedly different from the orthodox (and was partly responsible for his expulsion from the International Psychoanalytic Association), but which he would claim to be true to the spirit of Freud's original intentions. As well as having a following for his version of Freudianism in many other countries, he was the dominant influence in French psychoanalysis, becoming the pope of a new orthodoxy against which other radical psychoanalysts, such as Irigaray and Kristeva, had to rebel (see Chapter 9). His influence is felt, not only in narrowly psychoanalytic circles, but in the wider French culture, in literature, and even in politics (his thought had a significant effect on the events of May 1968 in France). Lacan died in 1981.

Lacan's interpretation of Freud, originally influenced by Husserlian phenomenology, took an increasingly 'structuralist' form in the 1950s and 1960s, and in its turn had an influence on the way in which structuralism developed. It was structuralist in the sense that it followed the 'linguistic turn', the new preoccupation with language and the social rather than with thought conceived of as something internal, private, 'mental'. Whereas Freud himself had thought of the 'unconscious' in biological terms, a repository for primitive, animal 'drives', Lacan conceived of the unconscious rather as being structured like a *language*. It is equally true for him, however, that the 'conscious self' is to be understood in linguistic terms. Human subjectivity in general does not exist, in Lacan's view, apart from language.

This is crucially important philosophically, since it means that one does not exist as a subject independently of relations to other subjects (since language is inseparable from relations with others). Even the very formation of a self is a social construct: one becomes a subject when one learns to say 'I', which is a term in a shared language and one which is learned through relations with others. This is the significance of the 'mirror stage' which was spoken of earlier in connection with Lacan's 1936 paper. At an early stage in a child's development (from the age of six months, Lacan tells us), the child comes to recognize his own image in the mirror. (I deliberately use Lacan's masculine pronoun here, since, as we shall see in a later chapter, this was one focus of the later feminist critique of his views.) So too can a chimpanzee; however, Lacan goes on, there is an important difference:

This act, far from exhausting itself, as in the case of the monkey, once the image has been mastered and found empty, immediately rebounds in the case of the child in a series of gestures in which he experiences in play the relation between the movements assumed in the image and the reflected environment, and between this virtual complex and the reality it reduplicates—the child's own body, and the persons and things around him.'[2]

This paragraph incorporates a number of Lacan's central themes, all of crucial philosophical importance. There is the formation of the subject through a relation to something external to oneself (the mirror image): thus the subject is no longer, as in Descartes, something which is immediately present to oneself when one separates oneself from everything external and looks within. In a later work, Lacan comments that Descartes's 'I think' (in the 'I think, therefore I am') 'certainly cannot be detached from the fact that he can formulate it only by *saying* it to us, implicitly—a fact that he forgets.'[3] Secondly, there is the role of the imagination in the acquisition of language—the child acquires the sense of self and the ability to use 'I' by 'experiencing in play' the relation between this *virtual* image and himself. Thirdly, the child's sense of self is inseparable from his awareness of his own *body* (cf. Merleau-Ponty's concept of the 'body-subject').

Imagination is fundamental to Lacan's thought. We discover ourselves in an *image*—a reflected image as in the mirror, or a statue by which our identity is projected before us in an imaginary form, or a dream image of ourselves, and so on. The acquisition of a sense of oneself, the ability to use the word 'I', is bound up with an ability to look upon oneself from the outside, by means of such an image. In this sense, becoming a 'self', becoming fully human rather than merely natural, and so becoming able to gain control over one's desires, is inseparable from becoming socialized. But it is also, by the same token, becoming alienated from one's own desires. Becoming a self is coming to see those desires as essentially a *threat* to one, in a way which they could not have been when one did not have a self to be threatened. It is a characteristic of human desire, as opposed to the merely animal variety, that it is seen in relation to the self, and so is essentially given a linguistic form.

The roots of the kinds of problems with which psychoanalysis later deals are seen as lying here, in the difficulties of coping with the threats to the child's selfhood presented by his own desires, as in the Oedipal desire of the male child for his mother and the resulting experience of 'castration', or deprivation of the phallus, by the father. But it is precisely the effort to deal with such threats, above all in the Oedipal situation, which for Lacan constitutes the process of forming a self, an identity. The aim of analysis, for Lacan, is not to achieve human happiness, in the bourgeois sense of the achievement of certain 'goods'. It has an ethical end, but 'that ethics implies the dimension that is expressed in what we call the tragic sense of life'.[4] Lacan cites a number of actual tragic dramas—*King Oedipus* itself, *King Lear*—to illustrate the way in which the tragic hero gives up the 'service of goods' and 'enters the zone in which he pursues his desire'.[5] Psychoanalysis makes possible a form of ethical judgement which 'gives this question the form of a Last Judgment: Have you acted in conformity with the desire that is in you?'[6]

In order to see how psychoanalysis is supposed to achieve this end, we need to look more closely at what Lacan says about language. What Lacan says is notoriously obscure, but it seems that what he thinks about language is as follows. If we accept the structuralist view that the meaning of any sign depends on its relation to other signs, rather than on any relation to a referent (in other words, that the signifier is *autonomous*), then it follows that language is essentially metaphorical, or at least that no sharp distinction can be drawn between the 'literal' and the 'metaphorical'. For any such distinction would have to be based on the criterion that 'literal' language simply refers to the facts, while 'metaphorical' language embroiders on the facts. The breakthrough of metaphor into literal language, however, can be seen as the breakthrough of the repressed into expression.

The language which we normally use as adults is the language which our membership of society requires: it expresses the socialized 'self' which we have acquired in the process of becoming adapted to society. But the desires which have been repressed in order to allow that socialized self to be formed can always express themselves in indirect ways. This particularly happens, as Freud saw, in dreams, slips of the tongue, and so on. The psychoanalyst's job is thus to interpret these metaphorical expressions, in order to allow the unconscious to find a more direct expression and the uncompleted task of self-formation to be completed. Lacan quotes Freud's famous dictum, 'Where id (it) was, there Ego (I) shall be,' and glosses it by saying that 'Freud addresses the subject in order to say to him the following, which is new—*Here, in the field of the dream, you are at home.*'[7]

Psychoanalysis is thus interpreted as a transaction in what Lacan calls 'the symbolic order', a linguistic transaction between therapist and client. Freud himself, of course, had spoken of psychoanalysis as the 'talking cure', but because of his own medical training, of the biological preoccupations of the time, and of the desire to present psychoanalysis as something 'scientific' in the nineteenth-century sense of that term, it was more usual, both for Freud and for his followers, to conceive of it on the lines of medical treatment. Lacan's linguistic interpretation of psychoanalysis cuts right across any attempt to assimilate it to bodily medicine or to a scientific theory as understood in positivist philosophy of science. The whole notion of a 'science' is anyway much harder to define than the positivists thought, and 'it is in no way necessary that the tree of science should have a single trunk.'[8] The central Western idea of science as a disinterested pursuit of knowledge is called in question by Lacan: the desire for knowledge is seen by him as simply a sublimated version of other desires which have been repressed in Western culture: 'I think that throughout this historical period the desire of man, which has been felt, anesthetized, put to sleep by moralists, domesticated by educators, betrayed by the academies, has quite simply taken refuge or been repressed in that most subtle and blindest of passions, as the story of Oedipus shows, the passion for knowledge.'[9]

The value, both theoretical and practical, of Lacan's interpretation of Freud is not our concern here. But in the course of developing it he propounds a number of philosophical theses which have had a profound effect on much subsequent French philosophy, and so have to be taken seriously in such a work as this. First of all, just by offering a psychoanalytic account of the construction of the self, he helped to legitimize the idea that psychoanalysis could enter the domain of philosophy. Once philosophers themselves had questioned the assumption that there is a transcendental ego to be reached as the conclusion of a priori reasoning, of course, it was natural to conclude that the way was open for empirical accounts of how the self was formed. But to give such an account in *psychoanalytic* terms, as Lacan did—that is, in terms of non-rational desires and infantile relationships—gave a particular character to much structuralist and post-structuralist French philosophy, as we shall see. The 'subject' was not just seen as constructed, but as a construction which received its character from non-rational human desires.

Lacan's treatment of language has also been enormously influential. He completed the structuralist dissociation of language from literal reference or meaning, making the meaning of what was said or written a function, not of any relation between the words and an 'objective world', but rather of the speaker's or writer's unconscious thoughts and motives. This conception of language as essentially metaphorical, though originally developed as an account of the Freudian unconscious in its role in psychoanalytic theory, became increasingly pervasive, as an account of *all* uses of language. It was a natural extension to apply it to the language of imaginative literature: but, as we shall see in the next two chapters, it has come to be applied even to the apparently sober language of philosophical texts.

Finally, we should not ignore Lacan's cynicism about the pretended disinterestedness of 'science'. Here we see an example of the influence of Nietzsche on recent French thought. Nietzsche too rejected the whole idea of a disinterested pursuit of knowledge: the passion for truth for him concealed a whole number of much baser passions, all of them incorporated in a 'will to power'. In this case, Lacan is probably important only as an *example* of such Nietzschean patterns of thought, rather than as a channel for Nietzschean influence on others: other recent French thinkers who show the same patterns seem to have been independently affected by their reading of Nietzsche. Nevertheless, Lacan's powerful association of Nietzschean and Freudian themes does seem to have played some part in the recent course of French philosophy.

There is undoubtedly an internal coherence between these three elements in Lacan's thought. If the subject of thought and knowledge is to be equated with the self as formed in the course of individual experience (in ways which psychoanalysis purports to describe), then the concepts employed by that subject to make sense of the world will have to be explained in terms of the manner of that formation. A person's concepts and language will be those formed by the particular character of early childhood experience: they will express the needs and desires of the infant self, rather than the character of the world independently of that self. Language will indeed be 'metaphorical' in the sense of describing things in images shaped by the demands of human need rather than in terms of rational concepts. And then we can conclude that the vaunted objectivity of science, which depends on such a rational and dispassionate way of describing the world, is a myth in the way that Nietzsche says.

What particularly strikes an analytically trained philosopher about all this, however, is the lack of any serious argumentative support for the starting-point, the equation of the subject of thought with the self of psychoanalysis. Even if we accept the abandonment of a 'transcendental' subject in favour of a subject whose being is 'in-the-world'—which necessarily looks out on the world from a position within space, time, and history—it by no means follows that the structures of that subject's thought are determined by the accidents of individual human development, as described in a Freudian theory for which Lacan offers little or no empirical evidence. This failure to offer empirical evidence for what looks like an empirical account, however, depends on Lacan's Nietzschean suspicion of the whole notion of objective science; and this in turn depends on Lacan's conception of language and its relation to the world, to which I shall return, in a critical spirit, at the end of the chapter.

4. Michel Foucault

One other French philosopher who has certainly been influenced by Nietzsche, and who can be classified, at least in his earlier work, as a 'structuralist' (in the same loose sense as Lacan) is Michel Foucault. Foucault was born in Poitiers in 1926, the son of a doctor. After early education at a Catholic school, he became a boarder at the Lycée Henri IV in Paris, and then entered the École Normale Supérieure to study philosophy. Among his teachers were Maurice Merleau-Ponty, Jean Hyppolite, and Louis Althusser. He was a member of the Communist Party for a short time, but left it in 1951. After graduating, his interests quickly moved away from philosophy as normally conceived (though I hope to show that he remained a philosopher throughout his major writings), and towards psychiatry and history: his work for his doctorate was in fact a study of the history of madness. This was to provide the basis for his first major work, *Folie et déraison: histoire de la folie à l'âge classique*, published in 1961 (an abridged version was published in 1964 and subsequently translated into English as *Madness and Civilization*[10]).

In 1960, Foucault was appointed head of the department of philosophy in the University of Clermont-Ferrand, and it was while he was there that he wrote the work which first really attracted wider attention to him, *Les Mots et les choses* (*The Order of Things*[11]). The publication of this in 1966 was partly responsible for his call to the University of Paris (Vincennes), where he was teaching during the student rebellion of 1968. In 1970, he was appointed to the chair of the history of systems of thought at the Collège de France. From then until his death in 1984, he continued to teach, to write further works, both scholarly and more journalistic, and to campaign for a number of leftist causes and for gay rights.

The first question which is liable to arise in the mind of someone brought up in the Anglo-Saxon tradition in philosophy is whether Foucault was a philosopher at all. Almost all his major works are either collections of essays and interviews on political and social issues or else what look to Anglo-Saxon eyes like studies in intellectual history. Even his more methodological works, such as *The Order of Things* and *The Archaeology of Knowledge* devote a good deal of space to the discussion of empirical historical questions. There is no doubt of Foucault's interest to students of the areas of history in which he worked, but I want to suggest, as I remarked earlier, that he is nevertheless in an important sense a philosopher. His studies of cultural history incorporate a number of important philosophical theses, though some of the most characteristic of them belong to that strange genre which could be called 'anti-philosophical philosophy'.

The very concentration on historical studies is in itself the adoption of this kind of anti-philosophical stance. Foucault turned to studying ideas in their historical context because of a typically modern scepticism about the possibility of metaphysics or grand over-arching theories of 'philosophical anthropology'— the formation of general a priori accounts of an unchanging 'human nature'. Connected with this was an equal suspicion of general theorizing in the human and social sciences, which always presupposes such accounts of human nature. Studying the historical changes in conceptions of human beings, and seeking to show that there was no sense in which one such conception was any 'truer' than any other, was one way in which to undermine grand metaphysical theories. It was this modern suspicion of large-scale abstract theorizing which he seems to have meant by 'structuralism': he says, 'Structuralism is not a new method; it is the awakened and troubled consciousness of modern thought.'[12]

It is in the light of this rejection of philosophical anthropology that we have to understand Foucault's opposition to 'humanism'. He was not expressing misanthropy, or a belief in the replacement of human beings by something else, such as machines or another species, when he said, at the very end of *The Order of Things*, that, 'As the archaeology of our thought easily shows, man is an invention of recent date. And one perhaps nearing its end.'[13] Rather, as the context shows, he was suggesting that the concept of human nature with which we currently operate is a product of a particular historical situation, a 'change in the fundamental arrangements of knowledge', which arose at the time of the Enlightenment. As he goes on, 'If those arrangements were to disappear as they appeared . . . then one can certainly wager that man would be erased, like a face drawn in the sand at the edge of the sea.'[14]

Foucault reveals his 'structuralism' in his earlier writings, not only by his suspicion of a priori theorizing, but also in the grounds for that suspicion. Underlying his historicism is the same kind of 'linguistic turn' which we have already seen in Lacan. The fundamental unit of his analyses is the 'discourse', or 'discursive practice', which is a rule-governed set of statements in which a community of human beings embodies what it thinks of as 'knowledge' (in the words of the quotation above, a set of 'fundamental arrangements of knowledge'). He defines a 'discursive practice' as follows: 'it is a body of anonymous, historical rules, always determined in the time and space that have defined a given period, and for a given social, economic, geographical, or linguistic area, the conditions of operation of the enunciative function.'[15]

The rules are 'anonymous': that is, they are not the rules of which a particular speaker may be consciously aware, but are shared by all members of the relevant community equally. Although Foucault indignantly denies, in the foreword to the English edition of *The Order of Things*, that he is a 'structuralist',[16] his discursive practices are *like* 'structures' in being unconscious: they are 'a positive unconscious of knowledge: a level that eludes the consciousness of the scientist and yet is part of scientific discourse.'[17] Furthermore, these practices are 'historical'—they are not found in all communities at all times and in all places, but belong to a particular phase in the historical development of a particular community.

Finally, they are 'conditions of operation of the enunciative function': in other words, they are the rules by which we can make statements which can be either true or false, and so are capable of embodying knowledge. They must therefore above all include rules for distinguishing true statements from false ones. But if such discursive practices are 'historical' in the sense explained, then that implies that the rules for distinguishing truth from falsity must be confined to particular communities at particular times in their historical development. There are no criteria for truth and falsity which apply outside a particular discursive practice, no universal standards of logic or rationality. There is some similarity here to the arguments of the later Wittgenstein to the effect that words such as 'truth' can be given meaning only in the context of a particular 'language-game', which forms part of a particular 'form of life'.

If truth is relative to particular discursive practices in this way, then it follows that different discursive practices are *incommensurable*: that they cannot be compared in respect of their truth and falsity. There can be no such thing as 'absolute' or 'object-ive' truth. And if different discursive practices are found at different periods in history, then we cannot see history as a progress towards objective truth:

I am not concerned, therefore, to describe the progress of knowledge towards an objectivity in which today's science can finally be recognised; what I am attempting to bring to light is the epistemological field, the *episteme* in which knowledge, envisaged apart from all criteria having reference to its rational value or to its objective forms, grounds its positivity and thereby manifests a history which is not that of its growing perfection, but rather that of its conditions of possibility.[18]

The appropriate method for bringing to light these 'epistemological fields', Foucault is quite clear, is *not* that of 'phenomenology', as conceived of by Husserl and even as practised by Merleau-Ponty. Phenomenology went back to the 'knowing subject', to our own consciousness of ourselves as 'scientists', or knowledge-seekers, in which the 'objects' of knowledge were 'constituted'. Foucault wants to play down the centrality of the notion of the 'subject'. He does not want to deny that 'science' cannot be considered entirely independently of 'scientists', and their conscious thoughts about what they are doing. But he does want to question whether such a 'phenomenological' analysis is enough to capture 'the immense density of scientific discourse.'[19] To do justice to that, he suggests, we need to take into account all those unconscious rules which determine what particular 'subjects' can count as 'scientific discourse'—the rules which distinguish between 'true' and 'false' statements in their particular discursive practice. In order to unearth those rules, we need a different discipline, which he calls 'archaeology'.

As Foucault's thinking developed, however, he came to play down the importance of 'archaeology', the (typically structuralist) concern with the purely formal analysis of rules of discourse, and to emphasize much more the Nietzschean concept of 'genealogy'. The notion of 'genealogy' is much more *political* than that of 'archaeology'. Genealogy is not a science, Foucault says: it is rather: 'the insurrection of knowledges that are opposed primarily not to the contents, methods or concepts of a science, but to the effects of the centralising powers which are linked to the institution and functioning of an organised scientific discourse within a society such as ours'.[20]

He had been mistaken, he came to think, to conceive of discursive practices as little more than 'paradigms' (he seems to be using the term in its Kuhnian sense), rather than in terms of 'the effects of power peculiar to the play of statements'.[21] The emphasis was now much more on knowledge as something which is not the product of some timeless human 'essence', manifested in individuals taken singly, but which is generated in social institutions, existing in a particular historical setting and embodying relations of power and 'hierarchization'.

Genealogy could thus unearth, not just the unconscious rules which lead members of a community to accept some statements as true and reject others as false, but the subtle historical and social conditions which bring about the institutions in which those rules are accepted. The particular set of unconscious rules which most interested Foucault were those which constitute the discursive practice of modern, or post-Enlightenment, society, the society of 'science', of 'reason', and of 'humanism'. For it is a distinctive characteristic of this discursive practice that those who follow its rules believe that their view of reality is objectively correct, an expression of human progress. If he could show by reference to the historical origins of this practice that it has no more claim to objectivity or rationality than any other, then he would have justified his suspicion of allegedly objective views in general, and would have liberated human beings to explore the actual diversity of their natures.

This is the motivation for Foucault's various historical studies, from *Madness and Civilization* onwards. He seeks to show how, in the modern world, since the 'Classical' period of the seventeenth and eighteenth centuries, varieties of human behaviour which previously were simply accepted as such, and controlled if need be by the naked apparatus of State power, have come to be subjected to control by 'experts', acting in the name of 'science'. Madness, for instance, has been redescribed as 'mental illness', and so subjected to medical control; many forms of crime have been reclassified as the expression of a 'sick personality', similarly in need of expert management by 'scientifically' trained people. Bodily illness itself has become the province of experts. Even our very sexuality has been taken over by science and is talked about and theorized about incessantly. In short, the idea has grown up since the Enlightenment that human beings do not simply have to obey the law in their external behaviour, but have to be 'normal', healthy, well-adjusted people. Deviations from this norm are policed, not by violence, but by scientific management which is accepted because 'it induces pleasure, forms knowledge, produces discourse'.[22]

In an important sense, what Foucault is doing here is turning the Enlightenment's own weapon of critique on to the 'humanist' consequences which have been derived from that same Enlightenment—the idea that there are certain human goods, happiness, health, reasonableness, which are the necessary pursuit of all human beings to the extent that they are truly human. Foucault explores this tension in his late essay, 'What is Enlightenment?', which was published only posthumously.[23] The essay is a commentary on Kant's famous essay of the same name, published in 1784, in which Kant described Enlightenment as humanity's coming of age, and as having as its motto *Sapere aude* (roughly, 'Dare to think for yourself'). This makes the essence of Enlightenment, according to Foucault, 'a critique and a permanent creation of ourselves in our autonomy'.[24] But this aspect of Enlightenment is in tension with humanism, which consists in fixed concepts of human nature, which are not subjected to critique.

Foucault aims to continue the Enlightenment project of 'critique and permanent creation of ourselves' by using his 'genealogical' method. Unlike humanism, which restricts the possibilities of what we can be as human beings, this genealogical critique 'will not deduce from the form of what we are what it is impossible for us to do and to know'.[25] Rather, it will liberate us to new possibilities:

it will separate out from the contingency that has made us what we are the possibility of no longer being, doing, or thinking what we are, or do, or think. It is not seeking to make possible a metaphysics that has finally become a science; it is seeking to give new impetus, as far and wide as possible, to the undefined work of freedom.[26]

By showing us that there is no objective truth, Foucault thus aims to liberate us from the idea that humanism is objectively true, and so make it possible to explore new ways of 'being, doing and thinking'. His social critique of modernity leads, not to an alternative general theory of human nature, but to an abandonment of all such theories and an opening to the possibility, in Lacan's words, of 'living in conformity with the desire that is in you'.

5. Conclusion and Critique

Lacan and Foucault differ in important respects. Above all, philosophy is much less central to Lacan's thought, in which psychoanalysis takes the primary place, than it is to Foucault's. Nevertheless, there is a good deal in common between them. Both express, as has been said, a typically twentieth-century suspicion of the excessive ambitions (as they would see it) of traditional Western philosophy and science, which they see as culminating in the Enlightenment project of conducting both our thought and our lives in accordance with universal principles of pure reason. This suspicion, and the reaction against the Enlightenment which it leads to, clearly embody a widespread current mood, and it is not surprising that so many have been attracted to their thought as a result, especially since they are both subtle thinkers who raise a number of probing questions about the philosophical tradition which demand an answer.

The basic ground for the suspicion in the case of both Lacan and Foucault is a certain view about the referential function of language, the capacity of language to say objectively true things about the world. In Lacan's case, as we saw, this is a view about *meaning*, which separates off meaning from all considerations about reference and makes the meaning of any given term depend entirely on its relations with other terms. The consequence of this, as we also saw, is the abandonment of any distinction between metaphorical and literal uses of language, since the idea of a 'literal' meaning is tied up with that of reference to some really existing thing or state of affairs, while 'metaphorical' meaning is much more indirect and nonreferential. Lacan, in effect, makes all meaning 'metaphorical' (or at least non-literal). In Foucault's case, the thesis is more about the *truth-conditions* of our statements, the conditions under which the things we say are true or false, which he claims to be necessarily relative to particular 'discursive practices'.

Lacan's conception of meaning is open to the objection that it makes it impossible to make certain distinctions which seem unavoidable—for instance, between saying 'She is a cat', in reference to my feline pet now reclining on the rug in front of the fire, and saying the same words as a way of describing a woman's agility and athleticism. We could perhaps make this distinction by saying that the first use is a standard use in English of the word 'cat', whereas the second is an adaptation of that standard use for a particular descriptive purpose. But that would not really get round the difficulty, since the first use is standard only because it is the use to refer to a naturally existing species of animals, while the second use can only function as it does because the first use literally *refers* to animals of that species. This is the familiar point that metaphorical uses are parasitic on literal, so that it would be impossible for *all* uses to be metaphorical. Even for Lacan's own purposes this is important: he cannot give his account of the distinctive features of the unconscious, as a use of language to conceal what people are really feeling, without presupposing a use of language to express feelings and thoughts directly. If psychoanalysts are to be able to decipher the language of the unconscious, they can do so only if they have a 'language of consciousness' into which to translate it.

One difficulty in Lacan's case is that his own language is frequently so obscure that it is difficult to know whether such objections really hit the mark. The same cannot be said of Foucault: his language is much more pellucid than Lacan's, and the view about truth-conditions in particular is clearly stated on a number of occasions. The *point* of his claims, however, and so the possibility of certain kinds of objection to them, is much more liable to variant interpretations. If we take Foucault, in proposing this view, to be offering a generalized critique of general theories, then he might be thought to be open to a familiar objection to all such attempts, namely, that they are self-defeating. If all attributions of truth and falsity are relative to discursive practices, the objection would go, then the truth-claims of Foucault's own thesis will be equally relative to a particular discursive practice. That is, he will not be able to claim that his own thesis is objectively true, or such that it ought to be accepted by any rational being. Foucault could, however, defend himself against such objections by, for example, presenting his enterprise as not so much a general theoretical critique of theories as a piecemeal liberation of his readers from the harmful influence of the belief in the need for general theories to be accepted by any rational being.

Very similar points can be made about Foucault's critique of 'humanism'. It is one thing, objectors might say, to criticize a particular conception of human nature and the human good, such as the liberal bourgeois conception that the good life for human beings is one of healthy 'normality'. But we can do this, they might say, only if we presuppose an alternative, and more *correct*, general account of what the good for human beings is, in terms of which the limitations of liberal humanism can be criticized. Foucault, however, could simply reject that latter claim: the alternative to liberal humanism is not, he could say, a different sort of humanism, resting on a different general conception of human nature, but a life open to diverse conceptions of our own humanity. Foucault's project is not so easily dismissed as all that, even if one may feel a lingering suspicion that it is fatally flawed.

CHAPTER EIGHT

After Structuralism: Lévinas, Derrida, and Lyotard

1. The Aftermath of Structuralism

The revolution in French philosophy unleashed by the influence of structuralism still continues. More recent French philosophers are sometimes described as 'post-structuralist', but this is an even more misleading label than usual, since it implies that they constitute a separate 'school', distinct from the 'structuralists' and later in time than them. But there never was, strictly speaking, a 'structuralist school', at least in philosophy proper, only a number of philosophers whose thinking responded to particular elements in the structuralist approach to language and anthropology and gave those elements their own philosophical 'twist'. And the philosophers called 'post-structuralists' are largely concerned with taking further that philosophical 'twist', rather than with developing a whole new style of philosophizing. In particular, they continue with the theme of the questioning of the philosophical tradition and with its associated critique of the 'modernism' derived from the Enlightenment (for which reason, they are sometimes associated with the more general intellectual movement known as 'post-modernism').

A number of recent philosophers could have been taken as representative of the current intellectual climate, but, partly for reasons of space, I propose to concentrate in this chapter on three: Emmanuel Lévinas, Jacques Derrida, and Jean-François Lyotard. An account of the thought of these three men both follows on naturally from that discussed in the preceding chapter and forms a coherent narrative which makes it easier to understand the present state of French philosophy more generally. (Though it is worth saying that Lévinas has been philosophically active since the late 1920s and has consistently pursued his own very individual line.) In the next, and final chapter, the narrative will be rounded off by considering some recent feminist thinkers who have taken the themes of structuralism and post-structuralism and applied them to their own concerns.

2. Emmanuel Lévinas

Emmanuel Lévinas has already appeared in this book, in connection with the discussion of existential phenomenology in Chapter 4. He figured then as the man whose book on Husserl introduced Sartre to phenomenology; but he could equally be described as the man who more than any other individual introduced phenomenology, in both its Husserlian and Heideggerian forms, to French philosophy generally. (He himself saw Bergson as a major early influence on his own thought, and describes Bergson's emphasis on temporality as having 'prepared the soil for the subsequent implantation of Heideggerian phenomenology into France'.[1]) He was born in 1906 in Kaunas, Lithuania (at that time part of the Russian Empire), the child of orthodox Jewish parents. His father owned a bookshop, and Emmanuel early became an avid reader, mainly of the Hebrew Bible and of the great Russian writers of the nineteenth century. In 1923 he left Lithuania for France, to study philosophy in Strasbourg. The political freedom which he encountered there persuaded him in 1930 to seek French citizenship and he has subsequently made his life and career in France.

One major philosophical influence on Lévinas's early thought was Husserlian phenomenology, which he began to study in 1927/8. So impressed was he by Husserl that he decided to write his dissertation on the fundamental concepts of phenomenology, and this work, *La Théorie de l'intuition dans la phénoménologie de Husserl*, in 1930 both received a prize from the Académie Française and was published in book form.[2] Through his interest in phenomenology, Lévinas made a discovery which was to be even more important for his own philosophical development, namely, the thought of Heidegger. Knowing that Heidegger was lecturing in Freiburg im Breisgau, Lévinas decided to spend the academic year 1928/9 there and to attend the lectures. It was the influence of the Heidegger of *Sein und Zeit* (*Being and Time*) which started Lévinas on his own course (even though he has significant disagreements with Heidegger), and which shapes Lévinas's interpretation of Husserlian phenomenology.

After his return from Germany in 1929, Lévinas taught philosophy at a Jewish college in Paris, but he published little in philosophy during the 1930s. Clearly, as a Jew, he was concerned by the rise of Nazism in Germany, and especially by the degree of support which Heidegger appeared to give to the Nazi party, which led him to become more critical in his attitude to Heidegger's thought. At the beginning of the Second World War, Lévinas was mobilized into the French Army, and with the fall of France was captured and confined in a prisoner-of-war camp, where he was made to do forced labour as a member of a Jewish work group. It was only after the war that he was able to return to philosophical activity, and it was at this time that he really began to develop a philosophy of his own, as opposed to commenting on the thought of others. He still, however, did not have a regular academic position, and he published only a short book, *De l'existence à l'existant*,[3] some articles, and a contribution to a collection of lectures by various authors until, in 1961, he produced his first major expression of his own original philosophy, *Totalité et infini*.[4] This was his main thesis for the *doctorat d'état*, which at last, at the age of 55, enabled him to obtain a full academic post, as a professor at the University of Poitiers, and brought him to the attention of a wider philosophical public. A stream of publications has followed—philosophical and Jewish religious books and articles, translations, and interviews. At the time of writing, he remains intellectually active, though by now almost 90, and says that he is still, at least in his conception of philosophical method, a phenomenologist.[5] Like Heidegger, however, he sees phenomenology as more than a method—rather as 'a way of becoming aware of where we are in the world'.[6]

Lévinas's thought is profoundly original, and has, as already noted, been developing over a long period, with its roots both in his response to Heidegger's preoccupation with Being and in Jewish religious thought (though he objects to being classified as a 'Jewish thinker'). But he has been enormously influential on later generations of French philosophers, even those with whom, on a superficial view at least, he has very little in common. If we consider his own thinking in more detail, however, we can begin to see just why that is indeed a *superficial* view.

Ethics lies at the heart of Lévinas's philosophy. The Western tradition of philosophy seems to him to have gone wrong because it has based metaphysics on ontology, the study of Being as such, rather than on ethics. The difference is that ontology is 'a reduction of the other to the same by interposition of a middle and neutral term that ensures the comprehension of being'.[7] That is, the distinction between myself and what is other than myself is blurred: the other is neutralized into a mere 'object' of my consciousness. Metaphysics based on ontology seeks a 'transcendence' which is nothing more than a 'totality', a systematic and objective comprehension of the whole of being, such that all apparent differences are resolved in the system.

Ethics, on the other hand, is the 'calling into question of my spontaneity by the presence of the Other':

The strangeness of the Other, his irreducibility to the I, to my thoughts and my possessions, is precisely accomplished as a calling into question of my spontaneity, as ethics. Metaphysics, transcendence, the welcoming of the other by the same, of the Other by me, is concretely produced as the calling into question of the same by the other, that is as the ethics that accomplishes the critical essence of knowledge.[8]

This passage can be interpreted as follows. Ethics begins not with the sense of myself as a spontaneous or autonomous being, but (and here is Lévinas's point of departure, as he sees it, from the philosophical tradition) with a sense of myself as in relation to an Other, a being who is not myself (not 'the same') and who sets limits to, and so calls into question, my spontaneity or capacity for free action. It is the awareness of otherness, that reality transcends my own consciousness of it and so is irreducibly independent of me, that is essential both to the possibility of knowledge and to metaphysics.

It is the *face* (*le visage*) which epitomizes most completely what Lévinas means by 'the Other': it is in the face, Lévinas says, that the Other's 'epiphany' is produced.[9] The 'face' here means, not simply the physiognomy, but the means which that physiognomy provides to make possible communication between the Other and myself. Communication does not abolish the distinction between persons, but affirms their difference: in engaging in discourse with another person, I am, after all, aware of that person as having his or her own thoughts, distinct from mine, thoughts which may thereby disturb my egoistic world. 'For the ethical relationship which subtends discourse is not a species of consciousness whose ray emanates from the I; it puts the I in question. This putting in question emanates from the other.'[10]

The initial encounter with the Other is, of course, in our dealings with other human beings. But, as the references to 'metaphysics' show, the otherness of other human beings points beyond itself, towards *absolute* Otherness. The encounter with the absolutely Other takes us beyond all possibility of encompassing the totality of things in a single system: such a totalizing system denies the distinction between 'the same' and 'the other'—in effect reducing everything to the same. Recognition of absolute Otherness, by contrast, is recognition of genuine transcendence, beyond Being or, in the title of one of Lévinas's later works, 'otherwise than Being' (*autrement qu' être*).[11] This absolutely Other, or Infinity, cannot in its very nature be *comprehended*, as traditional metaphysics sought to do: metaphysics is not a matter, therefore, of comprehension, but of discourse. 'Better than comprehension, *discourse* relates with what remains essentially transcendent.'[12] And, as in conversation with other human beings, this discourse, in preserving the difference between 'same' and 'other', does not *negate* oneself, but preserves the 'I' in its individuality.

This relation to the Other is described by Lévinas as one of *being responsible for* the Other. In encountering the Other as a 'face', we recognize our responsibility for him or her. In one of the conversations with Philippe Nemo recorded in his work *Ethics and Infinity*,[13] Lévinas says: 'meeting the face is not of the order of pure and simple perception, of the intentionality which goes toward adequation. Positively, we will say that since the Other looks at me, I am responsible for him, without even having *taken* on responsibilities in his regard; his responsibility *is incumbent on me.*[14] It is in this way that our relation with the Other is essentially ethical, since it takes us beyond egoism, even the kind of transcendental egoism which characterizes the Western philosophical tradition since Socrates—an egoism which, paradoxically, works against real individuality, since it blurs the distinction between the 'same' and the 'Other'. The demands which the Other makes on us are said by Lévinas to be unlimited: our relation with the other is not one of simple reciprocity, in which I acknowledge the demands of the Other in return for the Other's acknowledgement of my demands upon him or her.

The absolute Other to whom we are infinitely responsible in this way sounds remarkably like the Judeo-Christian God, and Lévinas does indeed make this identification. 'For every man', he says, 'assuming responsibility for the Other is a way of testifying to the glory of the Infinite, and of being inspired. . . . This responsibility prior to the Law is God's revelation.'[15] It is thus in the relation with the Other, beginning in the relation with other human beings, that we encounter God. Traditional metaphysics, in its primary concern with ontology and with our knowledge of Being, saw our relation with God as essentially *cognitive*: it produced theology, a 'thematisation' of God, that is, a treatment of God as one kind of object of knowledge. But this sort of religious metaphysics is in Lévinas's view really 'atheistic', since it denies God's intrinsic Otherness and our consequent responsibility towards Him (it is in this sense that Lévinas saw Heidegger's thought, in its preoccupation with Being, as essentially atheistic).

A truly religious metaphysics will thus be far from religiosity, since it will root religion in our concern with our fellow human beings: 'Hence metaphysics is enacted where the social relation is enacted—in our relations with men. There can be no "knowledge" of God separated from the relationship with men. The Other is the very locus of metaphysical truth, and is indispensable for my relation with God.'[16] The religion spoken of here is an 'ecumenical' religion: it contains what is common to all the great religions, and it is written in great literature as well as in the sacred books of those great religions.[17] Lévinas himself, of course, remains committed to Judaism as such, distinguishing between 'philosophy', which is rooted in ethics, and 'religion', which is able to give 'consolations' which philosophy cannot necessarily bring.[18]

The atheism of the Western tradition in philosophy has its own social consequences. It leads to a 'humanism' which, in Lévinas's view, is profoundly anti-human, an 'individualism' which is deeply hostile to real individuality. In denying, or at least playing down, the distinction between 'the same' and 'the Other', both traditional metaphysics and the traditional anti-metaphysics of empiricism or positivism seem to him to classify all human individuals as simply instances of 'humanity', parts of the 'totality'. The human subject becomes effectively the expression of an essential human reason, looking out upon a world of objects to be classified and so understood in general terms. And ethics becomes, not the unlimited responsibility of each person towards the Other and the attempt to communicate between the 'same' and the 'Other', but a matter of observing general rules of conduct dictated by this same universal human reason.

Few, if any, of the recent leaders of French philosophy share Lévinas's attachment to a traditional religion, so that it is not there that we should look for the source of his influence upon their thought. That influence lies rather in his attack on the mainstream tradition of Western philosophy and its alleged association with scientific attempts to understand the world in objective terms and with the species of optimistic rational humanism which goes along with such attempts. Lévinas's critique has helped to reinforce the already-existing sense that philosophy itself, at least as previously understood, was in crisis.

The 'structuralists' had already 'decentred' the subject, shifted our inner self-consciousness from centre-stage to a more marginal position away from the real drama of the operation of unconscious structures. They had rejected the comfortable Enlightenment version of humanism, which claimed to make humanity essentially at home in the world by showing how human beings could have technological mastery of things. Their criticisms of the referential view of language as transparently revealing the nature of objective reality, and their analysis of the role of irrational subconscious forces or power-structures in determining the things we say, led them to suspect the scientific view of the world on which that claim to technological mastery rested. The Enlightenment opposition of a 'subject' to a world of 'objects' seemed to them to imply an alienation of human beings from their world which was contrary to the easy claims of Enlightenment 'humanism'.

To reject Enlightenment thought and traditional philosophical conceptions of a universal reason in this way, however, is necessarily also to reject the sorts of rational argument on which the conclusions of that tradition were supposed to rest. The very heart of this sort of critique of 'humanism', indeed, lies in a suspicion that the allegedly 'rational arguments' themselves were merely a mask concealing something far less respectable—in Lévinas's case, an 'egoism' or forgetfulness of the Other. Lévinas's own thought, as one commentator expresses it, 'does not develop through a series of carefully reasoned arguments but rather by semi-poetic, rhapsodic and grammatically elusive meditations around certain central intuitions and metaphors'.[19] While one reads him, one is carried along by the flow of this poetry and prophecy: it is exciting and often illuminating.

But it could be suggested that there is an inescapable paradox about rejecting the structure of neutral, impersonal argumentation by which philosophers in the past sought to establish conclusions which any rational being could accept, since it deprives thinkers of at least one means by which they could hope to persuade opponents of the validity of that rejection itself. Poetry and prophecy can persuade without argument, but only those who are halfway to being persuaded anyway. Apart from this, it could be said that there is a serious danger in basing metaphysics on ethics, as Lévinas does, rather than on logic. It implies (and it is irrelevant from this point of view whether Lévinas himself would endorse this implication) that those who reject the metaphysical conclusions do so not because of an excusable deficiency in their reasoning powers, but because of a moral fault, a lack of willingness to accept the claims of the Other. Furthermore, it seems to remove Lévinas's extremist account of the extent of those claims from all possibility of rational criticism. The suggested problems are, when presented in this form, specifically for Lévinas himself; but similar problems could also be seen as confronting those much younger thinkers who have been influenced by him.

3. Derrida and Deconstruction

One result of the developing crisis of philosophy just described was the view which has come to be known as 'deconstruction', of which the leading exponent has been Jacques Derrida. Derrida acknowledges the influence of Lévinas on his own thinking, speaking of being 'fascinated and attracted by the intellectual journey of Lévinas' because he was 'the philosopher working in phenomenology and posing the question of the "Other" to phenomenology'.[20] As his essay 'Violence and Metaphysics' (included in his volume *Writing and Difference*[21]) shows, the influence of Lévinas is, however, much wider than that would suggest, posing as it does the whole question of the continued viability of the philosophical tradition derived from the Greeks.

Derrida is the most recently born of the philosophers we have considered so far (he was born of Jewish parents in Algeria, then a French *département*, in 1930) and (apart from Lévinas) the only one who is still alive. After primary and secondary education in Algeria, he went to France, where he enrolled as a student of philosophy in the École Normale Supérieure. Here he studied Hegel, Husserl, and Heidegger, all major influences on his own thinking. His reading of Husserl, however, led him to discover problems in phenomenology, and indeed in the philosophical tradition more generally. Philosophical writing, he came to think, though it presents itself as plain, unvarnished, logical argumentation, is as full of metaphors and images as any 'literary' text, and its meaning and force depend at least as much on these 'literary' elements as on the formal argumentation.

Although he abandoned, for these reasons, the thesis which he was writing for the *doctorat d'état* (the qualification needed to become a university teacher), Derrida did in due course return to the École Normale Supérieure as a teacher and has taught both there and at the École des Hautes Études en Sciences

Sociales, as well as lecturing at universities in the United States and being Professor of Humanities at the University of California at Irvine. In many ways, indeed, his fame is even greater in the United States than in his own country. His influence in the Anglo-Saxon world, however, has mainly been amongst literary critics and sociologists rather than amongst philosophers: indeed, when it was recently proposed to award him an honorary degree at the University of Cambridge, the proposal came largely from the literary side and was vehemently opposed by a number of philosophers, who described Derrida as a charlatan.

The strong feelings of hostility about Derrida aroused amongst some philosophers in the analytic tradition seem to reflect a mixture of bafflement and anxiety about the challenge which he presents, not just to particular philosophical positions which they hold, but to the whole conception of the philosophical project on which their work is based. Analytic philosophers can feel comfortable with challenges to the philosophical tradition on the grounds of *method*: Descartes, Kant, Husserl, and the early Wittgenstein, for example, have all, in their different ways, proposed new and allegedly more effective ways of pursuing the philosophical project than those used in the past, but without calling in question the validity of that philosophical project itself. The Logical Positivists of the Vienna Circle challenged the project at a more fundamental level: their verificationist criterion of what was meaningful made much of what had been accepted as philosophical discourse into plain nonsense, or at best a kind of poetry or rhetoric, and reduced philosophical activity to a merely subordinate discipline, the 'logic of science'. But the Positivists' very emphasis on logic and science, and on the avoidance of empty rhetoric, made them into allies of analytic philosophy (still sometimes confused with 'logical positivism'). Again, therefore, this was a kind of challenge to philosophical tradition with which analytic philosophers have found it easy to live.

Even some of the twentieth-century 'Continental' philosophers who have aroused the ire of many in the analytic tradition because of the alleged 'pretentiousness', 'empty rhetoric', or 'needless obscurity' of their language and general demeanour have come in the end to be accepted, at least by the more liberal-minded representatives of analytic philosophy. We may think of Bergson, Jaspers, Husserl, Sartre, Merleau-Ponty—to name but a few. At least it could be admitted (by the more open-minded) that what these thinkers were engaged upon, however pretentious or obscure their manner of proceeding, was recognizably the same task as their more sober analytic counterparts.

In the case of Derrida, however, something much more radical *seems* (and that 'seems' should be stressed) to be going on. It seems to be that he is calling in question the philosophical project itself as traditionally conceived, not just the method or the style in which that project has been carried on; and he is not calling it in question on the grounds of lack of logical clarity or scientific rigour. (The later work of Wittgenstein embodies a very similar attitude of suspicion to the philosophical tradition, and arouses similar hostility amongst some analytic philosophers, however much it may be treated as a paradigm of analytic philosophy in other circles). This sort of questioning may inspire bafflement: what then is the *point* of the work which Derrida himself is doing? The sense of obscurity which may strike the analytically trained reader when confronting Derrida's works is not, or not entirely, a result of the strange terminology which is used or the contorted syntax of his sentences: it is much more a result of uncertainty about what it is exactly that is going on. What is he up to? What he writes does not belong to any of the genres of philosophy which the analytic philosopher has been brought up to recognize. And the sense that what may be going on is something which might undermine the very *raison d'être* of analytic philosophy itself naturally turns that bewilderment into hostility.

So what is Derrida up to? His own view of what he is doing has naturally developed over the years, but it is possible to see a common thread running through his work. He continues to describe himself as a philosopher, both in the trivial sense that that is the title of his post at the École Normale, and in the more important sense that he considers himself to be still engaged in the essential philosophical task of fundamental questioning.

Where he sees himself as differing from the tradition of philosophical enquiry is, first, in the *style* of his questioning; secondly,
in putting philosophy itself to the question; and thirdly in
refusing to make the traditional philosophical distinction between philosophy proper and other forms of human thought.
(The third difference is in many ways a consequence of the
second).

Probably the best way to try to understand Derrida's project
is to consider his fundamental questioning of philosophy itself
(remembering that to question the philosophical tradition is not
necessarily to be hostile to philosophy as such, only to explore
ways in which the philosophical project may need to be
renewed). One important way in which traditional philosophy
has gone astray, in Derrida's eyes, is that it has been too
'logocentric': that is, it has proceeded too much on the basis of
the Aristotelian logic of identity and non-contradiction. The
metaphysics which has been based on this logic is the Platonistic
metaphysics of an eternally self-identical Being, a metaphysics of
sameness or 'presence'. Against this, Derrida wants to affirm the
centrality of otherness, or to use his preferred term *différance*.
(The influence of Lévinas here is obvious.) *Différance* is a
Derridean coinage, a kind of pun which combines the ideas of
différence (with an 'e'), the French word for 'difference' and
'*differer*', the French word for 'defer'. Combining these two ideas
in a single term, and marking the combination by the invented
spelling with an 'a', is Derrida's way of expressing his view that
reality is to be understood both in terms of difference, rather
than self-identity, and in terms of perpetual deferment, rather
than eternal presence.

The philosophical centrality of *différance* means for Derrida,
not an alternative kind of metaphysics to the metaphysics of
presence, but the abandonment of metaphysics altogether (this is
one way in which he disagrees with Lévinas). As with Foucault,
the move away from the philosophical tradition is a move away
from the grand metaphysical theories which were meant to make
rational sense of reality as a whole. What remains of philosophy
will be, not the construction of such general theories, but the
simple activity of fundamental questioning as such. And this

fundamental questioning will clearly not, given the rejection of 'logocentrism', take the form of logical assessment of arguments, but of a probing of modes of presentation of positions in terms of features other than their logical validity.

This suggests something more like literary criticism than philosophical argument as it has been traditionally understood. Another consequence of the opposition to 'logocentrism', then, is an assimilation of philosophy to literature, and of philosophical critique to the critical analysis of literary texts. This is a step which Derrida explicitly takes. For example, in his essay 'Qual Quelle', which is included in his collection *Margins of Philosophy*,[22] Derrida cites with approval Paul Valéry's reminder that philosophy is *written*, and the conclusion which he (Valéry) draws from this, that philosophy is 'a particular literary genre' consisting of texts which have to be analysed like any other text. A philosophical text has to be studied

in its formal structure, in its rhetorical organization, in the specificity and diversity of its textual types, in its models of exposition and production—beyond what previously were called genres—and also in the space of its mises en scène, in a syntax which would be not only the articulation of its signifieds, its references to Being or to truth, but also the handling of its proceedings, and of everything invested in them.[23]

Shortly afterwards, Valéry's reading of Descartes's *cogito* argument along these lines is referred to, with obvious expressions of Derrida's approval. 'Valéry', says Derrida, 'very quickly suggests that truth is Descartes's last concern' but does describe the 'I think, therefore I am' as having a 'very great value', in that it lays 'a trap into which generations of servile fetishists will come to be caught, thereby acknowledging the law of the master, of I, René Descartes'.

Derrida's approval of Valéry's concentration on the *written text* in this passage expresses a central theme in his deviation from the philosophical tradition. One thing which has marked that tradition since Plato, in Derrida's view, is its prioritizing of *speech* over *writing*. The first main part of his work *Dissemination*[24] is devoted to a discussion of Plato's thought, and in particular of Plato's dialogue *Phaedrus*, in which Socrates gives preference to *logos* or speech over *graphe* or writing. The invention of writing, Socrates there says, encouraged those who aspired to wisdom to rely on what had been said in the past, by themselves or by others, rather than to develop their own fresh thoughts. Moreover, writing can circulate promiscuously among all sorts of readers, both those who can understand what it says and those who cannot: the result is that garbled and confused ideas gain currency. Wisdom comes rather from what Phaedrus calls 'the living and animate speech of a man with knowledge, of which written speech might fairly be called a kind of shadow'.[25] True wisdom, in other words, comes, as Socrates sees it, from oral instruction given by a wise man to a suitable pupil.

It does seem to be true that this model of the quest for wisdom, the Socratic dialectic, has been a central part of the *image* of what philosophy is about. What is important, Derrida thinks, is to see that this is a false and misleading image. It is false because most Western philosophy has in fact been written: philosophy has not been transmitted by means of an oral tradition, but in the form of written texts (including the texts of Plato's dialogues themselves). And it is misleading because it creates the illusion that we can go back to the source of thought in order to get it at its freshest. There is then the further illusion that this source will consist in the pronouncements of some authoritative individual, expressed directly and without the distortions of thought inherent in the attempt to express it in a written language. For written language is more impersonal than spoken and so further removed from the unambiguous expression of what a thinker consciously wishes to say. The expression of the truth is 'deferred' (cf. what was said earlier about the meaning of Derrida's term *différance*) rather than an immediate 'presence'.

Once one accepts that what we have to deal with is a written text, therefore, one can see at least the possibility of a gap between what a philosopher consciously believes himself to be saying—the ordered, rational argument which he thinks he is presenting—and what is actually contained in the text, which will embody certain assumptions of which the author is not conscious. It is into this gap that 'deconstruction' can step, offering a way of reading philosophical texts other than by attending to the surface logic (or lack of it) of their arguments. Since philosophical texts have in the past claimed a special status for themselves precisely because they operate by means of rigorous logical argument rather than, for example, the kinds of imagery whose meaning is never fully explicit which are characteristic of works of literature, to approach them in this way is to deny that special status. So we come back to the point made earlier, that Derrida's approach blurs the distinction between philosophy and other kinds of writing, such as literature.

The assimilation of philosophy to literature in this way is also by simple logic an assimilation of literature to philosophy. Derrida is not *reducing* philosophy to 'mere literature', but expanding the field of philosophy to include the whole of human intellectual activity. To include philosophy itself within the scope of philosophical questioning is certainly to step beyond the bounds of *traditional* philosophy, which saw itself as occupying a position above that of other areas of human thought, from which the foundations of those other areas could be assessed. In this sense, it is to reduce *traditional* philosophy to the same level as those other areas. But by the same token it is to make the fundamental project of philosophy coextensive with human thought itself. If so, then it is, as Derrida acknowledges, impossible to step outside philosophy in the latter sense. 'The notion of the limit and boundary of metaphysics', he says, 'is itself highly problematic.'[26] We can, therefore, think about 'our inherence in the language of metaphysics' only from a 'non-place' which would be the 'other' of philosophy.

This non-place, he goes on to say, may be provided by literature, in the sense of 'certain texts which make the limits of our language tremble, exposing them as divisible and question-able'[27] (the examples cited are Blanchot, Bataille, and Beckett). Derrida, in attempting to subject philosophy itself to fundamental questioning, is thus faced with fundamentally the same problem which has confronted other philosophers, such as Kant and Wittgenstein, who have attempted to define the limits of our language—that to set limits is to step beyond those limits, but what is beyond the limits of language is necessarily unsayable and so unthinkable. What the present passage indicates is that Derrida sees the answer to that problem in that kind of literature which itself runs up against the limits of language, that is, which strains to say the unsayable and so 'makes the limits tremble'. That very trembling may (to use a Wittgensteinian mode of expression) *show* what cannot be *said*.

Where Derrida differs from, say, Wittgenstein in the *Tractatus* is that he does not equate the 'limits of our language' with the limits of meaningful (true-or-false) propositions, since he does not equate language with statements which can be true or false. To make that equation would be to fall victim to that same 'logocentrism' of which he accuses traditional metaphysics. He has inherited from structuralism a view of meaning as distinct from reference: 'the meaning' of any particular expression in any text is not to be identified with its 'referent', what it refers to, supposed to be immediately given and therefore completely determinable. Words are thus not given meaning by their one-to-one relation to non-linguistic things, but by their relations, within the language, to other words (including their 'differen-ces'—*différance* again—from other words). (See the discussion of Saussure in the preceding chapter.) To try to determine what any particular expression 'means' therefore involves examining the indefinite number of relations in which it stands to other expressions, which is to say that we can never fully determine its meaning at all. If that is true of the constituent expressions of a statement, then it follows that we can never speak of any statement as a whole as true or false, since to say that would imply that what was said in the statement had a determinate meaning which could be compared with 'the facts' to decide on the assertion's truth or falsity.

We have now, perhaps, said enough to be able to give some kind of a connected account of 'deconstruction'. 'Deconstruc-tion' clearly cannot be *defined*, any more than any expression can. We can, however, say some things about what it is *not*. It is not a matter of exposing some statements, made by a philo-sopher or by anyone else, as 'meaningless' or 'logically ill-founded': that much clearly follows from what has been said so far. Nor can it be a matter of debunking someone's views by showing them to be expressions of personal interests rather than of objective truth: if there is no such thing as a statement of 'objective truth', then no particular kinds of statements can be picked out for debunking in this way. In general, it cannot be a method or procedure for carrying out in any way the logocentric aims of traditional philosophy. Rather, it must be a matter of undermining that logocentricity itself: by treating philosophy as a literary genre, it shows its content, like that of any work of literature, to be found at least as much in its style, in its choice of metaphors, even in its physical manner of presentation, as in the logical structure of its arguments. It is a matter of reading a work of philosophy (or any other work which aspires to the condition of philosophy) simply as a *text* like any other, an expression of its author, rather than as a formal and impersonal piece of argumentation.

If we interpret 'deconstruction' in this way as a way of *reading philosophical (and other) texts*, then we shall have to accept (as Derrida certainly would) that there can be more than one illuminating reading of any given text: to put it differently, there is no such thing as the one *correct* reading. But it is easy to imagine the objection that, if that is all there is to say about deconstruction, then the fuss about it, both for and against, seems rather exaggerated. It sounds like something which is merely parasitic on real, original, philosophical activity, which may have some value as a tool for historians of philosophy, but can hardly advance philosophical enquiry itself. What Derrida seems to mean by 'deconstruction', however, is neither as parasitic as this objection imagines nor as purely negative as the form of the word itself might suggest.

The image conjured up by the word 'deconstruction' is indeed a negative one—that of the dismantling of some building or other structure. That image, as such, contains no suggestion that the dismantling of the structure might reveal something new about the structure itself which had previously been hidden. If we take the deconstruction of a text as a way of reading it in order to bring out its hidden content, however, then that sounds much more positive. The deconstruction of a traditional philosophical text, for instance, might reveal possibilities of meaning, and of answers to philosophical questions, which went far beyond what was contained in its manifest, prosaic, logocentric, surface. And if that were achieved, then deconstruction could be seen as something more than a tool for interpreting philosophy's past: it could be taken as a means of adding something new to the enterprise of philosophy. What it would add would be a new *kind* of answer to the philosophical questions: something which would be offered more as an illumination of the issues than as a 'true answer' to be supported by evidence and logical argument. Furthermore, it would offer the possibility of something more than a way of reading the texts of others: of presenting new ways of thinking, not by formal logical argument, but by skilful exploration of metaphors and imagery.

Derrida himself lends some support to this view of deconstruction in the dialogue with Richard Kearney which has already been cited several times in this chapter. Speaking in that interview of deconstruction as the attempt 'more and more systematically to find a non-site, or a non-philosophical site, from which to question philosophy', he goes on: 'But the search for a non-philosophical site does not bespeak an anti-philosophical attitude. My central question is: from what site or non-site (*non-lieu*) can philosophy as such appear to itself as other than itself, so that it can interrogate and reflect upon itself in an original manner?.'[28]

It is tempting to find parallels here with Richard Rorty's recent suggestions, from within the Anglo-American philosophical tradition, that the age of what he calls 'Philosophy with a capital P', in which philosophers claimed to be able to sit in judgement on all other areas of human thought, is now past and discredited, because of the work of such thinkers as William James, Dewey, Heidegger, and Wittgenstein. What must replace 'Philosophy', Rorty argues, is 'philosophy (with a lower-case p)', which will simply be a part, along with literature and art, of the 'conversation of mankind', concerned to produce, not 'truth', but images of how we might live our lives. It is not surprising that Rorty sees Derrida as an ally.[29] In an important respect, however, Derrida differs from Rorty, or at least from the image of himself which Rorty often projects: namely, that his deconstruction of the metaphysical tradition is more a matter of turning the philosophical enterprise in a new, and more ethically responsible, direction than of ironizing it out of existence. (This is true despite the frequent irony and playfulness of his tone, on which Rorty has commented.)

A good example of this can be seen in Derrida's complex attitude to 'humanism', a consideration of which will also provide an illustration of Derrida's method of deconstructive reading of texts at work. His paper 'The Ends of Man'[30] offers a reading of a number of philosophers. Humanism, he says, is a characteristic feature of all the French philosophy of the earlier part of the twentieth century, even that of someone like Sartre, who was at pains to satirize humanism (for example, in the character of the Autodidact in his novel *Nausea*). Sartre, Derrida argues, misread Heidegger when he took the German philosopher to be concerned with specifically *human* consciousness:

The transcendental structures described after the phenomenological reduction are not those of the intraworldly being called 'man'. Nor are they essentially linked to man's society, culture, language, or even to his 'soul' or 'psyche'. Just as, according to Husserl, one may imagine a consciousness without soul (*seelenlos*), similarly—and a fortiori—one may imagine a consciousness without man.[31]

Heidegger, Derrida claims, as his post-war *Letter on Humanism* showed, was never a humanist in that sense: his concern, like Husserl's, was not with the consciousness of human beings as such, which is always affected by history, culture, and language, but with 'consciousness as such', no matter whose consciousness it was.

The humanism which Heidegger opposed, however, was, according to Derrida, that associated with metaphysics. What Heidegger is centrally concerned with, Derrida maintains, 'is not simply the man of metaphysics'.[32] Nevertheless, it is '*nothing other* than man. It is, as we shall see, a repetition of the essence of man permitting a return to what is before the metaphysical concepts of *humanitas*.'[33] The metaphysical version of humanism depends on a certain conception of the 'essence of man' which is linked to particular historical circumstances in which our humanity was connected with our ability to impose technological mastery upon nature—a concept which Heidegger sees as inimical to true humanity. We become *truly* human, in fact, by 'meditating' and 'caring', by recognizing ourselves primarily in our relation to 'the truth of Being', in our harmony with Being as a whole. This view of true humanity is expressed, Derrida says, in Heidegger's characteristic imagery of 'home' and 'homelessness'.

Derrida's clear sympathy with this sort of critique of metaphysical humanism is connected with his political and moral objections to Western ethnocentrism. His 'deconstruction' of the philosophical tradition is meant to expose the tension between the surface attachment to Enlightenment ideals of universal humanity and rationality and the underlying sense that these ideals in fact inhere only in the particular values of a particular historical culture, that of Western Europe and the other parts of the world which have been influenced by Europe. (His own Algerian origins are clearly not irrelevant to the passion which he feels about this.) What it is important to realize, however, is that this does *not* imply that Derrida rejects those Enlightenment ideals themselves, if properly understood.

In his paper 'Cogito and the History of Madness',[34] Derrida discusses and criticizes Foucault's book *Histoire de la folie* (the longer original version of *Madness and Civilization*). Foucault, Derrida claims, tries in that work to do something impossible, namely, to subvert the discourse of reason from a position outside it. But even to understand the history of madness, Derrida points out, involves the use of reason. Foucault bases his position, he argues, on a misreading of Descartes's argument for the 'cogito' (the 'I think, therefore I am'), and in particular Descartes's consideration in that argument of the possibility of madness. Descartes and the post-Cartesian tradition, as Derrida reads them, do not seek to *exclude* madness from the domain of reason, as Foucault had claimed, but to face up to the threat which madness poses to reason in order to incorporate that threat within our very concept of rationality. It is impossible, Derrida concludes, to escape from the discourse of reason itself.

This conclusion is very illuminating about the meaning of Derridean deconstruction. The aim of Derrida's reading of the philosophical tradition is not to subvert the attachment of that tradition to concepts of humanity and reason, but to rescue those very concepts from their distortions by other subterranean influences which have been at work in the tradition. These subterranean influences have expressed themselves, like Lacan's unconscious, not in the surface prose and logic of the philosopher's manifest arguments, but in the metaphors and imagery which inevitably creep in even to the most sober philosophical writing. The task of deconstruction is to expose the tensions between these images and what they express and the prosaic logic and what it purports to express. The very seriousness of purpose of deconstruction, as so interpreted, is enough in itself to constitute a defence of Derrida against the absurder claims of charlatanry directed against him by some Francophobic analytical philosophers.

Nevertheless, the claims made for deconstruction depend on the very questionable assumption that the 'logocentrism' which Derrida criticizes has been shown to be flawed. That philosophical texts often contain *more* than impersonal logical argument, and that they can in such cases only be fully understood by taking into account that 'something more', is something which is inherently plausible and which is confirmed by Derrida's own deconstructive analyses. It is arguable, however, that it does not follow that philosophical texts do *not* contain impersonal argumentation, or that the tenability of their overt claims does not depend entirely on the logical validity of that argumentation. That would be like saying that, because the character of our experience of a football match can be influenced by such things as the character of the turf, the behaviour of the spectators, the colours of the players' shirts, etc., we should not say that it has a result which depends on the number of goals scored by each side.

We could accept that the logic of a philosopher's arguments and the truth of his statements do not affect the acceptability of what he says as a philosopher only if we could show that statements are neither true nor false, and so that logic (which investigates how truth can be preserved in passing from one statement to another) can have no purchase. Has Derrida shown that to be the case? As we have seen, he insists very strongly, following the structuralists, that the meaning of individual expressions is a matter of their relation to other expressions within the language, rather than to anything non-linguistic; and it would follow, as we have also seen that the meaning-content of whole statements made up of these expressions would be equally indeterminate. But this view of meaning cannot simply be dogmatically asserted, and it is at least arguable, as was suggested in the previous chapter, that it is untenable. If that argument can be sustained, then Derrida's whole programme of deconstruction, at least in its full-blooded form, rests on a mistake.

It might still be argued that Derrida has performed a useful service in insisting on a close reading of the *whole* text of a philosopher, including the images used, the literary form (dialogue, treatise, aphorisms, etc.), and even the presentation of the text on the page. To cling to the notion of philosophy as a rational activity, assessable by rational criteria, is not the same as insisting that the form which rationality takes in a proof in mathematics or formal logic is the only one possible. Rational arguments can be presented in many ways, sometimes by the use of images or metaphors, or by the presentation of insights in literary forms which make them readily acceptable as self-evident. Derridean deconstruction could be seen, less excitingly, perhaps, but more promisingly, rather as the addition of a new weapon to the armoury of philosophical criticism than as a radical change in direction for philosophy.

4. Lyotard and Post-modernism

One important type of philosophical criticism made popular by the deconstructionists (though it is not new—Nietzsche, for instance, makes much of it) is the objection that a philosopher presents as an insight into eternal truth what is in fact simply the expression of a particular set of cultural attitudes. In the discussion of Derrida's critique of humanism, we saw how this kind of criticism of philosophy can also have a bearing on practical social or political arrangements. In ways like this, the deconstruction of traditional Western philosophy implies a critique of traditional Western culture generally, since the shape of that culture has been given to it above all by the philosophical tradition descended from Plato. The 'modern' period, running from roughly the Enlightenment (with its predecessors such as Descartes, Locke, Newton, and Galileo) to fairly recent years, is particularly liable to this sort of criticism. Theoretical justification for thus picking on 'modernism' might be found by saying that it represents the ultimate fulfilment of the potentialities which had always been present in Western culture since the Greeks. Their Platonic, mathematicized, view of the world has been filled out with empirical detail in the last few centuries, and this, it might be claimed, has led, philosophically, to the idealization of the human subject and the denial of meaning in nature, and practically to the technological manipulation of our world. We can react against modernism conservatively (by attempting to retreat to a 'pre-modern' state) or more adventurously by seeking to go beyond modernism to what is often called, rather vaguely, 'post-modernism'. (Though post-modernism is often a rather ambiguous phenomenon, combining a conservative nostalgia and a desire to break with the past.)

The Derridean deconstruction of traditional metaphysics and recommendation of a whole new non-metaphysical attitude to philosophy could thus be seen as the philosophical underpinning of post-modernism. Derrida himself is unhappy with the idea of 'modernity'. 'I believe', he says, 'that what "happens" in our contemporary world and strikes us as particularly new has in fact an essential connection with something extremely old which has been covered over.'[35] Nevertheless, while accepting that, we could still hold, as suggested just now, that what is particularly new about 'modernity' is precisely that certain 'extremely old' features of our culture have come to full fruition only in relatively recent times.

'Post-modernism', as already stated, is a very vague term which can be used to cover a variety of rather different developments and ideas, in society and the arts as well as in philosophy proper, which do not always seem to have much of a connection with each other. Indeed, it seems to have been first used in relation to the arts, and only later entered into philosophy. For present purposes, it is plainly more appropriate to take it in its narrowly philosophical sense. In so far as it is possible to give it a precise philosophical sense, it refers to the movement which seeks to go beyond the philosophical inheritance of the Enlightenment and the cultural attitudes and values which have been supported by that inheritance. Of those in France who have developed the notion in this philosophical sense, the best-known is probably Jean-François Lyotard, who has a good claim to be the person who was responsible for introducing the term 'postmodern' into philosophical discussion. Although the purely philosophical interest of Lyotard's work is limited, it is worth some consideration because of the way he tries to apply philosophical conceptions to social critique.

Born in 1925, Lyotard has taught philosophy at the University of Paris at Vincennes and more recently at the University of California at Irvine. For many years in the 1950s and early 1960s, he was associated with a non-Communist but fundamentally Marxist left-wing group called *Socialisme ou barbarie,* and was active in left-wing politics in those years. However, the 'events' of May 1968, in which he himself participated, led him to think again about the role of large-scale theories of history such as Marxism in political activity. The students who acted in 1968, he saw, were not inspired by any such theory, but acted out of pure opposition to the established order. It was his growing sympathy with their attitudes which led him to his critique of 'modernism' and his analysis of the intellectual and social framework which, in his view, has succeeded it.

'Post-modernism' is a concept which straddles the gap between empirical sociological description and philosophical interpretation (and that, as we shall see, may be the source of most of the problems in the concept). In either case, it refers to 'what comes after modernism'. From a sociological point of view, the suggestion is that there have been important changes in widely held values, social institutions, and technological development in the relatively recent past. Philosophy plays a part, both in helping to provide the *explanation* for these changes and in giving reason for thinking that there is a *justification* for them in the inadequacies of modernist thought. Lyotard, in his principal work on the subject, *The Postmodern Condition*,[36] clearly thinks the concept to be both philosophically and sociologically illuminating.

It would be as well to begin by saying a little bit more in detail than has been said so far about what is meant by modernism. Philosophically speaking, modernism is the set of views and values developed by the philosophers of the Enlightenment—Leibniz, Hume, Kant, and the French Encyclopaedists, together with their seventeenth-century precursors, Descartes, Locke, and Newton. These philosophers, both those called 'empiricists' and those called 'rationalists', shared a particular conception of reason: rationality was the capacity which all human beings possessed, simply in virtue of being human beings, and so independently of their particular individual, cultural, or historical characteristics. It was manifested most obviously in the human capacity to think logically and mathematically. Because reason was universally human, its deliverances reflected, not the particular subjective ways of thinking and seeing of limited individuals, but the objective facts about the world. Thus, the supreme example of reason at work was pure mathematics itself and the application of mathematics in the physical sciences. These disciplines were purely objective, and mathematical natural science depicted the world as it really was (or at least, Kant would say, as it really was when viewed from a rational human perspective).

Once a fully developed natural science was available, including especially a natural science of human beings and human behaviour, then it could be applied, in the form of technology, to make human life perfectly happy, with all human needs supplied by the most efficient method which science could devise. What we needed to do, therefore, was to organize our social arrangements in such a way that science could be applied to all areas of human life, to make sure that all benefited equally from the capacities which an increasingly sophisticated science would make available. A rationally organized society, based on scientific principles, could also ensure that people behaved rationally, in such a way as not to make either themselves or others unnecessarily unhappy. It was such a 'science of society', of course, that Marxism claimed to provide.

The watchwords of modernism were thus reason, science, objectivity, and happiness. Sociologically, Lyotard would argue, we have moved into a period where modernism in this sense is in deep crisis: there is a rise in irrationalism and subjectivism, people are suspicious of science and the pursuit of happiness seems more and more like a fading dream of the past. Art and culture generally reflect this mood. If it were merely a sociological phenomenon, however, then it would be evaluatively neutral—in itself, it would neither be a good thing nor a bad thing, just a new phase in human history. On the other hand, if this change of mood is a response to the philosophical defects in modernism, then it can be seen as an improvement: it is 'after' modernism, not just in the temporal sense, but in the sense of going beyond it to something with a sounder intellectual foundation.

What could these philosophical defects in modernism be? The most obvious place to look is to arguments which seem to cast doubt on the Enlightenment concept of universal reason. Lyotard finds such arguments in part in the structuralist and post-structuralist tendency towards a linguistically based cultural relativism which we have just been considering, and partly in the later work of Wittgenstein and J. L. Austin's theory of 'speech-acts'. These two lines of development, one in French and one in Anglo-Saxon philosophy, point in much the same direction; so that, since some space has already been given to the French developments, we should say something about Lyotard's use of Wittgenstein.

It is Wittgenstein's notion of 'language-games' which Lyotard employs most. Wittgenstein's conception was that philosophers had gone astray by asking for 'the meaning' of any given expression, which implied that the expression got its meaning in one and only one way, presumably by being correlated with the thing to which it referred. What we should ask for was not 'the meaning', but 'the use' of the expression in the particular human activities in which it functioned. Language was something used by human beings in the course of particular activities ('language-games'), and expressions took on different 'meanings' as used in different language-games.

Lyotard understands Wittgenstein to be referring, by the term 'language-game', to the different uses of language, such as making statements, giving commands, uttering 'performatives' (in Austin's sense of 'doing something by saying something', such as making a promise by saying 'I promise'), giving a literary description, telling a story, and so on. Each of these language-games is different from every other; each is governed by its own set of rules, just as the game of chess is governed by a different set of rules from the game of football. Given this view of language, of course, no particular language-game can claim to be specially privileged as a 'representation of what things are actually like' or as making possible 'objectively true statements'. Therefore, the use of language in mathematical natural science cannot make such claims to privilege. The Enlightenment view of science as the paradigm of objectivity and rationality is called in question. Science becomes just one 'language-game' among others, developed for certain specific purposes.

If we cannot simply accept the peculiar objectivity and rationality of science as rationally self-evident, then we have to look elsewhere for an explanation of why modern society generally accepts this view of science. The peculiar feature of the scientific language-game which marks it out from all others is that it aims at truth alone, in the sense of statements which can be agreed upon as correct by all relevant 'players', following the particular rules for determining what is true and what is false which apply in the scientific game. Most other language-games, by contrast, are what Lyotard calls 'narrative': they have different criteria of truth and falsity from science, and, even more important, they incorporate other criteria of assessment than 'truth' alone (though the satisfaction of these other criteria is equally guaranteed by consensus). In narrative uses of language, moral and aesthetic criteria as well as purely cognitive are interwoven. For these reasons, in a scientifically dominated culture such as modernism, these other uses of language are given a lower value.

Popular myths and stories are obvious examples of narrative uses of language. We assess such myths by their own, non-scientific, standards of truth and falsity, and we assess them also by other criteria—aesthetic pleasure, moral uplift, social function, etc. The social function of such myths is mainly to *legitimize* institutions, types of activity, and individuals within the society, as the myth of the descent of the king from Adam, the father of humankind, was intended to legitimize the king's role as 'father of his country'. Modernism presents science as legitimizing itself in virtue of its objectivity and rationality. But the analysis of meaning, and of the variety of possible relations between the things we say in language and the world we talk about, cuts through that attempt at legitimation. Ironically, science too needs to be legitimated by myth. He cites two principal myths, though each takes several forms: the myth of science as the liberator of humanity and the Hegelian myth of science as the total system of all human knowledge.

These myths, however, have lost their credibility in contemporary society, so that science is 'delegitimated'. Modernism, which is based on the assumption that scientific thinking alone is legitimate, is thereby itself discredited. The myths are not credible because we can no longer accept such large-scale justificatory stories (society and knowledge have become too complex for that). The reason for pursuing science must therefore cease to be the idea that it is objectively true, and must become its simple pragmatic usefulness.

Modernism must thus be replaced by post-modernism, because we can no longer follow through the Enlightenment project of basing our lives on scientific rationality. The value of scientific rationality is now open to question: we cannot oppose it to, or think it superior to, simpler 'narrative' forms of thinking, since we now see that its own legitimacy depended on just such narratives. At the same time, we cannot accept the narratives in question, since they are on too large a scale for us to comprehend them or believe in them. We must therefore settle in to a post-modern culture in which there are no big overarching 'myths', no promises of transforming human society and making it happy by science, and in which science is pursued only for narrow utilitarian purposes.

Post-modernism, as so conceived, clearly has implications for politics and general culture. In politics, it implies suspicion of what Lyotard calls the 'politics of redemption', the kind of universalist political theory, such as Marxism, which seeks to create a perfect human society in which at last humanity will find fulfilment. Even the more sophisticated versions of such theories, such as Jurgen Habermas's concept of the ideal speech-community, are open to similar objections. Such utopian visions seem to Lyotard to be just another product of the modernist delusion that scientific rationality, applied to human life, will be able to make human beings happy. What is needed in post-modern society are rather local initiatives, on a small scale, informed by local traditions and seeking reform of concrete injustices.[37] Culturally, Lyotard favours pluralism and a lack of state interference in the arts, a situation in which individual artists are left to do their own thing in their own way, rather than conscripted in the service either of some great ideal or of commercial interests.

As was said in the previous chapter, this sort of suspicion of large-scale theory undoubtedly captures a widespread mood in contemporary society. If we are to speak of a 'post-modern condition', however, then we need more than what might be only a passing emotional reaction to the uncertainties of modern life. We do in fact need, as Lyotard realizes, a philosophical analysis which will show that there was such a thing as 'modernism' and that it *deserved* to fail because of its logical incoherence. Lyotard, however, does not in fact present us with such an analysis. Instead, he offers us a mixture of a sociological or historical account of human thought since the eighteenth century (which seems to fail to do justice to the richness of the historical reality) and a philosophical critique of what he takes to be 'Enlightenment ideals' (which does not appear to rest on any sound philosophical arguments).

To equate modern thought with a view that the only form of reasonableness is mathematical and scientific rationality seems to be historically false. It may be true that this has been one important strand of European and American thinking since the eighteenth century, but it is only one. Other philosophers have advocated contrary views, which have equally become a part of the popular consciousness. We need only think of Hume's denial that moral and practical thought could be conducted in terms of mathematical reason ('reason is and ought to be the slave of the passions') and of Rousseau's advocacy of a life lived in accordance with nature and simple emotions.

As for Lyotard's philosophical rejection of alleged 'Enlightenment' ideals (more correctly, positivist modes of thought), this is based, not on argument, but on the unsupported claim that scientific modes of thought derive their legitimacy only from a myth, and that this myth has now been discredited. Even if that latter claim were true, it would not follow that, because people now find it hard to accept large-scale justificatory stories, they were *justified* in refusing to accept them. Society might, in other words, find it hard to believe in science any more, without its being true that science was unbelievable.

Given that, it is possible that we can abandon some of the more utopian schemes of social improvement without necessarily abandoning either a belief in science as the pursuit of truth or a commitment to ideals of humanity and rationality derived from the Enlightenment. However useful it may be from the point of view of sociological analysis of contemporary society to have the concept of a 'post-modern condition', there seem to be no philosophical grounds for distinguishing between 'modernism' and 'post-modernism'. Lyotard's claim that there are seems to rest on a confusion between what people can as a matter of fact accept and what are adequate grounds for believing something.

CHAPTER NINE

Recent French Feminists

1. Feminism and Philosophy in France

As in most European countries, there is a long tradition of campaigning for women's rights in France, though women succeeded in obtaining the vote only in 1945. After that triumph, there was a lull in feminist activity until the late 1960s, when the modern movement for women's liberation really began to take off. Inevitably, the style of the women's movement in any particular country will reflect the peculiarities of that country's culture, in respect both of the nature of the relations between men and women in the society in question, and of the general character of its political life. From what has been said of French culture in this book, it will come as no surprise that French feminism (at least in its more radical forms) tends to be more philosophical in tone than does feminism in the English-speaking world. The critique of patriarchal society is often expressed, not in merely sociological or political terms, but as a philosophical analysis of the whole tradition of thought which allegedly supports patriarchy. Philosophy itself is seen as central to patriarchal culture, and the developments in structuralist and post-structuralist French philosophy which have been considered in the preceding chapters are pressed into service in order to deconstruct that patriarchal tradition.

The form which recent feminist thought has taken in France owes a great deal to the brave pioneering efforts of Simone de Beauvoir in her essay *The Second Sex*, first published in 1949.[1] De Beauvoir has been mentioned already, in Chapter 4, as Sartre's lifelong companion and collaborator: but, as was said there, it would be quite wrong to give the impression that she was somehow important only in relation to him. She was a distinguished thinker and novelist in her own right. And *The Second Sex* was an epoch-making book, exploring women's own thoughts about sexuality, children, the family, and their relationships with men in a depth and with a subtlety which had not been found earlier and which is still hard to find today. It was a brave book in the sense that it inevitably, in the climate of the time, brought down upon de Beauvoir's head a torrent of vile abuse from male journalists and intellectuals. François Mauriac, for instance, wrote of it in *Le Figaro littéraire*, 'We have literally reached the limits of the abject. This is the ipecac they made us swallow as children to induce vomiting.'

What inspired this abuse seems to have been simply de Beauvoir's rejection of the conception of women which exists in patriarchal society. She argued that in that society 'humanity' is equated with 'masculinity', so that male human beings do not need to reflect on their difference as males. Women, on the other hand, are regarded as 'the Other', to be defined only in terms of their difference from men. The idea of an 'essence' of femininity, somehow based on women's distinctive biological functions, still persists. In terms of the existentialist concepts which she and Sartre had developed, she argued that this was because women are not regarded as *subjects* in their own right, merely as *objects* in the world of men.

She thereby also distinguished her own thought from that of Sartre, who consistently, in *Being and Nothingness*, adopts an exclusively male point of view in which women are objectified by the male gaze, especially in his discussion of sexuality in part 3, chapter 3, 'Concrete Relations with Others'. In this sense, Sartre was not consistent in his humanism, since half the human race was effectively excluded from the domain of 'being-for-oneself'. It is de Beauvoir's simultaneous emphasis on sexual difference and on the denial of subjectivity to women in patriarchal culture which she has transmitted to the more recent French feminist thinkers to be discussed in the present chapter: principally Luce Irigaray and Julia Kristeva, with some reference also to Michèle Le Dœuff. The recognizably philosophical concerns of these writers, especially of the first two, are usually inextricably interwined with other which seem, at least to someone reared in the analytic tradition, to have nothing to do with philosophy. Furthermore, to some of their critics many of their major contentions seem false, or even nonsensical. All the same, I hope to show that, even where one disagrees with them, what they have to say deserves to be thought about: and, that apart, it would hardly be possible to give a complete account of French philosophy at the end of the twentieth century without giving at least a brief account of their views.

2. Luce Irigaray

Luce Irigaray has been particularly influential. She was born in Belgium in 1939, though she now lives and works in France. Since 1964 she has worked in research at the Centre National de Recherches Scientifiques in Paris, where she has more recently become a Director of Research in Philosophy. She trained as a psychoanalyst, and was greatly influenced in her approach to psychoanalysis by Jacques Lacan who, as was said in Chapter 7, saw the psychoanalytic encounter as the decipherment of the client's *language* by the analyst. Her work with schizophrenic and dementing patients suggested that the patients lacked identity because they were 'overwhelmed' by language. They were unable to construct an identity, a subjectivity, for themselves because the language, and the culture it reflected, did not make it possible. In particular in the case of those patients who were women, it seemed to her that the masculine bias of the language made it impossible to construct a distinctive identity for themselves. Sexual difference was, paradoxically, both concealed and emphasized: concealed in one way, emphasized in another. This led her on to wider reflections about the patriarchal character of the language and the culture of Western society, and about the consequences for both women and men of this patriarchal distortion.

Because of the centrality of philosophy to Western culture (it is 'the master discourse . . . the discourse on discourses'[2]), what that means is above all reflection on certain features of the history of Western philosophy. Thus, in her book *An Ethic of Sexual Difference*,[3] which was originally a series of lectures

given at the Erasmus University of Rotterdam in 1982, she says
(p. 6):

A revolution in thought and ethics is needed if the work of sexual
difference is to take place. We need to reinterpret everything concerning
the relations between the subject and discourse, the subject and the
world, the subject and the cosmic, the microcosmic and the
macrocosmic. Everything, beginning with the way in which the subject
has always been written in the masculine form, as *man*, even when it
claimed to be universal or neutral.

The language itself, Irigaray suggests, embodies this masculine bias,
even in such simple and relatively trivial ways as the use of the
masculine pronoun in cases where no specific gender is intended.
But this trivial feature of grammar only reflects something much
deeper, which runs through the whole history of philosophy and
which is expressed in the last sentence of the quotation given above:
'the subject has always been written in the masculine form . . . even
when it claimed to be universal or neutral'.

   This is the heart of Irigaray's critique of patriarchal philosophy: the 'subject' talked about in philosophy, whether it is the
'subject of knowledge' or the 'subject' in an ethical sense, is
alleged to be gender-neutral (as it is neutral in other senses). It
is claimed to be a 'transcendental subject', distinguished from
any individual's subjectivity, and certainly distinct from anything
bodily, and so to be neither masculine nor feminine. However, a
deconstructive reading of the great works of philosophy, according to Irigaray, will show that the subject of philosophy is in fact
always *masculine*, and so that women have been denied full
subjectivity and reduced to the status of objects of a male gaze.

   The deconstruction which Irigaray practises makes use of
psychoanalytic concepts derived from both Freud and Lacan: in
effect, she psychoanalyses the great Western philosophers in
order to show the male fears and anxieties which underlie the
apparently rational and neutral surface of their arguments. Her
attitude to psychoanalysis, however, is ambivalent. In the case of
Freud, and even more in that of Lacan, she sees psychoanalytic
theory and practice as itself part of the patriarchal culture. In
Freudian and Lacanian theory, women are, she claims, treated

simply as defective men, lacking a penis rather than having positive attributes of their own. The concentration is all on the problems of men, on the relations between mothers and their sons, in which the sons have to establish their male identity by rejecting their mother and identifying with their father. The balance needs to be corrected by a greater emphasis on the mother–daughter relationship and the problems of establishing a female identity. Nevertheless, Irigaray still sees the psychoanalytic method, with its attention to the 'imaginary', the world of fantasies and repressed wishes, as a useful instrument in her own consideration of patriarchal culture.

Thus, Plato's myth of the cave in the *Republic*, in which the philosophers have to ascend from a cave, in which they see only shadows cast against a wall by the fire, into the upper world where they see real objects illuminated by the sun, is given a psychoanalytic reading by Irigaray in the last section of her *Speculum of the Other Woman*.[4] The 'logocentric' reading of the myth is that the ascent from the cave into the sunlight is the move which must be made if one is to become a true philosopher, to see things as they really are, in the light of the Form of the Good, rather than as the mere appearances of an underlying reality. The psychoanalytic reading which Irigaray offers is meant to show that there is more going on in Plato's thinking than appears on the surface. The cave is seen as an image of the womb, and the ascent from the cave into the sunlight as the (male) child's assumption of an identity by escaping from identification with his mother, and by identifying with the father (the Form of the Good). If this reading is accepted, then what Plato is really saying is that truth and rationality are to be found only by repudiating the mother, the female. The ability to apprehend the truth and so to be a philosopher, a rational being, a subject, is thereby defined as an exclusively male characteristic, while the female is identified with all those forces which seek to prevent rationality and the pursuit of truth—nature, emotion, imagination, etc.

Western philosophy has been described by Whitehead as a series of footnotes to Plato. If that is so, then Irigaray would claim that the whole of subsequent Western philosophy is dis-

torted by patriarchal thought. It will be permeated by dicho-
tomies between subject and object, intellectual and sensory,
abstract and concrete, the mental and the bodily, the human and
the natural. The apparently impersonal and transcendental subject will in fact be male. Given the structuralist and post-
structuralist doctrine that the subject of philosophy is not
discovered a priori but constructed by human beings, the subject
will be seen as constructed as an expression of male identity. And
that male identity will be based on a fear of the female, which it
seeks to overcome by achieving both physical and intellectual
mastery over the female principle (and hence over actual
women). What is female will be denied subjectivity: it will be
reduced to an object over which the subject has to assert his (*sic*)
mastery. Only abstractions, apprehended by the pure intellect,
will be really real: the concrete, bodily, sensuous world will not
be real at all.

Thus, the subject comes to be represented as gender-neutral,
while women cease to be subjects, to have an identity of their
own. It is in this way that we arrive at the paradoxical situation
mentioned earlier, in which sexual difference is both affirmed and
denied. It is affirmed in that women are regarded as essentially
different from anything human (i.e. male): they exist only as a
species of objects to serve the needs of males. But this also means
that sexual difference is denied, in that the difference between
male and female is not seen as one between two sorts of human
being, two sorts of subject, but as the difference between the
human and the non-human, between subjects and objects. The
only truly 'spiritual' relations must be those between men, since
men alone have 'spirits', or subjectivity. Relations between men
and women, or between women and women, are reduced to a
lower level of pure carnality.

If the denial of sexual difference has, in Irigaray's opinion, had
such consequences for the whole of philosophy, then one can see
why she says, at the beginning of her *Ethics of Sexual Difference*:
'Sexual difference is one of the major philosophical issues, if not
the issue, of our age.'[5] And, given that philosophy is the 'master
discourse' in culture, the consequences of the neglect of sexual
difference in Western philosophy will be all-pervasive: they

include, as she goes on to say, 'the consumer society, the circularity of discourse, the more or less cancerous diseases of our age, the unreliability of words, the end of philosophy, religious despair or regression to religiosity, scientistic or technical imperialism that fails to consider the living subject'. Thus, she says, if we were to think the issue of sexual difference through, it could be our 'salvation'.

The aim is not to replace domination by men with the domination of men by women; but to get rid of all domination of one group of human beings by another. But how is this idyllic society to be achieved? Both men and women would have to play their part in this, but especially women. Irigaray follows Lacan's view that language is primary: that the construction of an identity is the construction of a language of one's own. Women are denied identity in patriarchal society, she contends, because the language of that society excludes them. Thus, a major task for women is to create a language of their own, fitted to female subjectivity and recognizing sexual difference as existing between subjects. Such a language will be capable of expressing specifically female experience. The patriarchal tradition in philosophy must also be deconstructed, along the lines suggested earlier. The myth that the subject of philosophy is gender-neutral and that the criteria of rationality are genuinely universal must be exposed as what it is, a fiction. This is one place in which there is a role for male philosophers, who must bring themselves to admit that the 'subject' of which they have been talking all along is in fact male. We need, she says, to: ' "reopen" the figures of philosophical discourse—idea, substance, transcendental subjectivity, absolute knowledge—in order to pry out of them what they have borrowed that is feminine, from the feminine, to make them "render up" and give back what they owe the feminine'.[6]

To base such sweeping conclusions as these on such a flimsy basis as a purely speculative psychoanalytic interpretation of some of Plato's myths is clearly unacceptable, and it is not surprising, therefore, that unsympathetic critics should want simply to dismiss what Irigaray has to say. Furthermore, any fair reading of Western philosophy as a whole would suggest that Irigaray's identification of it with patriarchal modes of thinking is, to say the least, greatly exaggerated. It does not follow, however, that there is *nothing* in what she says: it would hardly be surprising if, in such a thoroughly patriarchal culture as ours, philosophy were to escape entirely from masculine bias. Given that it is an essential part of our conception of philosophy that it must be self-critical, it is as well to be put on our guard against such bias. Is the 'subject' of philosophy always a gender-neutral being of pure reason as it purports to be, and as philosophy itself requires it to be? The feminist turn given by Irigaray to the general deconstructive attitude of suspicion towards philosophical pretensions to transcendence is in part a natural development of the philosophical tradition itself, though I shall argue later that it is something much more, and more disputable, than that.

3. Julia Kristeva

Of equal centrality with Irigaray in current French feminist thought is Julia Kristeva, who is not, in fact, French at all in origin, having been born in Bulgaria in 1941. Since her arrival in Paris in 1966, however, she has been increasingly absorbed, as many immigrants are, into French culture and intellectual life, so that her contributions can certainly be considered as part of twentieth-century French philosophy. At the same time, she has brought a non-French outsider's viewpoint to bear on the structuralist and post-structuralist theorizing which she encountered on arriving in France. Her thinking is influenced not only by these French currents but also by her deep knowledge of Marxism and of Soviet thought, and by her reading of Hegel.

Like Irigaray, she has combined an interest in linguistics, on which she worked under Roland Barthes, with Lacanian psychoanalysis: she trained as a psychoanalyst in the early 1970s. In view of what was said in earlier chapters about Lacan's concept of the Freudian unconscious as structured like a language and about the structuralist and post-structuralist emphasis on the unconscious background to linguistic signification, it should be easier to see how such interests could be meaningfully combined. The influence of both disciplines is found in her doctoral thesis *La Révolution du langage poétique*, published in 1974, which led to her appointment to a Chair in Linguistics at the University of Paris VII which she still holds. It is probably best to begin exploring Kristeva's thought, and especially her complex relationship to feminism, with this work.

In it, she brings to bear the 'outsider's' viewpoint on structuralism and other French intellectual currents which was mentioned above. The trouble with structuralism, in her view, is that it focuses too exclusively on the static formal structures of language, leaving out of account the fact that language is spoken by people and so is subject to change and development. Signifying is something which people *do*, though it is not necessarily something which they do *consciously* or *intentionally*. In terms of psychoanalytic theory, Kristeva distinguishes between '*the semiotic*' and '*the symbolic*'.[7] The language which we speak as adults in non-specialist contexts combines both 'modalities' in an inseparable dialectical unity, but the semiotic modality originates in the early, 'pre-Oedipal', phase of infant development, before we are capable of verbal language at all. It consists in an 'uncertain and indeterminate articulation' of drives, which is not yet a form of discourse, although our discourse 'simultaneously depends upon and refuses it'.[8]

Kristeva borrows a term from Plato's *Timaeus* to designate this articulation. The term is *chora* (literally, 'place' or 'space'), which Plato describes as 'nourishing' and 'maternal', and which Kristeva also associates with the space provided for the infant by its mother. The *chora* is not supposed to be either a sign or a signifier—it does not *represent* something other than itself. It is, however, a precondition for signification, and it is a modality of what Kristeva calls *signifiance*. The articulation of the drives in the *chora* is *quasi*-signifying, in that its 'vocal and gestural organization is subject to what we shall call an objective *ordering*, which is dictated by natural or socio-historical constraints such as the biological difference between the sexes or family structure'.[9] It relates to objects functionally, even if it does not *refer* to them as true signs do.

This 'pre-verbal functional state' must, however, be distinguished 'from symbolic operations that depend on language as a sign-system—whether the language is vocalized or gestural (as with deaf-mutes)'.[10] Thus, the difference between the 'semiotic' and the 'symbolic' seems to correspond to the difference between the pre-linguistic conditions for language, some kind of ordering of drives in relation to objects, and the development of language proper, a rule-governed social system of communication, in which signs *refer* to objects. In true Freudian style, Kristeva sees the pre-Oedipal drives as chaotic and predominantly destructive: the semiotic *chora* is both the place where the subject is generated and where there are forces tending to destroy it, to produce disintegration. The subject's identity is only fully established, however, with the development of the 'symbolic' modality: verbalized, propositional language containing terms such as the first-person pronoun 'I' without the use of which a subject in the full sense cannot exist. The symbolic modality is superimposed on the semiotic in the process of the child's integration into the wider society, governed by the Law of the Father. In this sense, the subject is a social construction, though its construction depends on a pre-social and pre-linguistic basis.

The paradox underlying Kristeva's distinction between the 'semiotic' and the 'symbolic' modalities in language is that the 'semiotic' *chora* is supposed to be a pre-linguistic stage in an individual's development, but one which can only be *described* in language. In particular, the peculiar way in which the semiotic 'signifies' (through a functional, but not a representational, relation to objects) can only be taken into account once we do have the power to represent objects through rule-governed signs. In that sense, the semiotic only comes into its own once it has been superseded by the symbolic: it is as dependent on the symbolic order as the latter is dependent on it. Thus Kristeva says: 'Once the break instituting the symbolic has been established, what we have called the semiotic *chora* acquires a more precise status. Although originally a precondition of the symbolic, the semiotic functions within signifying practices as the result of a transgression of the symbolic.'[11]

The interest of this from a psychoanalytic point of view, of course, is that in the adult human being both 'modalities' exist in necessary tension with each other. The individuals with whom analysts primarily deal are those in whom this uncertain coexistence has broken down, with the result that they cannot function satisfactorily within the social order. These tensions also have a wider philosophical relevance. In the language of science and technology, the 'symbolic' modality is supposed to predominate, and the chaotic, anarchic, irrational 'semiotic' modality is repressed. 'Scientific discourse . . . aspiring to the status of meta-language, tends to reduce as much as possible the semiotic component.'[12] In the language of poetry, or at least of avant-garde poetry, however, this is reversed. In poetry, the semiotic bursts through the constraints of the symbolic order: the poet is no longer, as the user of purely 'symbolic' language is, master of his or her language. Avant-garde writers such as Mallarmé and Joyce introduce 'ruptures' into language: 'All of these modifications in the linguistic fabric are the sign of a force that has not been grasped by the linguistic or ideological system. This signification renewed, "infinitized" by the rhythm in a text, this precisely is (sexual) pleasure (*la jouissance*).'[13] In this sense, this sort of radical literary creation is a way of allowing what has been 'repressed' to come to the surface and play its part in revitalizing our consciousness.

This raises the question of what the point of psychoanalysis is. People only have a subjectivity and an identity in the full sense once they have entered the symbolic order and so put behind themselves (repressed) the semiotic *chora*. At the same time, however, this semiotic *chora* is a necessary precondition for the development of subjectivity and identity, and certainly its repression poses a constant threat to the stability of that identity. The task of the analyst is therefore somehow to enable her patient to develop an identity into which that pre-personal self can be integrated, which will be stable enough to allow patients to express themselves and to act in the law-governed social order, but not one which is rigidly defined in terms of the concepts of the symbolic order alone.

This is of central importance to understanding both Kristeva's general philosophical position (as it has developed since the early 1970s) and in particular her uncertainties about feminism. On the one hand, she sees the existing symbolic order as in need of destabilization: it exalts law, order, rationality to an exclusive status, and in this way creates *technocracy*, the rule of those who are masters of the language they speak, the purely propositional language of science. This also involves, of course, legitimizing the dominant position of males, the 'phallocracy'. This applies as much, Kristeva has come to think, to the so-called 'left-wing' totalitarianism of the Communist states before their collapse as to the right-wing or Fascist states. The destabilization, however, is in Kristeva's opinion already taking place: those who are marginal to technocratic society, including the artists spoken of earlier, are disrupting the symbolic order: 'the master discourses begin to drift and the simple rational coherence of cultural and institutional codes breaks down'.[14]

We need to remember, however, what was said earlier: the breakdown of a *particular set* of cultural and institutional codes need not and must not become the breakdown of cultural and institutional codes as such. Not only can the semiotic not exist without the symbolic, but it represents on the Freudian perspective, as we have seen, forces of destruction and disintegration as well as of life and sensual enjoyment. The anarchy of avant-garde poetry is not, as some 'formalists' have claimed, simply the free play of signifiers when freed from any relation to the signified, but the expression of dark instinctual forces released from their repression. Without some restraint from symbolic ordering, the disruption is likely to lead to the breakdown of any kind of social order.

In this way, Kristeva's psychoanalysis of the present social order needs to be distinguished from 'deconstruction'. The attempts at 'deconstructing' phenomenology, she says, perform an important task in circumscribing 'the metaphysics inherent in the sciences of signification and therefore in the human sciences', but they reveal their limitations in that they 'refuse ... what constitutes one function of language though not the only one: to express meaning in a communicable sentence between speakers'.[15] That is, Kristeva, unlike the deconstructionists, recognizes the value of the 'logocentric' function of language, even though only as one among a number of functions. The task is not to eliminate the transcendental subject, but to develop a 'subject of enunciation' which includes in its 'operating consciousness not only logical modalities, but also interlocutory relationships'.[16]

The exaggerated emphasis on sexual difference in certain kinds of feminism is in Kristeva's view, 'metaphysical' in that it is linked to the idea of a fixed subjectivity, rigid because it is rooted in biology. On Kristeva's account, as we have seen, the subject, although it has its roots in biological drives, only comes to fulfilment in the symbolic order, so that its identity is social and changeable rather than biological and fixed. The consequence of this is that all notions of rigidly defined personal and sexual identities disintegrate in their very nucleus. Such rigid definitions of sexual identity amount to sexism, whether indulged in by men or by women. 'The answer to Spinoza's question ["Are women subject to ethics?"] can be affirmative only at the cost of considering feminism as but a *moment* in the thought of that anthropomorphic identity which currently blocks the horizon of the discursive and scientific adventure of our species.'[17]

There is a clear sense, therefore, in which Kristeva is a very different kind of feminist from Irigaray, and some would deny that she is a feminist at all. What is of much more importance from our point of view, however, is the difference in her *philosophical* approach and conclusions. Her aim, unlike Irigaray, is not to deconstruct the philosophical tradition by revealing the patriarchal subtext beneath the gender-neutral surface. Rather, she offers an account of two modes of language and of their interaction in the formation of human identity, whether male or female. Her use of this distinction to formulate a feminist critique of contemporary culture can be seen as essentially separate from her purely philosophical analysis of the distinction itself. That is, feminism and philosophy are divisible for Kristeva in a way that they cannot be for Irigaray.

From a purely philosophical point of view, therefore, any criticism must centre on the value of Kristeva's contrast between the 'semiotic' and the 'symbolic'. Is there a clear distinction to be made between the 'rational', 'fact-stating', language of science and the 'imaginative', 'expressive' language of poetry and the subconscious? There is a long tradition of making such a distinction, which suggests that in broad terms at least it is worth making: but it is extraordinarily difficult to make it clear exactly where the difference lies. Kristeva herself makes suggestive use of the distinction, both in her accounts of the nature of psychonalysis and in her critique of contemporary society, but in the end its sheer diffuseness leaves it uncertain whether it can provide the basis for anything more than suggestions.

4. Michèle Le Dœuff

Michèle Le Dœuff is both the youngest of the figures considered in this chapter (she was born in 1948) and the most purely philosophical. She is indeed a professional philosopher: she previously taught philosophy at the École Normale Supérieure and now holds a research post at the CNRS (Centre National de la Recherche Scientifique). Her main field of research interest also marks her out amongst French philosophers, in that it is English philosophy of the Renaissance, especially Francis Bacon and Sir Thomas More. Because of her interest in British philosophy and her acquaintance with English life, it is tempting to see in her thinking about feminism traces of an almost Anglo-Saxon caution and distrust of rhetoric.

Not only, therefore, does Le Dœuff not have the background in either linguistics or psychoanalysis which both Irigaray and Kristeva have, but she has a positive aversion to the introduction of such extraneous theories as psychoanalysis and Marxism into philosophy, partly because she sees them as a potential source of new dogmatic orthodoxies. In general, her feminism is much more narrowly focused on philosophy itself and on the ways in which women are excluded from it. This exclusion is both practical, in the sense of the small number of posts for women philosophers and the not unconnected domination of the profession by men, and theoretical, in that the traditional discourse of philosophy effectively ignores or denigrates women. The practical exclusion is a political matter, and therefore outside the scope of a book such as this; but the theoretical exclusion is directly relevant to a study of the development of French philosophy in the twentieth century.

In her studies of the history of philosophy, Le Dœuff quickly became aware of the importance of images in philosophical discourse. Philosophy represents itself traditionally as a purely rational and intellectual pursuit, seeking to convince only by the logical force of its arguments: on this view, any images which a philosopher might use were only psychological or pedagogic devices, means of illustrating abstract ideas in order to make them more accessible to readers, with no part in the actual process of argument itself. Le Dœuff, however, came to the conclusion that this was a deception: that the images used by a philosopher were (or at least could be) a crucial part of his argument (the use of the male pronoun here is deliberate). In an interview, Le Dœuff says: 'Any form of rational discourse proceeds from, or originates in, things which can't be sustained or produced through reason, things such as beliefs for example. In philosophy, these beliefs are set forth in the form of myths, or "exempla", comparisons, images or pictorial writing.'[18] The role of images and myths thus seems to be to set out and make plausible the basic premisses from which reasoning must start, and which therefore reasoning itself cannot establish.

Next (and this is where the connection with feminism comes in) Le Dœuff noticed that many of these images in the philosophical tradition expressed hostility towards women and the feminine. In her study of Bacon, for instance, she found that he describes nature as a woman, with whom false knowledge deals as with a prostitute, but true knowledge as with a lawful wife. This is hostile to women, in that it clearly takes for granted that the knower must be male, and that knowledge can be compared to male sexual penetration of women, and so excludes by the very form of the image the possibility that women might be capable of knowledge or of reason (and so capable of being philosophers).

Another, much more recent, instance, and one of a rather different kind, is that of Sartre's philosophical examples. 'In his philosophical writings', Le Dœuff says, 'I have nowhere come across a female character involved in a historical situation (the war or the Resistance, for example), nor even in a workplace scene (in the fashion of, for example, the café waiter). Woman is always seen only as a body, and a sexed body.'[19] Here the hostility to women takes the form of reducing them to mere sexual objects, and thus again excluding them from the domain of rational philosophical discourse. This particular case has a special relevance for French feminism because of Sartre's relationship with Simone de Beauvoir. Throughout that relationship, as Le Dœuff points out using quotations from de Beauvoir's writings, it was assumed by both partners that the philosophy would be left to Sartre, even though de Beauvoir had been a brilliant student of philosophy and showed her capacity to write original works of her own. De Beauvoir, in short, was not able in her own case to achieve that liberation which she recommended to other women. (None of this, incidentally, diminishes Le Dœuff's admiration either for de Beauvoir or for *The Second Sex*.)

Because she does not relate this use of anti-female imagery by philosophers to any psychological or sociological framework, such as psychoanalysis or Marxism, Le Dœuff is able to be reasonably optimistic about the chances for improvement. Male philosophers can, she thinks, be persuaded, at least in principle, to change both the character of their imagery and the institutions of the philosophical profession. Then philosophy can pursue its true destiny of being rational discourse amongst equals, both men and women. There is thus nothing in Le Dœuff's conception of philosophy which makes it intrinsically patriarchal and so in need of a radical upheaval which would fundamentally change its character. To the extent that philosophy is central to Western culture, the same could be said of that culture as a whole. In that sense, then, Le Dœuff's feminism is reformist, rather than revolutionary.

Just because of that, it can hardly be described as 'feminist philosophy'. The way in which images figure in philosophical writing is something that can be recognized by anyone at all, whatever their views on feminism. On the other hand, the claim that a large number of philosophical images express hostility to women deserves attention; but it is, as far as Le Dœuff shows, one which, if true, is only contingently so: it is not derived from any a priori philosophical principles. That is, Le Dœuff's philosophy is not particularly feminist, and her feminism is not particularly philosophical.

5. Is There a Feminist Philosophy?

The three thinkers discussed in this chapter are all feminists, and all have made some contribution to philosophy. But the link between their feminism and their philosophy is different in each of the three, as we have seen. In the case of Irigaray, her feminist perspective provides the basis for a deconstruction of the whole Western philosophical tradition as an expression of patriarchy. The very centrality of impersonal and gender-neutral rationality in that tradition's understanding of itself is seen by her, in psychoanalytic terms, as a repression of the real roots of traditional philosophizing in the (male) child's fear of womanhood. To accept her conclusions, therefore, would be to change the essential character of philosophy itself: her feminism and her philosophy, in short, are inextricably interlinked.

The connections between philosophy and feminism in Kristeva's case are much more complex. She certainly links her philosophical distinction between the two types of language to a critique of an excessively scientistic culture, which is in turn seen as based on patriarchal concepts. But the links are in the end contingent: logically speaking, there is no reason why scientism *must* be regarded as an expression of male domination. Moreover, the critique of scientistic culture is not wholesale, as we have seen: Kristeva allows a place for scientific concepts of rationality. As for Le Dœuff, it has already been said that her philosophical activity is not in any sense essentially feminist: her feminism affects her philosophy only in the sense that it leads her to criticize certain kinds of argument used by some philosophers as infected by patriarchal imagery.

This raises the question of whether a genuinely feminist philosophy is possible. It would be hard to deny that feminist emphases can provide a useful new perspective on many of the traditional problems of philosophy and on the interpretation of philosophical texts. It is salutary to be reminded of the possibility that the apparently impersonal discourse of the philosopher may conceal fundamentally masculine conceptions of the subject and its relation to the world of objects. A truly feminist philosophy, however, would need to go much further than that. In the way that Irigaray attempts, it would have to show that genuinely impersonal and gender-neutral discourse was ruled out in principle. The problem then is that the notion of rational argument depends on the possibility of impersonal discourse: a rational argument is one which can appeal to a human (or indeed any rational) being as such, regardless of gender, nationality, or other particular characteristics. By denying the possibility of such discourse, Irigaray, or those who think like her, seems to be depriving herself of the use of rational argument even to defend her feminist readings of Plato and other philosophers. And if they cannot be defended by rational argument, then it seems as if they can be acceptable only to those who happen to accept Irigaray's own starting point already: she would always be preaching to the converted.

The opposition to logocentrism by feminists such as Irigaray does seem to depend, as Kristeva suggests, on an exaggerated emphasis on sexual difference, amounting, despite Irigaray's attempts to avoid it, to 'essentialism'. The equation of logical, impersonal, reasoning with the male, and of a looser, more personal, mode of thinking with the female both ignores what seem to be obvious cases in which men think intuitively and women logically and is potentially damaging from the feminist point of view itself. For it reinforces the male chauvinist myth that women are incapable of rational argument, that they are forever bogged down in the emotional, the sensuous, and the particular. It is paradoxical, to say the least, to see feminists appearing to propose, not just that all of us, men and women, need to recognize that there is a place for imagination and emotion in our thinking *as well as* impersonal logic, but that the whole tradition of logical philosophical thought ought to be abandoned.

To avoid any possibility of misunderstanding, I must end by making it absolutely clear that what has just been said is *not* intended as a criticism of feminism or the women's movement or a defence of patriarchy, only as a criticism of the confused thinking, as I see it, of some feminists. Anyone with an open mind should find it perfectly obvious that women have been excluded and ignored by Western culture (and other cultures) and that in philosophy itself there may often be found a tendency to represent as 'transcendental subjectivity' what has many elements of a purely masculine view of the world. Philosophy would be better if that were recognized: but it would be better just *because* we could then strive for concepts, categories, and patterns of thought which were genuinely universal, human, and rational, and nothing discussed in the last few chapters constitutes an argument that there is something in the nature of things which rules out the possibility of achieving such concepts and categories.

Retrospect and Prospect

Now that we are approaching the beginning of the twenty-first century, there is an obvious, though very superficial, sense in which the story of twentieth-century French philosophy is coming to an end. This is a *very* superficial sense: philosophy continues without regard to such conventional divisions of time. In a more profound sense, however, the last years of the twentieth century do mark an important turning-point in French philosophy. I have tried to show how the French philosophical tradition has developed in an intelligible fashion from the beginning of the century and on the basis of the foundations laid by Bergson. In many ways, however, what has been developing is a *crisis* in Western philosophy itself, in which philosophy has called itself in question. It is not the done thing in analytic philosophy to use expressions such as 'a crisis in Western philosophy': such 'rhetoric' is frowned on. In discussing French philosophy, it is much easier: the very involvement of philosophy in France with a wider literary, artistic, and political culture makes the use of such language by philosophers much more normal. Perhaps this is one way in which analytic philosophers could indeed learn from their French colleagues.

The growing crisis has been seen in earlier chapters to arise from the critique of Cartesian rationalism and dualism, paradoxically often using the tools supplied by Descartes himself. The stress on embodiment and so on historicity has called in question the whole notion of philosophy as a foundational discipline, pursuing universal a priori truths about the most basic elements of all other branches of human knowledge and wisdom. The 'linguistic turn' in French (as in Anglo-Saxon) philosophy has further fuelled a sense of crisis, since the development of a holistic theory of meaning has seemed to many to cast doubt on the referential relation of words to reality, and so on the possibility of saying things which are objectively true or false. This crisis in philosophy is also a crisis in the wider culture, since it casts doubt on objectivity in science, and so on the centrality of science in modern European civilization since the Enlightenment.

What I have tried to suggest in the last few chapters is not that there is no crisis in Western philosophy and culture, but that the nature of that crisis should not be misinterpreted. We do indeed need to face up to the fact that philosophers exist in history and can propose their views only from where they are. We need to accept also that the relation between what we say and the world that we talk about cannot be reduced to a simple one-to-one correspondence; nor can rationality be reduced, for the same reason, to the simple observance of formal logic. It does not follow, however, either that there is *no* relation between what we say and the world, such that it is the world which makes our statements true or false; or that formal logic does not form a central part of what we mean by rational thought.

What is required is not the abandonment of the philosophical enterprise, but an extension of our concept of philosophical rationality which takes account of the complexities of reference and the diversity of ways in which we can rationally justify our claims. Philosophers need also to accept with humility the fact that they will never transcend history to adopt a 'God's eye view', but nevertheless to seek to push human reason to whatever limits it can reach within their own time. I have tried to suggest that there are some hints of such a view of philosophy in Derrida; in the analytic tradition, similar conceptions (and some respect for 'Continental' philosophy) can be found in such figures as Hilary Putnam. It is always dangerous to predict, but it may well be that the most interesting philosophy in the twenty-first century will come from the convergence of the analytic and the French (or more broadly the 'Continental') traditions.

Notes

Chapter 1

1. Cf. St Augustine's remark, 'Return to yourself; truth resides in the inner man.'
2. Émile Durkheim, *The Rules of Sociological Method*, edited with an introduction by Steven Lukes, trans. W. D. Halls (London: Macmillan, 1982), 33.
3. Descartes, *Second Meditation* (in Cottingham, Stoothoff, and Murdoch (trans.), *The Philosophical Writings of Descartes*, ii (Cambridge: Cambridge University Press, 1984), 22 f.).
4. Maurice Merleau-Ponty, "Bergson in the Making", in his collection *Signs*, trans. R. C. McCleary (Evanston, Ill.: Northwestern University Press, 1964), 183.

Chapter 2

1. For a lively and thorough account of Bergson's influence on the wider culture see Mark Antliff, *Inventing Bergson: Cultural Politics and the Parisian Avant-garde* (Princeton: Princeton University Press, 1993).
2. Péguy, *Œuvres en prose, 1898–1908* (Paris: Bibliothèque de la Pléiade, 1959), 483; quoted in A. E. Pilkington, *Bergson and his Influence* (Cambridge: Cambridge University Press, 1976), 30 (my translation).
3. *An Introduction to Metaphysics*, by Henri Bergson, trans. T. E. Hulme (London: Macmillan, 1913).
4. Bergson, *Time and Free Will*, English trans. of his *Essai sur les données immédiates de la conscience*, F. L. Pogson (London: George Allen & Unwin, 1910), 161 f.
5. See ibid. 175 ff.
6. Bergson, *Matter and Memory*, trans. N. M. Paul and W. S. Palmer (New York: Zone Books, 1991), 9.
7. Ibid. 133.

8. Bergson, *Introduction to Metaphysics*, 6 (Bergson's own italics).
9. Bergson, *Creative Evolution*, trans. Arthur Mitchell (New York: The Modern Library, 1944) 3 f.
10. Ibid. 7 f.
11. Ibid. 19.
12. Bergson, *The Two Sources of Morality and Religion*, trans. R. Ashley Audra and Cloudesley Brereton (Garden City, NY: Doubleday & Co. Inc. (reprinted from the 1935 edition published by Henry Holt & Co. Inc.), 55.
13. English trans., C. Brereton and F. Rothwell, *Laughter* (London: Macmillan, 1911).
14. Bergson, *The Two Sources*, 212.
15. It is said that Proust may not actually have read any of Bergson's works before starting on his novel, and Proust himself explicitly denied that he was influenced by Bergson: but it is hard to believe that he (Proust) was not affected by ideas which were so much in the Parisian air at the time as a result of Bergson's fashionable lectures.

Chapter 3

1. Emmanuel Mounier, *Personalism*, trans. Philip Mairet, first published in English by Routledge & Kegan Paul (London, 1952); page references are to the paperback edition published by University of Notre Dame Press (Notre Dame, Ind., and London, n.d.).
2. Mounier, *Personalism*, 19.
3. Ibid. 70.
4. Gabriel Marcel, *Being and Having*, trans. K. Farrer (New York: Harper & Row, Harper Torchbooks edn., 1965).
5. English trans. Emma Crauford, with the title *Homo Viator: Introduction to a Metaphysic of Hope* (New York: Harper & Row, Harper Torchbooks edn., 1962).
6. In two vols. i (London: Harvill Press, 1950); ii (London: Harvill Press, 1951).
7. Published under the same title (Cambridge, Mass: Harvard University Press, 1963).
8. Marcel, 'Existence and Human Freedom', in *The Philosophy of Existentialism*, trans. Manya Harari (Secaucus, NJ: Citadel Press, 1956), 47, 85. It should be said, however, that Marcel himself is believed by many to have coined the term 'existentialism'.
9. Cf. *Mystery of Being*, i. 1.

10. Ibid. 8.
11. Marcel, *Philosophy of Existentialism*, 19.
12. Marcel, *Mystery of Being*, 83.
13. Marcel, *Homo Viator*, 13.
14. Ibid. 23.

Chapter 4

1. See Simone de Beauvoir, *The Prime of Life*, English trans. Peter Green (Harmondsworth: Penguin Books, 1965), 135 ff. Emmanuel Lévinas, the author of the book on Husserl referred to here (presumably his *La Théorie de l'intuition dans la phénoménologie de Husserl* (Paris: Alcan, 1930), continues even now, despite his advanced age, to be influential in French philosophy: see below, Ch. 8.
2. Edmund Husserl, *The Idea of Phenomenology*, trans. William P. Alston and George Nakhnikian (The Hague: Martinus Nijhoff, 1964), 11.
3. Ibid. 4.
4. Ibid. 7.
5. Originally in *La Nouvelle Revue française* (Jan. 1939), reprinted in Sartre, *Situations philosophiques* (Paris: Éditions Gallimard, 1990), 9–12: all translations from this essay given here are my own.
6. Sartre, *Situations philosophiques*, 9 f.
7. Ibid. 12.
8. Sartre, *Being and Nothingness*, trans. Hazel Barnes (London: Methuen, 1958), 73 (since 1989 this trans. has been published by Routledge: pagination remains as before).
9. An English trans. by Forrest Williams and Robert Kirkpatrick, 'The Transcendence of the Ego', has been published by Noonday Press (New York, 1957).
10. Sartre, *Situations philosophiques*, 12.
11. Sartre, *Being and Nothingness*.
12. Ibid. 623.
13. Ibid. 55 ff.
14. Ibid. 55.
15. Ibid. 56.
16. Cf. 'She does not notice because it happens by chance that she is at this moment all intellect. She draws her companion up to the most lofty regions of sentimental speculation; she speaks of Life, of her life, she shows herself in her essential aspect—a personality, a consciousness.' ibid. 56.

17. Ibid. 63.

18. Ibid. 64.

19. Trans. Philip Mairet as *Existentialism and Humanism* (London: Methuen, 1957).

20. Sartre, *Being and Nothingness*, 93.

21. Ibid. 628.

22. Sartre, *Cahiers pour une morale* (Paris: Gallimard, 1983); English trans. David Pellauer *Notebooks for an Ethics* (Chicago: University of Chicago Press, 1992).

23. Sartre, *Existentialism and Humanism*, 45.

24. Ibid.

25. E.g. the modern British philosopher P. F. Strawson, in his book *Individuals* (London: Methuen, 1959) and elsewhere. See, in particular, ch. 3.

26. Sartre, *Being and Nothingness*, 94.

27. Ibid. 93.

28. Cf. Sartre, *Existentialism and Humanism*, 47.

29. Sartre, *Being and Nothingness*, 429.

30. Ibid., pt. 3, ch. 3.

31. Cf. ibid. 3, 'The concrete is man within the world in that specific union of man with the world which Heidegger, for example, calls "being-in-the-world." '

Chapter 5

1. Merleau-Ponty, *Phenomenology of Perception*, trans. Colin Smith (London, Routledge & Kegan Paul, 1962), p. vii.

2. Ibid., p. ix.

3. Ibid., p. xi.

4. Cf. ibid. 83 f.

5. Alphonse de Waelhens, in his foreword to the second French edition of Merleau-Ponty's *The Structure of Behaviour*, describes Merleau-Ponty's philosophy as 'a philosophy of the ambiguous' (English trans. (London: Methuen, 1965), pp. xviii–xxvii.

6. Merleau-Ponty, *Phenomenology of Perception*, 88.

7. Quoted from Lewis S. Feuer (ed.), *Marx and Engels: Basic Writings on Politics and Philosophy* (Glasgow: Collins, The Fontana Library, 1969), 360.

8. Cf. Merleau-Ponty, *Phenomenology of Perception*, 436–7.

9. Ibid. 352.

10. Ibid. 449 f.

11. Ibid.
12. Merleau-Ponty, *Signs*, trans. with an intro. by R. C. McCleary (Evanston, Ill.: Northwestern University Press, 1964), *Sense and Non-Sense*, trans. with a preface by Hubert L. and Patricia Allen Dreyfus (Evanston, Ill. Northwestern University Press, 1964).
13. In *Sense and Non-Sense* 21.
14. Ibid. 27.
15. Ibid. 48–59.
16. Published after his death as 'Un inédit de Maurice Merleau-Ponty', in *Revue de métaphysique et de morale*, 4 (1962), 401–9; English trans. Arleen B. Dallery, in James M. Edie (ed.), *Maurice Merleau-Ponty, The Primacy of Perception* (Evanston, Ill: Northwestern University Press, 1964), 3–11. References are to the English trans.
17. *Primacy of Perception*, 3.
18. Ibid. 8.
19. Ibid. 9.
20. Ibid. 10.
21. English trans. John O'Neill, *The Prose of the World* (Evanston, Ill.: Northwestern University Press, 1973).
22. Merleau-Ponty, *Phenomenology of Perception*, 177.
23. Merleau-Ponty, *Prose of the World*, 36.
24. Maurice Merleau-Ponty, *Le Visible et l'invisible* (Paris: Gallimard, 1964), English trans. *The Visible and the Invisible*, trans. Alphonso Lingis, (Evanston, Ill.: Northwestern University Press, 1968). (References are to the English trans.).
25. Ibid. 137.
26. Ibid. 140.
27. Ibid. 125.

Chapter 6

1. Alexandre Kojève, *Introduction à la lecture de Hegel*, assembled by Raymond Queneau, 2nd edn., (Paris: Gallimard, 1947); English trans. James H. Nichols, Jr., *Introduction to the Reading of Hegel* (New York: Cornell University Press, 1980). (References are to the English trans.).
2. Cf. Descartes, *Discourse on the Method*, in *The Philosophical Writings of Descartes*, trans. Cottingham, Stoothoff, and Murdoch (Cambridge, Cambridge University Press, 1985), i. 113.
3. Kojève, *Introduction to the Reading of Hegel*, 3.
4. Ibid. 3–4.

5. Ibid. 7.
6. Ibid. 8–9.
7. Ibid. 20.
8. Sartre, *Critique de la raison dialectique* (Paris: Gallimard, 1960); English trans. *Critique of Dialectical Reason*, trans. Alan Sheridan-Smith (London: New Left Books, 1976). (References are to the English trans. in the revised version published in London in 1991 by Verso) (An unfinished second vol. of the *Critique* was published after Sartre's death: no account will be taken of vol. ii. here).
9. Sartre, 'Question de méthode', *Les Temps modernes*, 139 (Sept. 1957), 338–417 and 140 (Oct. 1957), 658–98; subsequently published as a prologue to *Critique de la raison dialectique* and as an independent vol. (Paris: Gallimard, 1967); English trans. Hazel E. Barnes, *Search for a Method* (in the UK, *The Problem of Method*) (New York: Knopf, 1963; London: Methuen, 1963).
10. Sartre, *Critique of Dialectical Reason*, 79.
11. Ibid. 80.
12. Cf. ibid. 711.
13. Ibid. 123.
14. Sartre, *L'Idiot de la famille*, i and ii (Paris: Gallimard, i and ii, 1971, iii 1972), *The Family Idiot*, trans. by Carol Cosman of first part of vol. i (Chicago: University of Chicago Press, 1981).
15. Louis Althusser, *Lenin and Philosophy and Other Essays*, trans. Ben Brewster (London: New Left Books, 1971), 69.
16. Althusser, *For Marx*, trans. Ben Brewster (London: Verso, 1990), 221.
17. Ibid. 171 n.
18. Ibid. 96.

Chapter 7

1. Lacan, *Écrits* (Paris: Éditions du Seuil, 1966), English trans. of selected papers by Alan Sheridan, *Écrits: A Selection* (London: Tavistock Publications and Routledge, 1977). (References are to the English trans.).
2. Lacan, *Écrits: A Selection*, 1.
3. Lacan, *The Four Fundamental Concepts of Psychoanalysis*, trans. Alan Sheridan (Harmondsworth: Penguin Books, 1991), 36.
4. Lacan, *The Ethics of Psychoanalysis, 1959–1960: The Seminar of Jacques Lacan Book VII*, trans. Dennis Porter (London: Tavistock Publications and Routledge, 1992), 313.
5. Ibid. 304.

6. Ibid. 314.
7. Ibid. 44.
8. Ibid. 8.
9. Lacan, *The Ethics of Psychoanalysis*, 324.
10. Foucault, *Madness and Civilisation*, trans. Richard Howard (London: Tavistock, 1971).
11. Foucault, *The Order of Things: An Archaeology of the Human Sciences* (London: Tavistock, 1970).
12. Ibid. 208.
13. Ibid. 387.
14. Ibid.
15. Foucault, *The Archaeology of Knowledge*, trans. A. M. Sheridan Smith (New York: Pantheon Books, 1972), 117.
16. Foucault, *The Order of Things*, p. xiv, 'In France, certain half-witted "commentators" persist in labelling me a "structuralist".... I have used none of the methods, concepts, or key terms that characterize structural analysis.'
17. Ibid. p. xi.
18. Ibid. p. xxii.
19. Ibid. p. xiii.
20. Foucault, 'Two Lectures', in Colin Gordon (ed.), *Michel Foucault: Power/Knowledge* (Brighton: Harvester Press, 1980), 84.
21. Foucault, 'Truth and Power', ibid. 113.
22. Ibid. 119.
23. Foucault, 'What is Enlightenment?', first published in P. Rabinow (ed.), *The Foucault Reader* (Harmondsworth: Penguin Books, 1986).
24. Ibid. 44.
25. Ibid. 46.
26. Ibid.

Chapter 8

1. Cf. Richard Kearney, 'Dialogue with Emmanuel Lévinas', in *Dialogues with Contemporary Continental Thinkers* (Manchester: Manchester University Press, 1984), 49.
2. Lévinas, *La Théorie de l'intuition dans la phénoménologie de Husserl* (Paris: Alcan, 1930); English trans. A. Orianne, *The Theory of Intuition in Husserl's Phenomenology* (Evanston, Ill.: Northwestern University Press, 1973). This is the work referred to above (Ch. 4), through which Sartre first became acquainted in detail with Husserl's phenomenology.

3. *De l'existence à l'existant* (Paris, Éditions de la Revue Fontaine, 1947); English trans. Alphonse Lingis, *Existence and Existents* (The Hague: Martinus Nijhoff, 1978).

4. *Totalité et infini: essais sur l'extériorité* (The Hague: Martinus Nijhoff, 1961); English trans. Alphonse Lingis, *Totality and Infinity: An Essay on Exteriority* (Dordrecht: Kluwer Academic Publishers, 1991).

5. Cf. Kearney, *Dialogues*, 50.

6. Lévinas, in Kearney, ibid. 51.

7. Lévinas, *Totality and Infinity*, trans. 43.

8. Ibid.

9. Ibid. 194.

10. Ibid. 195.

11. Lévinas, *Autrement qu'être ou au-delà de l'essence* (The Hague: Martinus Nijhoff, 1974); English trans. Alphonso Lingis, *Otherwise than Being or Beyond Essence* (The Hague: Martinus Nijhoff, 1981).

12. Lévinas, *Totality and Infinity*, 195.

13. Lévinas, *Éthique et infini* (Paris: Librairie Arthème Fayard and Radio France, 1982); English trans. Richard A. Cohen, *Ethics and Infinity* (Pittsburgh: Duquesne University Press, 1985): references are to the English trans.

14. Lévinas, *Ethics and Infinity*, 96.

15. Ibid. 113.

16. Lévinas, *Totality and Infinity*, 78.

17. See Lévinas, *Ethics and Infinity*, 117.

18. See ibid. 118.

19. Roland Paul Blum, 'Emmanuel Lévinas's Theory of Commitment', *Philosophy and Phenomenological Research*, 44 (1983), 146.

20. Derrida, in 'Dialogue with Jacques Derrida', in Kearney, *Dialogues*, 107 f.

21. Derrida, *Writing and Difference*, trans. Alan Bass. (London: Routledge & Kegan Paul, 1978).

22. Derrida, *Margins of Philosophy*, trans. Alan Bass (Chicago: University of Chicago Press, and London: Harvester Wheatsheaf, 1982).

23. Ibid. p. 293.

24. Derrida, *La Dissémination* (Paris: Seuil, 1972); English trans. Barbara Johnson, *Dissemination* (Chicago: University of Chicago Press; London: Athlone Press, 1981).

25. Plato, *Phaedrus*, 276 (quoted in the trans. by Walter Hamilton, *Plato: Phaedrus and Letters VII and VIII* (Harmondsworth: Penguin Books, 1973), 98.

26. Derrida, in 'Dialogue with Jacques Derrida', in Kearney, *Dialogues*, 111.
27. Ibid. 112.
28. Ibid. 108.
29. See especially Richard Rorty, *Philosophy and the Mirror of Nature* (Princeton: Princeton University Press, 1979).
30. Derrida, *Margins of Philosophy*, 109–36.
31. Ibid. 118.
32. Ibid. 124.
33. Ibid. 127.
34. Derrida, *Writing and Difference*, 31–63.
35. Derrida, in 'Dialogue with Jacques Derrida', in Kearney, *Dialogues*, 112.
36. Lyotard, *The Postmodern Condition*, trans. G. Bennington and B. Massumi (Manchester: Manchester University Press: 1984).
37. A selection of Lyotard's writings on particular political issues can be found in Jean-François Lyotard, *Political Writings*, trans. Bill Readings and Kevin Paul Geiman (London: UCL Press Ltd., 1993).

Chapter 9

1. Simone de Beauvoir, *Le Deuxième Sexe* (Paris: Gallimard, 1949); trans. H. M. Parshley as *The Second Sex*, (Harmondsworth: Penguin Books, 1978).
2. Luce Irigaray, *This Sex Which Is Not One*, trans. C. Porter and C. Burke (Ithaca, NY: Cornell University Press, 1985), 149.
3. Irigaray, *An Ethic of Sexual Difference*, trans. Carolyn Burke and Gillian C. Gill (London: Athlone Press, 1993).
4. Irigaray, *Speculum of the Other Woman*, trans. Gillian C. Gill (Ithaca: Cornell University Press, 1985).
5. Irigaray, *An Ethic of Sexual Difference*, 5.
6. Irigaray, *This Sex Which Is Not One*, 74.
7. See e.g. Kristeva, 'The Revolution in Poetic Language', trans. Margaret Waller, extract in Toril Moi (ed.), *The Kristeva Reader* (Oxford: Blackwell, 1986), 92.
8. Ibid. 93–4.
9. Ibid. 94.
10. Ibid. 95.
11. Ibid. 118.
12. Kristeva, *Desire in Language*, ed. Leon S. Roudiez, trans. T. Gora, A. Jardine, and L. S. Roudiez (Oxford: Blackwell, 1981), 134.

13. Kristeva, from an interview with Xavière Gauthier in *Tel quel* (Summer, 1974), reprinted in Elaine Marks and Isabelle de Court-ivron (eds.), *New French Feminisms* (New York: Harvester Wheat-sheaf, 1981), 165.

14. Kristeva, 'A New Type of Intellectual: The Dissident', in Moi (ed.), *Kristeva Reader*, 294.

15. Kristeva, *Desire in Language*, 131.

16. Ibid.

17. Ibid. 211.

18. Le Dœuff, in Raoul Mortley, *French Philosophers in Conversation* (London: Routledge, 1991), 87.

19. Le Dœuff, *Hipparchia's Choice*, trans. Trista Selous (Oxford: Black-well, 1991), 62.

Some Suggestions for Further Reading

The works listed are all cited in English-language versions, and as far as possible in editions which are still in print and readily available in libraries and/or bookshops: the edition cited is the most recent known.

1. General Histories

COPLESTON, FREDERICK, SJ, *A History of Philosophy*, ix (New York: Image Books, Doubleday & Co. Inc., 1977).

KEARNEY, RICHARD (ed.), *Continental Philosophy in the 20th Century*, Routledge History of Philosophy, 8 (London: Routledge, 1994).

KENNY, ANTHONY (ed.), *The Oxford Illustrated History of Western Philosophy* (ch. 4) (Oxford: Oxford University Press, 1994).

2. General Works about More Recent Philosophy

CADAVA, EDUARDO, CONNOR, PETER, and NANCY, JEAN-LUC (eds.), *Who Comes after the Subject?* (London: Routledge, 1991).

DESCOMBES, VINCENT, *Modern French Philosophy*, trans. L. J. Scott-Fox and J. M. Harding (Cambridge: Cambridge University Press, 1980).

FERRY, LUC, and RENAULT, ALAIN, *French Philosophy of the Sixties: An Essay on Antihumanism*, trans. Mary Schnackenberg Cattani (Amherst, Mass.: University of Massachusetts Press, 1990).

KEARNEY, RICHARD, *Dialogues with Contemporary Continental Thinkers* (Manchester: Manchester University Press, 1984).

—— *Modern Movements in European Philosophy*, 2nd edn. (Manchester: Manchester University Press, 1994).

MORTLEY, RAOUL, *French Philosophers in Conversation* (London: Routledge, 1991).

PHILLIPS GRIFFITHS, A. (ed.), *Contemporary French Philosophy* (Cambridge: Cambridge University Press, 1987).

SKINNER, QUENTIN (ed.), *The Return of Grand Theory in the Human Sciences*, Canto Books edn. (Cambridge: Cambridge University Press, 1990).

3. Bergson

(i) Major works by Bergson himself:

Creative Evolution, trans. A. Mitchell (New York: The Modern Library, 1944).

An Introduction to Metaphysics, trans. T. E. Hulme (London: Macmillan, 1913).

Laughter, trans. C. Brereton and F. Rothwell (London: Macmillan, 1911).

Matter and Memory, trans. N. M. Paul and W. S. Palmer (New York: Zone Books, 1991).

Time and Free Will, trans. F. L. Pogson (London: Allen & Unwin, 1910).

The Two Sources of Morality and Religion, trans. R. Ashley Audra and Cloudesley Brereton (Garden City: NY: Doubleday Anchor Books, n.d.).

(ii) Some useful writings about Bergson:

ANTLIFF, MARK, *Inventing Bergson* (Princeton: Princeton University Press, 1993).

CARR, H. WILDON, *The Philosophy of Change* (London: Macmillan, 1914).

DELEUZE, GILLES, *Bergsonism*, trans. Hugh Tomlinson and Barbara Habberjam (New York: Zone Books, 1991).

KOLAKOWSKI, LESZEK, *Bergson*, Past Masters Series (Oxford: Oxford University Press, 1985).

LACEY, A. R., *Bergson* (London: Routledge, 1989).

4. Mounier and Marcel

(i) Writings by Mounier and Marcel themselves:

MOUNIER, EMMANUEL, *Personalism*, trans. Philip Mairet (London: Routledge & Kegan Paul, 1952; repr. Notre Dame, Ind.: University of Notre Dame Press, n.d.).

MARCEL, GABRIEL, *Being and Having: An Existentialist Diary*, trans. K. Farrer, Harper Torchbooks edn. (London: Fontana Library, and New York: Harper & Row, 1965).

—— *Homo Viator: Introduction to a Metaphysic of Hope*, trans. E. Crauford, Harper Torchbooks edn. (New York: Harper & Row, 1962).

MARCEL, GABRIEL, *Metaphysical Journal*, trans. B. Wall (Chicago: Henry Regnery Co., 1967).

—— *The Mystery of Being*, 2 vols.: i, trans. G. S. Fraser; ii, trans. R. Hague (London: Harvill Press, and Chicago, Henry Regnery Co., 1950 and 1951).

—— *The Philosophy of Existentialism*, trans. Manya Harari (Secaucus, NJ: Citadel Press, 1956).

(ii) Some useful writings about Mounier and Marcel:

O'MALLEY, J. B., *The Fellowship of Being: An Essay on the Concept of Person in the Philosophy of Gabriel Marcel* (The Hague: Martinus Nijhoff, 1966).

RICOEUR, PAUL, 'Emmanuel Mounier: A Personalist Philosopher', repr. in Ricoeur, *History and Truth*, trans. Charles A. Kelbley (Evanston, Ill.: Northwestern University Press, 1965), 133–61.

SCHILPP, P., and HAHN, L. (eds.), *The Philosophy of Gabriel Marcel*, Library of Living Philosophers (La Salle, Ill: Open Court, 1983).

5. Sartre as Existentialist

(i) Writings by Sartre himself:

Being and Nothingness, trans. Hazel Barnes, (London: Routledge, 1989).

Existentialism and Humanism, trans. Philip Mairet (London: Methuen, 1957).

Notebooks for an Ethics, trans. David Pellauer (Chicago: University of Chicago Press, 1992).

The Psychology of the Imagination, trans. B. Frechtman (London: Routledge, 1995).

Sketch for a Theory of the Emotions, trans. Philip Mairet (London: Routledge, 1971).

The Transcendence of the Ego, trans. Forrest Williams and Robert Kirkpatrick (New York: Noonday Press, 1957).

Truth and Existence, trans. Adrian van den Hoven (Chicago: University of Chicago Press, 1992).

(ii) Some useful writings about Sartre:

CAWS, PETER, *Sartre* (London: Routledge, 1979).

DANTO, ARTHUR C., *Sartre*, Fontana Modern Masters (London: Collins, 1975).

HOWELLS, CHRISTINA (ed.), *The Cambridge Companion to Sartre* (Cambridge: Cambridge University Press, 1992).

MCCULLOCH, GREGORY, *Using Sartre: An Analytical Introduction to Early Sartrean Themes* (London: Routledge, 1994).

MURDOCH, IRIS, *Sartre: Romantic Rationalist* (London: Collins, 1967).

SCHILPP, PAUL A. (ed.), *The Philosophy of Jean-Paul Sartre*, Library of Living Philosophers (La Salle, Ill: Open Court, 1981).

6. Merleau-Ponty

(i) Writings by Merleau-Ponty himself:

Adventures of the Dialectic, trans. J. Bien (Evanston, Ill.: Northwestern University Press, 1973).

Phenomenology of Perception, trans. Colin Smith (London: Routledge & Kegan Paul, 1962).

In Praise of Philosophy, trans. J. Wild and J. M. Edie (Evanston, Ill.: Northwestern University Press, 1963).

The Primacy of Perception and Other Essays, ed. J. M. Edie (Evanston, Ill.: Northwestern University Press, 1964).

The Prose of the World, trans. John O'Neill (Evanston, Ill.: Northwestern University Press, 1973).

Sense and Non-Sense, trans. Hubert L. and Patricia Allen Dreyfus (Evanston, Ill.: Northwestern University Press, 1964).

Signs, trans. Richard C. McCleary (Evanston, Ill.: Northwestern University Press, 1964).

The Structure of Behaviour, trans. A. L. Fisher (Boston: Beacon Press, 1963; London: Methuen, 1965).

The Visible and the Invisible, trans. Alphonso Lingis (Evanston, Ill.: Northwestern University Press, 1968).

(ii) Some useful writings about Merleau-Ponty:

BANNAN, J. F., *The Philosophy of Merleau-Ponty* (New York: Harcourt, Brace, & World, 1967).

LANGAN, T., *Merleau-Ponty's Critique of Reason* (New Haven: Yale University Press, 1966).

LANGER, MONIKA, *Merleau-Ponty's Phenomenology of Perception: A Guide and Commentary* (Basingstoke: Macmillan, 1989).

MALLIN, S. B., *Merleau-Ponty's Philosophy* (New Haven: Yale University Press, 1979).

O'NEILL, JOHN, *Perception, Expression and History: The Social Phenomenology of Maurice Merleau-Ponty* (Evanston, Ill.: Northwestern University Press, 1970).

RABIL, A., *Merleau-Ponty: Existentialist of the Social World* (New York: Columbia University Press, 1967).

WHITESIDE, K. H., *Merleau-Ponty and the Foundations of an Existential Politics* (Princeton: Princeton University Press, 1988).

7. Kojève, the Later Sartre, and Althusser

(i) Writings by these authors themselves:

KOJÈVE, ALEXANDRE, *Introduction to the Reading of Hegel*, trans. James H. Nichols Jr. (New York: Cornell University Press, 1980).

SARTRE, J.-P., *Critique of Dialectical Reason*, trans. Alan Sheridan-Smith (London: New Left Books, 1976), rev. edn. (London: Verso, 1991).

—— *The Family Idiot*, trans. Carol Cosman (Chicago: University of Chicago Press, 1981).

—— *The Problem of Method*, trans. Hazel E. Barnes (London: Methuen, 1963): published in USA as *Search for a Method* (New York: Knopf, 1963).

ALTHUSSER, LOUIS, *For Marx*, trans. Ben Brewster (London: Verso, 1990).

—— *Lenin and Philosophy and Other Essays*, trans. Ben Brewster (London: New Left Books, 1971).

—— *Reading Capital*, trans. Ben Brewster (London: New Left Books, 1970).

(ii) Some useful works about recent French Marxism and its background:

BENTON, T., *The Rise and Fall of Structural Marxism: Althusser and his Influence* (London: Macmillan, 1984).

COLLETTI, LUCIO, *Marxism and Hegel* (London: New Left Books, 1973).

GOLDMANN, LUCIEN, *The Human Sciences and Philosophy* (London: Jonathan Cape, 1969).

KELLY, M., *Modern French Marxism* (Oxford: Basil Blackwell, 1992).

MERQUIOR, J. G., *Western Marxism* (London: Paladin Books, 1986).

POSTER, MARK, *Existential Marxism in Postwar France: From Sartre to Althusser* (Princeton: Princeton University Press, 1975).

8. Lacan and Foucault

(i) Works by Lacan and Foucault themselves:

LACAN, JACQUES, *Écrits: A Selection*, trans. Alan Sheridan (London: Tavistock Publications and Routledge, 1977).

—— *The Four Fundamental Concepts of Psychoanalysis*, trans. Alan Sheridan (Harmondsworth: Penguin Books, 1991).

—— *The Ethics of Psychoanalysis, 1959–1960*, trans. Dennis Porter (New York: W. W. Norton & Co. Inc.; London: Tavistock Publications and Routledge, 1992).

FOUCAULT, MICHEL, *The Archaeology of Knowledge*, trans. A. M. Sheridan Smith (New York: Pantheon Books, 1972).

—— *Madness and Civilisation*, trans. Richard Howard (London: Tavistock, 1971).

—— *The Order of Things: An Archaeology of the Human Sciences* (New York, Vintage, and London, Tavistock, 1970).

GORDON, COLIN (ed.), *Michael Foucault: Power/Knowledge* (Brighton: Harvester Press, 1980).

KRITZMAN, LAWRENCE D. (ed.), *Michel Foucault: Politics, Philosophy, Culture: Interviews and other Writings, 1977–1984* (New York: Routledge, 1988).

RABINOW, P. (ed.), *The Foucault Reader* (Harmondsworth: Penguin Books, 1986).

(ii) Some useful works about Lacan and Foucault:

RAGLAND-SULLIVAN, ELLIE, *Jacques Lacan and the Philosophy of Psychoanalysis* (Urbana, Ill.: University of Illinois Press, 1986).

SAMUELS, ROBERT *Between Philosophy and Psychoanalysis: Lacan's Reconstruction of Freud* (New York: Routledge, 1993).

ARMSTRONG, TIMOTHY J. (trans.), *Michel Foucault, Philosopher* (Brighton: Harvester Wheatsheaf, 1992).

DREYFUS, HUBERT, L., and RABINOW, PAUL, *Michel Foucault: Beyond Structuralism and Hermeneutics* (Brighton: Harvester Press, 1982).

GUTTING, GARY (ed.), *The Cambridge Companion to Foucault* (Cambridge: Cambridge University Press, 1994).

—— *Michel Foucault's Archaeology of Scientific Reason* (Cambridge: Cambridge University Press, 1989).

HOY, DAVID COUZENS (ed.), *Foucault: A Critical Reader* (Oxford: Basil Blackwell, 1986).

MCNAY, LOIS, *Foucault: A Critical Introduction* (Cambridge: Polity Press, 1994).

9. Lévinas, Derrida, and Lyotard

(i) Works by these authors themselves:

LÉVINAS, EMMANUEL, *Ethics and Infinity*, trans. Richard A. Cohen (Pittsburgh: Duquesne University Press, 1985).

—— *Otherwise than Being or Beyond Essence*, trans. Alphonso Lingis (The Hague: Martinus Nijhoff, 1981).

—— *Totality and Infinity: An Essay on Exteriority*, trans. Alphonso Lingis (Dordrecht: Kluwer Academic Publishers, 1991).

DERRIDA, JACQUES, *Dissemination*, trans. Barbara Johnson (Chicago: University of Chicago Press; London: Athlone Press, 1981).
—— *Margins of Philosophy*, trans. Alan Bass (Chicago: University of Chicago Press; London: Harvester Wheatsheaf, 1982).
—— *Positions*, trans. Alan Bass (London: Athlone Press, 1987).
—— *Spectres of Marx*, trans. Peggy Kamuf (New York: Routledge, 1994).
—— *Writing and Difference*, trans. Alan Bass (Chicago: University of Chicago Press; London: Routledge & Kegan Paul, 1978).

LYOTARD, JEAN-FRANÇOIS, *Political Writings*, trans. Bill Readings and Kevin Paul Geiman (London: UCL Press Ltd., 1993).
—— *The Postmodern Condition: A Report on Knowledge*, trans. G. Bennington and B. Massumi (Manchester: Manchester University Press, 1984).
The Lyotard Reader, ed. A. Benjamin (Oxford: Basil Blackwell, 1989).

(ii)   Some useful writings about these authors:
BERNASCONI, R. and WOOD, D. (eds.), *The Provocation of Lévinas: Rethinking the Other* (New York: Routledge, 1988).
LLEWELLYN, J., *Emmanuel Lévinas: The Genealogy of Ethics* (London: Routledge, 1995).
PEPERZAK, ADRIAAN, *To the Other: An Introduction to the Philosophy of Emmanuel Lévinas* (West Lafayette, Ind.: Purdue University Press, 1992).
LLEWELLYN, JOHN, *Derrida on the Threshold of Sense* (London: Macmillan, 1986).
NORRIS, CHRISTOPHER, *Deconstruction: Theory and Practice* (New York: Methuen, 1982).
—— *Derrida*, Fontana Modern Masters (London: Fontana Library, 1987).
SALLIS, JOHN (ed.), *Deconstruction and Philosophy* (Chicago: University of Chicago Press, 1987).
WOOD, D. (ed.), *Derrida: A Critical Reader* (Oxford: Basil Blackwell, 1992).
—— and BERNASCONI, ROBERT (eds.), *Derrida and Différance* (Evanston Ill.: Northwestern University Press, 1988).

10. Feminist Philosophers

(i)   Writings by these authors:
BEAUVOIR, SIMONE DE, *Ethics of Ambiguity*, trans. B. Frechtman (Secaucus, NJ: Citadel Press, 1980).

—— *The Second Sex*, trans. H. M. Parshley (Harmondsworth: Penguin Books, 1978).

IRIGARAY, LUCE, *An Ethic of Sexual Difference*, trans. Carolyn Burke and Gillian C. Gill (Ithaca, NY: Cornell University Press; London: Athlone Press, 1993).

—— *Speculum of the Other Woman*, trans. Gillian C. Gill (Ithaca, NY: Cornell University Press, 1985).

—— *This Sex Which Is Not One*, trans. C. Porter and C. Burke (Ithaca, NY: Cornell University Press, 1985).

The Irigaray Reader, ed. Margaret Whitford (Oxford: Basil Blackwell, 1992).

KRISTEVA, JULIA, *Desire in Language*, trans. T. Gora, A. Jardine, and L. S. Roudiez (New York: Columbia University Press, 1980; Oxford: Basil Blackwell, 1981).

—— *Revolution in Poetic Language*, trans. M. Waller (New York: Columbia University Press, 1984).

The Kristeva Reader, ed. T. Moi (Oxford: Basil Blackwell, 1986).

LE DŒUFF, MICHÈLE, *Hipparchia's Choice: An Essay concerning Women, Philosophy, etc.*, trans. T. Selous (Oxford: Basil Blackwell, 1991).

—— *The Philosophical Imaginary*, trans. C. Gordon (London: Athlone Press, 1986).

(ii) Some useful works about these authors:

BURKE, CAROLYN, SCHOR, NAOMI, WHITFORD, MARGARET (eds.), *Engaging with Irigaray* (New York: Columbia University Press, 1994).

WHITFORD, MARGARET, *Luce Irigaray: Philosophy in the Feminine* (London: Routledge, 1991).

LECHTE, JOHN, *Julia Kristeva* (London: Routledge, 1990).

OLIVER, KELLY, *Reading Kristeva* (Bloomington, Ind.: Indiana University Press, 1993).

MOI, TORIL (ed.), *French Feminist Thought: A Reader* (Oxford: Basil Blackwell, 1988).

LLOYD, GENEVIEVE, *The Man of Reason: 'Male' and 'Female' in Western Philosophy* (London: Macmillan, 1984).

Index

8 +
128 : humanism def.
132 : Althusser's 'practices'.
138 : Marx + humanism
139 : structuralist abolition of subject.
142-3 : Lacan's mirror stages
("I" as external / linguistic / body)
146-7 { 144 : metaphor + repression (symbolic
+ ** { 145 : science + DESIRE order +
{ 149 : Foucault + 'invention of man' as recent.
+ 150 : F, Discourse + Truth self.)
151 : archaeology v. genealogy
152 : historical origins of 'values' as power
POLITICS + POWER-DRIVEN SCIENCE. Discourse
174 + 172 : différance — 126 : D + ethnocentrism
179 : D. on nothing New
197 : Kristeva, poetry, pleasure.